Understanding Innovation

Series Editors
Christoph Meinel
Larry Leifer

For other titles published in this series, go to
http://www.springer.com/series/8802

Hasso Plattner · Christoph Meinel · Larry Leifer
Editors

Design Thinking

Understand – Improve – Apply

 Springer

Editors

Hasso Plattner
Hasso-Plattner-Institut für
Softwaresystemtechnik GmbH
Prof.-Dr.-Helmert-Str. 2-3
14482 Potsdam
Germany
hasso.plattner@sap.com

Christoph Meinel
Hasso-Plattner-Institut für
Softwaresystemtechnik GmbH
Prof.-Dr.-Helmert-Str. 2-3
14482 Potsdam
Germany
meinel@hpi.uni-potsdam.de

Larry Leifer
Center for Design Research (CDR)
Stanford University
424 Panama Mall
Stanford, CA 94305-2232
USA
leifer@cdr.stanford.edu

ISBN 978-3-642-13756-3   e-ISBN 978-3-642-13757-0
DOI 10.1007/978-3-642-13757-0
Springer Heidelberg Dordrecht London New York

Foreword

In 2005, the Hasso-Plattner-Institute of Design at Stanford University in California began to teach Design Thinking to engineering students. The philosophy behind this venture was the conviction that it is possible to train engineers and scientists to become innovators. Design Thinking has since become a highly recommended course in the Stanford engineering curriculum. The method of Design Thinking melds an end-user focus with multidisciplinary collaboration and iterative improvement and is a powerful tool for achieving desirable, user-friendly, and economically viable design solutions and innovative products and services. In 2007, a second School of Design Thinking, operating under similar premises, was established at the Hasso-Plattner-Institute (HPI) for IT Systems Engineering in Potsdam, Germany. It has been equally successful in attracting students and external partners from industry, the public sector, and society, and producing innovative products and services solutions.

My motivation behind initiating the HPI-Stanford Design Thinking Research Program was the desire to understand why and how the Design Thinking method works on a scientific basis. Through joint research projects, we try to figure out which factors ultimately contribute to the success of this type of innovation in all areas of life. In order to implement innovation processes in industry and the public sector, we must strive to improve our understanding of them.

My main interest is to see the Design Thinking method used in IT/engineering and to understand how it inspires creative multidisciplinary teamwork across faculties; whether and how spatial, time, and cultural boundaries can be overcome; and how it can be meshed with traditional approaches in the field of engineering. We might also be able to propose different organizational structures for design teams in corporations.

It has also been a mystery to me for a long time why the structure of successful design teams differs so substantially from traditional corporate structures.

I am delighted and proud to see this transatlantic research cooperation thrive and develop into a potent academic force in the field of innovation research, and I am confident that answers to some of these questions can be found – and to an extent – have already been found. This volume presents the first comprehensive collection of the research studies carried out by the HPI-Stanford Design Thinking Research Program and is an excellent starting point for the new Springer series on "Understanding Innovation."

Potsdam/Palo Alto   *Hasso Plattner*
May 2010

Contents

Part III   Tools for Design Thinking

Part IV   Design Thinking in Information Technology

Contributors

Currano, Rebecca Center for Design Research, Stanford University, Building 560, 424 Panama Mall, Stanford, CA 94305, USA, bcurrano@stanford.edu

Dow, Steven P. Human-Computer Interaction Group, Stanford University, Gates Computer Science Building, 353 Serra Mall, Stanford, CA 94305, USA spdow@stanford.edu

Edelman, Jonathan Center for Design Research, Stanford University, Building 560, 424 Panama Mall, Stanford, CA 94305, USA, edelman2@cdr.stanford.edu

Gabrysiak, Gregor System Analysis and Modeling Group, Hasso-Plattner-Institute for IT Systems Engineering at the University of Potsdam, Prof.-Dr.-Helmert-Str. 2–3, 14482 Potsdam, Germany Gregor.Gabrysiak@hpi.uni-potsdam.de

Gericke, Lutz Hasso-Plattner-Institute, Campus Griebnitzsee, P.O. Box 900460, 14440 Potsdam, Germany

Giese, Holger System Analysis and Modeling Group, Hasso-Plattner-Institute for IT Systems Engineering at the University of Potsdam, Prof.-Dr.-Helmert-Str. 2–3, 14482 Potsdam, Germany, Holger.Giese@hpi.uni-potsdam.de

Gumienny, Raja Hasso-Plattner-Institute, Campus Griebnitzsee, P.O. Box 900460, 14440 Potsdam, Germany

Hinds, Pamela Department of Management Science & Engineering, Stanford University, Stanford, CA 94305–4026, USA, phinds@stanford.edu

Hirschfeld, Robert Software Architecture Group, Hasso-Plattner-Institute, University of Potsdam, 14482 Potsdam, Germany hirschfeld@hpi.uni-potsdam.de

Klemmer, Scott R. Human-Computer Interaction Group, Stanford University, Gates Computer Science Building, 353 Serra Mall, Stanford, CA 94305, USA

Kowark, Thomas Hasso-Plattner-Institute, University of Potsdam, 14482 Potsdam, Germany

Leifer, Larry Center for Design Research, Stanford University, Building 560, 424 Panama Mall, Stanford, CA 94305, USA, leifer@cdr.stanford.edu

Lincke, Jens Software Architecture Group, Hasso-Plattner-Institute, University of Potsdam, 14482 Potsdam, Germany, jens.lincke@hpi.uni-potsdam.de

Lindberg, Tilmann Hasso-Plattner-Institut, PO-Box 900460, 14440 Potsdam, Germany, tilmann.lindberg@hpi.uni-potsdam.de

LoBue, Peter Hasso-Plattner-Institute, Campus Griebnitzsee, P.O. Box 900460, 14440 Potsdam, Germany

Luebbe, Alexander Hasso-Plattner-Institute, University of Potsdam, 14482 Potsdam, Germany, alexander.luebbe@hpi.uni-potsdam.de

Lyon, Joachim Department of Management Science & Engineering, Stanford University, Stanford, CA 94305–4026, USA, jblyon@stanford.edu

Meinel, Christoph Hasso-Plattner-Institute, Campus Griebnitzsee, P.O. Box 900460, 14440 Potsdam, Germany, meinel@hpi.uni-potsdam.de

Noweski, Christine Hasso-Plattner-Institute, Campus Griebnitzsee, P.O. Box 900460, 14440 Potsdam, Germany

Quasthoff, Matthias Hasso-Plattner-Institute, Campus Griebnitzsee, P.O. Box 900460, 14440 Potsdam, Germany

Rauth, Ingo Hasso-Plattner-Institute, Campus Griebnitzsee, P.O. Box 900460, 14440 Potsdam, Germany

Reimann, Martin University of Southern California, Department of Psychology/Brain & Creativity Institute, Los Angeles, CA 90089, USA mreimann@usc.edu

Schilke, Oliver University of Southern California, Department of Psychology/Brain & Creativity Institute, Los Angeles, CA 90089, USA schilke@ucla.edu

Seibel, Andreas System Analysis and Modeling Group, Hasso-Plattner-Institute for IT Systems Engineering at the University of Potsdam, Prof.-Dr.-Helmert-Str. 2–3, 14482 Potsdam, Germany, Andreas.Seibel@hpi.uni-potsdam.de

Sirkin, David Stanford University, Center for Design Research, 424 Panama Mall, Stanford, CA 94305, USA, sirkin@stanford.edu

Skogstad, Philipp Center for Design Research, Stanford University, Building 560, 424 Panama Mall, Stanford, CA 94305, USA, skogstad@cdr.stanford.edu

Steinert, Bastian Software Architecture Group, Hasso-Plattner-Institute, University of Potsdam, 14482 Potsdam, Germany bastian.steinert@hpi.uni-potsdam.de

Thienen, Julia von Hasso-Plattner-Institute, Campus Griebnitzsee, P.O. Box 900460, 14440 Potsdam, Germany

Uflacker, Matthias Hasso-Plattner-Institute, University of Potsdam, 14482 Potsdam, Germany, matthias.uflacker@hpi.uni-potsdam.de

Wagner, Ralf Hasso-Plattner-Institut, PO-Box 900460, 14440 Potsdam, Germany

Weske, Mathias Hasso-Plattner-Institute, University of Potsdam, 14482 Potsdam, Germany, mathias.weske@hpi.uni-potsdam.de

Willems, Christian Hasso-Plattner-Institute, Campus Griebnitzsee, P.O. Box 900460, 14440 Potsdam, Germany

Zeier, Alexander Hasso-Plattner-Institute, University of Potsdam, 14482 Potsdam, Germany, Alexander.Zeier@hpi.uni-potsdam.de

Design Thinking Research

Christoph Meinel and Larry Leifer

"We believe great innovators and leaders need to be great design thinkers. We believe design thinking is a catalyst for innovation and bringing new things into the world. We believe high impact teams work at the intersection of technology, business, and human values. We believe collaborative communities create dynamic relationships that lead to breakthroughs." These are the visions of the first two schools of Design Thinking, the d.school at Stanford University in the Californian Silicon Valley and the D-School of the Hasso-Plattner-Institute in Potsdam, Germany. With overwhelming success these schools educate young innovators from different disciplines like engineering, medicine, business, the humanities, and education to work together to solve big problems in a human centered way.

The open and radical culture of collaboration practised there inspires both intellectually and emotionally, and creates an environment where people from different areas such as big companies, start-ups, schools, nonprofits and the government can participate in working and learning with us on projects. But what is the intellectual basis for this successful educational approach? Exactly these types of questions are scientifically approached in our HPI Stanford Design Thinking Research Program, whose first results are presented in this volume.

1 The Philosophy of Design Thinking

Everyone loves an innovation, "an idea that sells." Unfortunately, this is an outcome, not a process for achieving the goal. How does one go about increasing the probability of successful innovation from the research, development, and marketing investments one makes?

For the last years we have asked one guiding question: "What are designers and engineers really thinking and doing, when they create products, services, and enterprises?" Building on insights from our research we have designed new tools, activities, and values that improve the individual, team, and enterprise-wide capacity for design innovation.

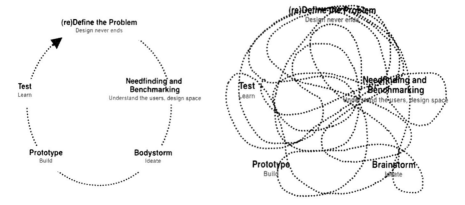

Fig. 1 Design thinking is commonly visualized as an iterative series of five major stages. To the left we see the standard form. To the right we see something closer to reality. While the stages are simple enough, the adaptive expertise required to chose the right inflection points and appropriate next stage is a high order intellectual activity that requires practice and is learnable

We have seen that a powerful methodology for innovation has emerged. It integrates human, business, and technological factors in problem forming, -solving, and -design: "Design Thinking." Its human-centric methodology integrates expertise from design, social sciences, engineering, and business. It blends an end-user focus with multidisciplinary collaboration and iterative improvement to produce innovative products, systems, and services. Design thinking creates a vibrant interactive environment that promotes learning through rapid conceptual prototyping (Fig. 1).

Design Thinking is about the creation of, as well as adaptive use of a body-of-behaviours and values. This goal stands in sharp contrast to, while complimentary to, the predominant disciplinary model based on the creation and validation of a body-of-knowledge.

2 Rules of Design Thinking

We now have evidence in support of several design thinking activities that have long been considered important, but were lacking an explanation and understanding for their truth. Of these, the most global truth lies in the fact that every physical product delivers a service; that every service is manifested through physical products; and that without an insightful enterprise strategy, it matters little that one has products or services. Findings include the following four "rules of design thinking."

2.1 The Human Rule: All Design Activity Is Ultimately Social in Nature

There are studies that substantiate the assertion that successful innovation through design thinking activities will always bring us back to the "human-centric point of view." This is the imperative to solve technical problems in ways that satisfy human needs and acknowledge the human element in all technologists and managers.

2.2 The Ambiguity Rule: Design Thinkers Must Preserve Ambiguity

There is no chance for "chance discovery" if the box is closed tightly, the constraints enumerated excessively, and the fear of failure is always at hand. Innovation demands experimentation at the limits of our knowledge, at the limits of our ability to control events, and with freedom to see things differently.

2.3 The Re-design Rule: All Design Is Re-design

The human needs that we seek to satisfy have been with us for millennia. Through time and evolution there have been many successful solutions to these problems. Because technology and social circumstances change constantly, it is imperative to understand how these needs have been addressed in the past. Then we can apply "foresight tools and methods" to better estimate social and technical conditions we will encounter 5, 10, or even 20 years in the future.

2.4 The Tangibility Rule: Making Ideas Tangible Always Facilitates Communication

Curiously, this is one of our most recent findings. While conceptual prototyping has been a central activity in design thinking during the entire period of our research, it is only in the past few years that we have come to realize that "prototypes are communication media." Seen as media, we now have insights regarding their bandwidth, granularity, time constants, and context dependencies.

The "make it tangible" rule is one of the first major findings of the design thinking research program documented in this book.

2.5   HPI-Stanford Design Thinking Research Program

The HPI-Stanford Design Thinking Research Program was started in 2008 and is financed by the Hasso Plattner Foundation.

Program Vision.   The research program engages multidisciplinary research teams to investigate the phenomena of **innovation** in all its holistic dimensions scientifically. In particular, researchers are encouraged to develop ambitious, long-term explorations related to the innovation method of design thinking in its technical, business, and human aspects.

The HPI-Stanford Design Thinking Research Program is a rigorous academic research applied to understanding the scientific basis for how and why the innovation method of design thinking works. Researchers in the program study e.g. the complex interaction between members of multidisciplinary teams requested to design innovations. Beyond understanding, here the goal of the program is to discover metrics that predict team performance and facilitate real-time team performance management. The program invites to design, develop and evaluate innovative (analogue and digital) tools that support teams in their cooperative creative work eventually even bursting time and space boundaries. Another program interest is to explore the use of design thinking methods in the field of information technology and IT systems engineering. An important feature of the domain is the need for creative collaboration across spatial and temporal boundaries. In the context of disciplinary diversity, how do design thinking methods mesh with traditional engineering and management approaches, specifically, why does the structure of successful design teams differ substantially from traditional corporate structures.

The Program engages multidisciplinary research teams with diverging backgrounds in science, engineering, design, humanities, who are passionate about developing ambitious, long-term explorations related to design thinking in its technical, business, and human dimensions.

Program Priorities.   Following the strong cooperation in offering the first design thinking education programs, the two d.schools, at Stanford University in Palo Alto, California, and at the Hasso-Plattner-Institute in Potsdam, Germany, the focus of the design thinking research program is on collaboration between researchers of Stanford University and the Hasso-Plattner-Institute, Potsdam, Germany. Multi-year funding favours projects that set new research priorities for this emergent knowledge domain. Selection is based on intellectual merit and evidence of open collaboration. Special research interests are in the following points-of-view and their guiding questions:

- What are people really thinking and doing when they are engaged in creative design innovation? How can new frameworks, tools, systems, and methods augment, capture, and reuse successful practices?
- What is the impact on technology, business, and human performance when design thinking is practiced? How do the tools, systems, and methods really work to get the innovation you want when you want it? How do they fail?

3   The Program Book

Design Thinking: Understand – Improve – Apply. As the title of the book stresses, a system's view is taken that begins with a demand for deep, evidence-based understandings of design thinking phenomena. Given new knowledge and the body-of-behaviours needed to apply that knowledge we strive to improve design thinking and adapt its processes to the evolving socio-technical context of our education and business worlds.

Part I: Design Thinking in Various Contexts. The first chapter explores the usefulness of design thinking in IT development processes. The authors Tilmann Lindberg, Christoph Meinel, and Ralf Wagner from the Hasso-Plattner-Institute provide a comprehensive description of the design thinking process and its various steps and elements and analyze how design thinking helps to obtain a multi-perspective comprehension of a complex and ambiguous problem. They explain the interdependency and iterative alignment of problem space and solution space. The authors explore how comprehension of a problem along design thinking principles can help overcome the familiar problems that arise from a traditional, predominantly technical perspective in the development process. The most blatant and well-known of said problems is the creation of technically perfect and highly sophisticated products or services which turn out to be either incomprehensible or undesired by the user. The integration of the user's perspective – which ultimately defines the economic viability of a development – is critical. The chapter also outlines how organizational structures might need to be modified in order to successfully incorporate design thinking principles into development processes in the IT industry.

The **second chapter** by Philipp Skogstad and Larry Leifer presents an innovation process model which elucidates the way engineering designers and managers interact and under which circumstances they succeed. The authors' research emphasizes the crucial importance of experimentation. The model chain "plan => execute => synthesize" can be seen as a variation of important elements in the design thinking process, in particular problem research, rapid prototyping, and iteration. Based on their experiments the authors show how the feedback process is expressed either as approval/feedback or as censorship and delineate how these options influence the further design process.

The authors of the **third chapter**, Martin Reimann and Oliver Schilke of Stanford University, explore the psychological and neurological dimension of the design thinking process and the role of aesthetics and creativity within the process. The goal is to understand the underlying neural processes of the increased creativity which has been proven to manifest itself when the design thinking process has been applied. This chapter's outstanding practical relevance lies in the exploration of potential strategies and methodologies that firms can implement to foster greater creativity among their designers and product managers.

Part II: Understanding Design Thinking. Another important element for understanding design processes is an exploration of the role of media in said processes. In the **fourth chapter** Jonathan Edelman and Rebecca Currano of Stanford University evaluate a media-model framework which categorizes types of media and provides a guide to discerning the major characteristics and differences between them. Thus, design teams are enabled to make a more economical and purposeful choice of media used in the various stages of their design process. The research shows how media-models can help navigate the variety of shared media available to designers and provide a new approach to successful Business Process Modelling, an application which is explored in detail in chapter eleven.

In the subsequent **fifth chapter**, Julia von Thienen, Christine Noweski, Ingo Rauth, and Christoph Meinel from the Hasso-Plattner-Institute explore the relationship between theory and practice in design thinking. This inquiry lies at the heart of design thinking research and its advancement as an academic discipline with sound methodological approaches and empirical validity. Design thinking research should constantly question and refine design thinking theory, much in the same way iterative prototyping constantly improves design solutions. The authors have conducted experiments in order to test two common assumptions design thinkers entertain: (1) that multidisciplinary teams are more innovative than mono-disciplinary teams, and (2) that designer teams with training in the design thinking process are more innovative than untrained teams. While these assumptions proved to be largely correct in terms of design solutions, a different picture emerged with regard to utility deliberations. In combination with an assessment of communication within design teams, the research identified certain contradictions which should stimulate refinements in design thinking theory.

Another significant parameter of understanding the design process and the applicability of design thinking is national culture. This relationship between design practice and innovation on the one hand, and culture on the other hand, is explored in the **sixth chapter** by Pamela Hinds and Joachim Lyons of Stanford University. The authors apply ethnographic research methodologies and arrive at their conclusions through extensive field interviews and observation of designers. In their multiple case study design, they juxtapose American and Chinese designers and in addition to that, make a broader comparison between Europe, Asia, and the US. One of the preliminary results is a confirmation of the idea that there are no universal "best practices" for the design process, or – by extension – for the implementation of design thinking in various cultural contexts.

Concluding the first two parts of the book that deal with understanding design thinking in various contexts and on multiple levels is a study on the efficacy of prototyping under time constraints. The **seventh chapter** by Steven Dow and Scott Klemmer of Stanford University pursues the question of whether repeated prototyping and re-design provides a tangible advantage opposed to quicker realization of a finished design with only one round of prototyping. The experimentation results showed that designers in the iteration condition, i.e. with multiple rounds of prototyping, outperformed those who only prototyped once. Prior experience with iteration proves to be a positive performance indicator as designers tend to discover more flaws and constraints and try new concepts. This is valuable data for design companies which always operate under tight time constraints in the race for early market entry with innovative products.

Part III: Tools for Design Thinking. Design thinking will never be optimal in the sense of an absolute compendium of natural science facts. It will always be subject to improvement and adaptation to changing circumstances, both human and environmental. There is always a better way and our talent, as design thinkers, will lie in our "adaptive expertise." The adaptive nature of design thinking is at the root of its value in confronting uncertainty and ambiguity, in confronting the future. Improvement is most often associated with the creation of better tools. Papers in Part III are focused on design thinking tool development and validation. Information technology plays a critical role. The space we work in is also a major determinant of our behavioural performance. The development of "metrics" is very important to human and technical systems performance improvement.

A major performance parameter is communication behaviour among design team members. Information and communication technology has the potential of constantly improving design performance and efficiency. The team of Matthias Uflacker, Thomas Kowark, and Alexander Zeier from the Hasso-Plattner-Institute has developed a software tool which collects data and analyzes communication processes in technology-enabled design spaces. In **chapter eight** the authors present their new insights into the complex characteristics of real-time online interactions among design team members and elaborate on the multiple dimensions of capturing design team communications. The research proves the notable differences of communication patterns between high-performance and low-performance design teams and introduces a reliable diagnostic tool for design team success, making it highly relevant for recruitment and process structuring in industry and research.

A newly developed tool for transporting the working mode and physical environment of design thinking into a remote collaboration environment is presented in **chapter nine**. The author team around Raja Gumienny and Christoph Meinel from the Hasso-Plattner-Institute has developed and tested a prototype, the "Tele-Board," that builds on a remote digital white board setup and integrates life-size video with the possibility of simultaneous manipulation of artifacts on a digital white board. Thus, essential elements of design thinking processes, like, for example, the clustering of ideas, are mirrored in a remote collaboration environment. In many ways this new tool allows for the combination of the advantages of analogue and digital design thinking practice. While maintaining the time-tested physical working mode of the design thinking process in a digital space, it adds digital functions, for example easy, systematic, and unobtrusive documentation by saving the various stages of the design thinking process.

The potential of communication robots for improving the design process of geographically distributed teams is introduced in **chapter ten** by David Sirkin of Stanford University. Similar to the "Tele-Board" research, this project also addresses the barriers of effective collaboration which usually requires physical presence, body language signals, and the ability to point to and act upon artefacts. The author shows how expressive tele-operated robotic avatars can be integrated into designers' workflow, mainly in the conceptual and the prototype development. The avatars can help in overcoming the sensory void usually impeding effective exchanges in globally distributed teams. They establish a resemblance of a physical presence and facilitate more direct communication.

The various tools developed in the HPI-Stanford Design Thinking Research Program have significant business potential and have, in part, already been patented. We expect that the desire for such tools will increase further as globalized design processes become more and more common.

Part IV: Design Thinking in Information Technology. Design thinking has always been about "practice," the real world creation and deployment of products, services, and enterprise systems. Our research program makes the difference between deploying last year's best practices and those informed by our research, to be next generation practices. They will come complete with evidence, real world metrics, and a program for continuous innovation and discovery. Papers in Part IV are focused on these applications and their validation.

The **eleventh chapter** explores the application of the design thinking process to business process management which is or should be a matter of concern for each and every company. The knowledge, analysis, and optimization of business processes are preconditions for efficient and successful operation and process modelling is the first step towards knowing and ultimately streamlining said processes. Alexander Luebbe and Mathias Weske from the Hasso-Plattner-Institute have used design thinking principles to develop a method for improving the modelling process. In their chapter they recount the iterative experiments with design thinking factors, such as physical elements (plastic building blocks as tangible prototypes), methodological guidance, and intensive end-user/participant involvement and present the results and relevance of this experimentation for successful application in real-world companies. Confirming what Steven Dow and Scott Klemmer have shown earlier in this book, the performance (in this case the optimization of a business process model) improved with iteration.

Another application area for design thinking is software development. In the **twelfth chapter** Robert Hirschfeld, Bastian Steinert und Jens Lincke from the Hasso-Plattner-Institute integrated design thinking elements in order to further improve the already advanced and progressive agile approaches to software development which are user and code centric and allow for instance problem solving due to a high-quality code base. Design thinking has much to offer in this context, not just to develop more innovative software, but also to aid distributed development which is getting more and more common. The research team integrated both the application *ProjectTalk* and the development environment extension *CodeTalk* into a platform which supports remote-collaborative software development, thereby facilitating independent yet simultaneous interacting with shared tools and improved communication among software design team members.

The final chapter of this section and our book also deals with the application of design thinking onto software development. In the **thirteenth chapter** Gregor Gabrysiak, Holger Giese, and Andreas Seibel from the Hasso-Plattner-Institute specifically address the problem that tangible prototypes are not feasible for complex software systems, in particular because of financial and time constraints. As an answer to this problem, the researchers have developed an innovative and cost-effective scenario-based approach to prototyping such systems. They generated interactive simulations for end users, thus exploring the application of two major pillars in design thinking: early and rapid prototyping and user involvement, even in a non-tangible environment.

4 In Summary

The heart of the design thinking process lies at the intersection of technical feasibility, economic viability, and desirability by the user. Accordingly, the inquiries of design thinking research extents to all aspects related to these three dimensions. With regard to the scope of the research presented in this book, we are confident that an important step has been made towards a thorough, scientifically viable exploration of the design thinking process.

We are thankful to all who have contributed to the book. These are not only the authors but also Dr. Karin-Irene Eiermann, Denise Curti, and Ingo Rauth. Karin-Irene and Denise successfully managed the program and various community building activities and workshops that have considerably contributed to the success of the HPI Stanford Design Thinking Research Program. We are particularly thankful to Karin-Irene Eiermann and Sabine Lang for her work in preparing this book.

We sincerely hope that you will enjoy and benefit from the content, format, and intent of this book. We hope to instigate and contribute to scholarly debates and strongly welcome your feedback. Your first opportunity to contribute directly is to submit papers to the newly launched "Electronic Colloquium on Design Thinking Research (ecdtr)". We invite you to visit this innovative platform of dynamic and rapid scholarly exchange about recent developments in design thinking research: http://ecdtr.hpi-web.de/

Part I
Design Thinking in Various Contexts

Design Thinking: A Fruitful Concept for IT Development?

Tilmann Lindberg, Christoph Meinel*, and Ralf Wagner

Abstract In our research project *Collaborative Creativity of Development Processes in the IT Industry*, we pursue the question how design thinking can help to enhance the innovativeness in IT development and which individual and organizational factors facilitate or encourage this. In this chapter, we outline what the contribution of design thinking to engineering thinking can be, how it is related to akin IT development approaches (e.g. agile development), and what our initial insights on the didactic and organizational implications are.

1 Introduction: On Problem Solving in Design and Science

"Most outsiders see design as an applied art, as having to do with aesthetics, unlike a solid profession unto itself, with technical knowledge, skills, and responsibilities to rely on. Insiders to design, by contrast, talk of innovative ideas, coordinating the concerns of many disciplines, being advocates for users, and trying to balance social, political, cultural, and ecological considerations."

Klaus Krippendorf (2006, 47)

It seems to be the nature of design that it is not always easy to understand what this term actually means. As the initial quotation exposes, people in design themselves have not only a broader view on their discipline, they also see themselves in a different role than outsiders do: not merely in the position of dealing with aesthetical aspects of forms and products, but of taking on a general role of coordinating disciplines, stakeholders, and the manifold environmental matters within product development processes. The following argumentation reduces this point to central differences in problem solving in design as well as in science and technology.

T. Lindberg (✉), C. Meinel, and R. Wagner
Hasso-Plattner-Institut, PO-Box 900460, 14440 Potsdam, Germany
e-mail: tilmann.lindberg@hpi.uni-potsdam.de; meinel@hpi.uni-potsdam.de

* Principal Investigator

H. Plattner et al. (eds.), *Design Thinking: Understand – Improve – Apply*,
Understanding Innovation, DOI 10.1007/978-3-642-13757-0_1,
© Springer-Verlag Berlin Heidelberg 2011

Comparing problems tackled in well-established sciences as astronomy, quantum mechanics, or computer science with those in design, it seems obvious that design problems are closer to the everyday life. What does a backache reducing office chair look like? What form should a computer interface have to be accessible for elderly people? What do we have to do to avoid injuries through battery acid in developing countries? The motivation to find answers to those questions is not to gain scientific knowledge or to discover new technical possibilities (even if design clearly takes advantage of both). Rather, it is the need to create ideas and find solutions (products, services, systems), which are as viable as possible for certain groups of users. By that, design intends to offer a very concrete solution to a complex problem that is socially highly ambiguous and hence neither easy nor certain to comprehend. Design problems thus – using a term by Horst Rittel – are close to *wicked problems*, blurred in character and not definitely definable (Rittel 1972).

People in design have developed problem solving skills that allow them to deal with such kind of problems successfully. This however calls for a dissimilar mode of thinking than taught in the curricula of the established sciences. Solving wicked problems does not acquire the analytical inductive/deductive scheme pursued in science that follows an epistemological logic to achieve knowledge about scientific truth, since designers only strive for enhanced viability and novelty of products (Dewey 1997, 79; Martin 2009, 63). Scientific problems generally will be answered by theories, concepts, taxonomies, or models, and only become finally accepted when they depict a problem analytically in all its dimensions. Still, this demands not only long-term efforts to put into research and analysis but also to reduce the complexity of a stated problem to such an extent that it is finally *non-wicked*, thus entirely describable. Yet for design problems, this would be a misleading approach: first, as designers have to deal with problems pragmatically and come up with solutions in much shorter periods of time than scientists do; second, as designers do not have the possibility to reduce the complexity of a problem because design problems are made up of exogenous perspectives that finally decide about the solution's viability: the user's, the client's, the engineer's, the manufacturer's, the law-maker's, the environmentalist's, the employee's, etc. (Lawson 2006, 83f).

It becomes obvious that design unavoidably has to take on a coordinating role within this context of multiple stakes, because they have to rely on the knowledge of others as long as they want to approach general viability of solutions. To do so, there emerged professional learning strategies in design: cognitive patterns to grasp multiple knowledge and multiple perspectives of others for the purpose of synthesizing and creatively transforming the knowledge to new service or product concepts. In contrast to analytical thinking in science, we call those strategies *design thinking* (Brown 2008; Dunne and Martin 2006; Lindberg et al. 2009).

To understand how those strategies work, it is useful to work with two fundamental pairs of terms: the problem and solution space on the one hand, and diverging/converging thinking on the other hand.

The distinction between the problem and solution space elucidates the dualistic approach of design thinking.[1] Whereas in science the focus lies in general on exploring the solution while the initial problem is given, design treats both the problem and the solution as something to be explored. This indeed characterizes design thinking as an approach for professional learning. The distinction between diverging and converging thinking however shows how designers approach both spaces (Lawson 2006, 142f). Learning alone, certainly, is not enough in design as the knowledge acquired is at the same time a means to come up with viable as well as novel solutions. Thus design thinking is always an interplay between diverging exploration of problem and solution space and converging processes of synthesizing and selecting. Contrary to thinking styles predominant in science, the knowledge processed in design thinking has to be neither representative (as in inductive thinking) nor entirely rationalized (as in deductive thinking), rather it serves to obtain an exemplary but multi-perspective comprehension in order to deal creatively with the ambiguity of wicked problems. Building upon this argumentation, design thinking can be put down to three basic characteristics (see also Fig. 1).

- *Exploring the problem space*: When exploring a problem space, design thinking acquires an intuitive (not fully verbalized) understanding, mainly by observing exemplary use cases or scenarios, as opposed to formulating general hypotheses or theories regarding the problem; and synthesise this knowledge to point of views.
- *Exploring the solution space*: Design thinking asks for a great number of alternative ideas in parallel and elaborates them with sketching and prototyping

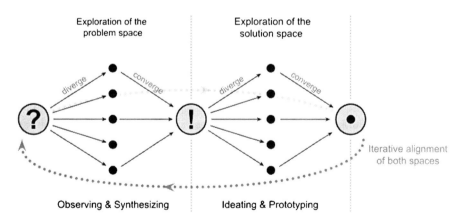

Fig. 1 Problem and solution space in design thinking

---

[1] A concept of the "problem space" was first introduced by Newell et al. (1967), although with a different meaning, as they locate the representation of possible solutions in the problem space without regarding a separate solution space. This conceptualization does not appear sufficient for our purpose, as the distinction between learning about the problem and learning about the solution in design thinking could not be depicted.

techniques. In this manner, ideas are being consciously transformed into tangible representatives.

- *Iterative alignment of both spaces*: These representatives of ideas and concepts facilitate communication not only in the design team, but with users, clients and experts as well. Thus, design thinking helps to keep in touch with the problem-relevant environment and can use this information for refining and revising the chosen solution path(s).

Accordingly, design thinking engenders a system of checks and balances to ensure that the conclusive solution will be both innovative and suitable for the social system that the design problem addresses.

2 Understanding the Problem: Overcoming the Dilemma of Analytical Thinking in IT Development by Design Thinking?

As outlined in the preceding section, there are crucial differences concerning the quality how problems are characterized and approached in design and in science. The paradigms of problem solving in science originated in epistemology, the studies of finding out what is true or not, and led to a strong focus on analytical thinking. The paradigms of problem solving in design though originate in finding out what novel solution fits best in a social or technical system. The discussion about how to bring both paradigms together is particularly valuable in areas with a strong tradition in analytical thinking but which are nevertheless related to design responsibilities.

In our research project *Collaborative Creativity of the Development Processes in the IT Industry*, we explore the capabilities of design thinking to broaden the problem understanding and problem solving capabilities in IT development processes. We pursue in particular the question in which cases the application of design thinking to IT development is valuable (or not) and what the individual and organizational implications for teams and organizations are. Hereby, we draw upon an in-depth case study research with international IT companies. In our first year, we conducted 36 qualitative guideline interviews with IT experts on the one hand and design thinking experts on the other who were involved in design thinking-based IT projects both in the United States and in Germany.

In the following section, we will discuss the background and the peculiarity of our research focus.

2.1 Why IT Development Tends to Take Place in an Engineering Expert's World

Within the IT industry – comparable to any other industry dealing with technical products and services – a technical perspective plays a central role in problem solving and solution development.

This seems to be necessary as the development process itself asks for highly trained professionals who are able to deal with complex technical issues, such as programming languages or software and hardware architecture. Competencies in engineering-centered areas used to be not only a condition for participating in the IT development process, but also in the developing process of the actual design of the software product itself. Getting a comprehensive understanding of what the product will look like, what solutions will work or not, and how the conditions of interaction between user and software can be shaped, generally presupposes the ability to communicate about those questions in technical terms. This is due to the situation that every decision about the software design unavoidably manifests at the level of architecture or code and, thus, cannot be solved without expert knowledge. Consequently, the educational background of hardware and software engineers has strong influence on mind-set building and decision-making and, as a result, IT development has the tendency to take place within an "exclusive" expert's world. Thus, in past and present times, these circumstances lead to the fact that technically and analytically trained IT engineers take on the designer's role as well, although they have not been professionally trained in that field. The word "software design" is, in fact, one of the few design terms that are almost exclusively associated with technical issues.

2.2 The Dilemma of a Predominantly Technical Perspective

Pursuing a dominant technical perspective in IT development however comes with its own set of problems. One basic problem, for instance, is that functionalities and user interfaces, albeit technically perfect, may shape up as incomprehensible or inappropriate from the user's point of view. Other features considered as meaningful and essential from a user's perspective may not be addressed. This problem, which is in these days e.g. approached by the research field of human-computer-interaction, can cause serious drawbacks: inefficiency and loss of effectiveness for the user, rejection of the product, and a loss of innovation prospects for the producer. Furthermore, those times in which the IT market grew mainly driven by technology push dynamics became a thing of the past. From home entertainment to web 2.0 applications and ubiquitous computing, IT products deeply depend on social life dynamics, which are primarily not the concern of engineering but of design. Since IT solutions became more and more part of people's everyday life, not only the demands on usefulness and usability have been growing continuously, but IT engineers must also learn to develop for highly competitive consumer markets, in which successful innovations are rather defined by the users point of view than by technical perfection. An isolated technical perspective entailing isolated analytical thinking can thus lead into an innovation trap: while spending much effort in the development of technically novel or reasonable solutions, the clients do not really see the solution's distinctive value.

2.3 Design Thinking as a Complementary Approach?

Overall, the challenges that IT development is faced with exceed the established focus of an expert's world and ask for the integration of further perspectives on problem understanding and solution finding in IT development. This problem actually is the focal point of the present debate of applying design thinking to IT. The thinking of IT engineers is mainly influenced by the deductive-rationalist approach as taught in mathematics and informatics – subsequent to the logic of having a given problem and deducing the right solution in accordance with rational rules of logic. Design thinking, by contrast, teaches to treat problems as wicked problems, thus more openly, with the purpose of embracing the blurred space of social ambiguity through which a successful design process should pass as well. Thus, the idea behind applying design thinking to IT development asks for setting up a complementary thinking style, which extends the problem solving abilities of IT development teams with the purpose of making their outcomes more innovative.

However, when we talk about design thinking, we do not use the term in a sense of how designers (may) think, but of how anyone "should" think while dealing with design problems (Lindberg et al. 2009).

In consequence, we do not look upon design thinking as a profession-bound concept of designer's cognitive strategies, but as a comprehensive meta-disciplinary concept that broadens disciplinary reasoning and helps for example engineers to forget about the 'drawers' for a moment that they have internalized in their academic training – until a problem has been defined precisely enough so that professional rationales and expert knowledge may suitably be applied. This understanding of design thinking actually characterizes the d.school's educational philosophy as well as the main focus of the HPI-Stanford Design Thinking Research Program (Plattner et al. 2009). Thus our project focus is how to relate design thinking to the structures, cultures and processes of IT development – in particular with regard to the following aspects:

- *Building on Diversity*: Facilitating strong team diversity and frequent interdisciplinary communication and collaboration throughout the design process
- *Exploring the Problem Space*: Supporting a comprehensive shared understanding of the problem addressed before the actual development process starts, in particular by learning about the user and its social context from different perspectives

- *Exploring the Solution Space*: Promoting a creative ideation and conceptualization process by pursuing many alternative ideas on a rough-sketch level in order to learn about the most viable solution path
- *Iterative Alignment of Both Spaces*: Enabling a highly iterative development process with an early and continuous integration of user feedbacks based on comprehensible prototypes

To deal with this issue in detail, we will consider three questions. First, what approaches do exist that try to solve similar problems like design thinking and how is design thinking related to them? Second, how can design thinking in IT development be conceptualized on an operational level? Third, what implementation hurdles are there and are there ways to overcome them? In the subsequent section, we outline existing IT development approaches and their relation to design thinking.

3 Discussing the Context: Waterfalls, Agility, and New Design Professions

There have been various models to organize IT development projects and each of them tackles the issue of problem solving and knowledge processing in a different way. "Old school" IT approaches used to follow linear process logic as known from milestone-based project management: The process passes through several phases in a predefined order, separated through milestones that describe particular preliminary goals and timelines, and require an extensive phase documentation. The prime example of those models is the "waterfall model" that divides IT development generally in the following basic phases: *Requirement and specification analysis*, *program design*, *coding*, *testing* and *implementation* (whereas different descriptions of the waterfall phases vary depending on how detailed they are) (Royce 1970; Davis et al. 1988). The waterfall model seeks to build up knowledge about problem and solution very systematically, so that each step can build upon the outcome of the preceding ones. Knowledge processing is rather formalized via an in-depth documentation as a core completion criteria of each stage, not only with the purpose of recording knowledge for future maintenance and changes in the software code, but also to advance knowledge in an explicit condition to the subsequent phases. Overall, the waterfall process facilitates strong process and resource control as well as a strong clarity of that what is being developed. It allows project planning which is very comprehensible from an ex ante perspective and thus easy to communicate to clients and customers.

Nevertheless, the waterfall model does not always have a good reputation due to several reasons. As Boehm points out, "document-driven standards have pushed many projects to write elaborate specifications of poorly understood user interfaces and decision-support functions, followed by design and development of large quantities of unusable code" (Boehm 1988, 63). Even if feedback loops between the stages are not excluded, their effect on product improvements is very low due to the rigid demand for documentation that slows down the feedback communication between the stages and makes the process, albeit potentially iterative, inflexible. Another problem is that cross-functional collaboration and mind-set building happens only on a poor level as there are mainly mono-disciplinary teams specialized in the respective stage's task. As a result, the waterfall model pursues a predominant technical perspective. The user perspective is considered only at the edges of the process: either by means of analyzing user or market demands and translating them into specifications *before* the actual development process starts, or by evaluating and testing the almost finished product by user feedbacks towards the end of the process. It has been shown that both ways of interacting with the user do not help to extend technical thinking, rather they have the opposite effect. While the translation of user or market demands into technical specifications helps to maintain a focal technical perspective throughout the development process, user feedbacks in the final stages mainly contribute to the elimination of discrete software errors. Changes of fundamental shortcomings in the general architecture would be extremely expensive at this late stage of development.

3.1 Overcoming the Waterfall with Agile Development

Further developments of the waterfall model pursue a more detailed view on software implementation in order to guarantee a better match between the initial specifications and the final system (V-model, see e.g. Höhn and Höppner 2008), or they integrate specific iteration phases that help to evaluate the progress continually throughout the process (Spiral model, see e.g. Boehm 1988). Yet, those concepts try to overcome the problems of the waterfall model by making the processes more complex and thus more difficult to handle. In contrast, with *agile development* (in particular *Scrum* and *Extreme Programming*), alternative approaches came up that bring in a fundamentally new perspective on organizing IT development (Beck 2003; Pichler 2008). The basic idea behind agile is to manage IT development not by rigid milestone-based process roadmaps that the team has to follow, but by a set of obligatory rules and roles in which the team can act flexibly in order to sustain learning about the project and adaptability to unexpected events. The requirement analysis is not a preceding step, but a parallel process to the actual development. The reason for this is one main feature of agile: the division of development circles into short iterative steps while the goal of each step is to produce an incremental intermediate solution that serves to generate feedback by users and specialists. These feedback loops, again, are the drivers of further development and refinement steps. Another feature is the strong focus on team collaboration and communication. For instance, in *extreme programming* there is (at least) an emphasis on programming in pairs, and *SCRUM* asks for an all-embracing one-team approach in which all disciplines involved in the development process (architects, developers, tester, documentation experts, ...) pool their resources all the way through.

In comparison with design thinking, agile shows some strong parallels: core features like "user-centricity", "iterative learning and development processes", and "extensive team communication" seem to suggest that design thinking methodology has been already introduced to IT development. On closer examination, however, one can see crucial differences. Primarily, agile rather concentrates on continuous incremental refinements than on exploring and comparing radically new solution paths. As one of the interviewees, a software designer, stated, this can lead to highly contradictory ways of progressing:

> "In agile, you downsize the problem so that they're actually small enough that people can deal with it and make progress and don't get lost. But that's a very constraining technology. (…) Agile is always looking to remove options from the table. Design thinking is always trying to keep options on the table a long as possible."

According to this, agile seems to have a tendency to avoid divergent thinking in order to maintain the overall view on what to do next. This also means that the whole aspect of problem understanding in design thinking is limited down to the trial and error approach of iterative prototyping. This is why the focal goal of design thinking to put divergent options on the table will hardly be achieved. One other difference is that there is less emphasis on interdisciplinary creative collaboration than in design thinking. Although there is a strong emphasis on team collaboration, the people involved still are technically trained thinkers. A real expansion of thinking styles within the team does not occur. Thus, the major matter of concern in agile development is to reconfigure the way in which IT development projects are managed. It is not the aim to diverge the disciplinary composition of the development team – the focus still lies on engineering teams developing the software from start to finish.

3.2 Adding New IT Design Specialists

There have been serious efforts to introduce new design specialists to IT development in order to overcome the mentioned restrictions and encourage more interdisciplinary collaboration. In general, those specialists are assumed to take on the role of the "user's advocate" within the development team. The precise role of those specialists however varies. For instance, while *user-interface designer* mainly work on user-friendly digital graphic interfaces (Mandel 2009), *interaction designer* look also on the dynamic aspects of human computer interaction (Dix et al. 2003). Designers following a *user-centered approach* intend to both generate and validate IT design decisions on the basis of comprehensive user research (general information as well as specific feedback) (Vredenburg et al. 2002), but *user-experience designers* try to design the whole experience a product conveys in a such way that current users may not even be able to imagine (Buxton 2007).

This variety of concepts shows that the possible roles of IT designers professionally dealing with user perspectives in the development process are highly divergent. For instance, in case of the user-interface or interaction design the role is clearly limited to what the software front-end actually should look and feel like. The role of user-centered design however is about both translating observable user needs into the software design and validating the software design through observable user feedbacks – as a kind of "coverage for user-friendliness" for the development team. In contrast, user experience design is much more wide-ranging because it embraces the whole software design process from specification to architecture. Accordingly, the demands on team collaboration highly vary. Whereas in user interface and interaction design, tasks can be clearly separated and carried out individually, user-interface and user experience design demand stronger collaboration between IT designers and IT engineers. In the last case, the designer would even gain a leading role in the whole process.

Those entire professional IT design concepts, and in particular user-experience design, show strong parallels to design thinking. They also emphasize learning about the user context in order to gain insights on novel solutions. They also pursue iterative and feedback-based learning, and they even apply similar techniques (e.g. observation techniques, ideation techniques, prototyping techniques). However, they differ from design thinking in so far as they concentrate on adding a new profession to the IT development team with the intention of bridging the gap between the potentials of technical thinking and a viable product by more man-power. It does not tackle the concept of collaboration or process management of the team itself. Having a user experience designer in the team would not mean that there is a guarantee for a shared problem understanding or a collaborative ideation process between design specialists, architects, and programmers. Thus, though concepts like user experience or user-centered design show strong similarities, those concepts still engender new *professional* disciplines added to the established team setting, whereas design thinking aims at influencing people meta-disciplinarily.

3.3   Design Thinking in the Context of IT Development Approaches

In sum, when comparing design thinking with the approaches to IT development discussed above, we see elementary differences:

- *Building on Diversity*: New IT design professions specialized on the user perspective mainly extend disciplinary diversity in IT development, whereas strong team-based collaboration is a core feature of agile development. Yet, a collaborative approach that tries to implement differing thinking styles in development teams as well as design thinking on a meta-disciplinary level is not explicitly addressed.
- *Exploring the problem space*: Understanding the user context has been professionalized by means of new design specialists. IT engineers still deal with the user's voice in a translated form: via specifications, which may be validated by user insights, but do not deliver the "full picture" needed for creative ideation.

Also, a team-based approach that uses a collaborative understanding of the user context to come up with radically new ideas has not been taken into account.

- *Exploring the solution space*: The whole issue of creative ideation is not explicitly included in IT development models. There could be a tendency in agile if the approach would not focus that much on incremental progress, which limits divergent thinking.
- *Iterative Alignment of both spaces*: There is a strong parallel between design thinking and agile concerning continuous iteration of user feedbacks based on prototypes throughout the process. However, a clear difference is that design thinking supports the iterative exploration of both spaces much more extensively than agile does.

4   Discussion: On the Challenges of Translating Design Thinking into Action

On a theoretical level, we have seen that design thinking can make valuable contributions to IT development and enhance the innovativeness of IT development. The question, however, how to apply it successfully to IT development is still an unsolved challenge and a central part of our ongoing research. In what follows, we will outline which elemental strategies to translate design thinking into action we have observed up to this point and will discuss essential conflicts and implementation hurdles.

Within the preceding discussion, we have conceptualized design thinking with four aspects: *exploring the problem space*, *exploring the solution space*, and *iterative alignment of both spaces* explain the workflow of design thinking from a knowledge-based viewpoint, while *building on diversity* aims predominantly at the team carrying out the workflow. One central insight of our research is that translating those aspects into practical action patterns can be carried out from two basic perspectives: the didactic perspective on the one hand, and organizational perspective on the other hand.

The guiding question of the didactic perspective is: How can one educate groups or individuals (in particular non-designers) in design thinking? We call those people who are both specialists in certain disciplines and trained in design thinking *t-shaped*, which means that one is able to look both horizontally on problems (going broad, looking for options, and being able to review the viable role of specialists within the development process) as well as vertically (bringing in the own disciplinary knowledge, solving aspects of the design problem which can be tackled through one's own expertise). In contrast, the guiding question of the organizational perspective is how one can shape those processes and structures in which people interact so that "designerly" product development will be supported. Thereby, we talk in particular about procedures and structures. While procedures in particular include the workflow triassic "observe & synthesize, ideate & prototype, and revise & refine" (see introduction), structures refer to the team diversity itself as well as to those multilayered organizational aspects that either enable or support the process, including as diverging facets as corporate cultures, reward and control systems, and supportive tools and techniques. Summing up, whereas the didactic perspective intends to foster design thinking abilities by educating people, the organizational perspective tries to adjust the contextual and managerial conditions of product development projects. Although we pursue in our research project an organizational focus and thus look mainly at the organizational factors and strategies supporting or obstructing the implementation of design thinking, we have learned that we cannot exclude the didactic perspective due to the fact that both perspectives strongly presuppose each other: An effective design thinking strategy needs well-trained people as well as an organization that supports them instead of slowing them down.

4.1   The Didactic Perspective: Educating Design Thinking Competencies

The basic methodology of design thinking didactics has been elaborated at Stanford's School of Engineering. The basic philosophy of design courses for instance at ME310 and the d.school pursues a strong project-based learning approach – following the rule: training people in problem solving beyond scientific thinking asks for an education without theory lessons. Thus, design thinking students learn in interdisciplinary teams how to tackle a given design problem by exploring its problem space with hands-on research (e.g. by inquiries, interviews, observations, self-experiments), exploring its solution space with various ideating techniques (e.g. by brainstorming, sketching, prototyping), and aligning the ideas with the reality through repeated feedback that helps to refine or revise the selected paths towards a solution. The didactic goal of this kind of training is not only to develop practical insights into the essentials of dealing creatively with wicked problems, but also to learn to build up a shared team-based understanding of the problem that is not bound or disrupted by disciplinary thinking. Design thinking education, thus, teaches to generate a mutual knowledge and experience pool that helps to facilitate team communication on a meta-disciplinary level. In the course of our first year's research, we interviewed a group of IT professionals who attended design thinking workshops within a company training program. In those workshops, the participants were asked to go into a problem space that is close to their everyday work experiences from an explicitly non-professional perspective (i.e. mainly from the user's perspective) and brought into a situation in which they had to leave technical thinking behind for a while in order to find a viable solution concept. We intended to gain several insights into the acceptance and effectiveness of design thinking trainings for IT specialists from them. We asked them how they experienced those trainings, how they value design thinking in IT development in general, and what they think about applying design thinking to their daily work routines. Conclusions from these interviews can be summarized as follows:

First, the majority of our interviewees were more skeptical about the benefit of design thinking before the workshop than afterwards. Most of them regarded the workshop experience as inspiring for their future personal work. In some cases, however, there was a tendency of reacting negatively to the use of too "flowery and cloudy" language when dealing with ambiguous situations. Also, some interviewees appreciated the creative openness of design thinking, but nevertheless doubted its viability as soon as a project is under time pressure, due to the fact that too much time would be spent *before* the development process for problem understanding. Second, almost all of our interviewees were interested in particular in the diverging aspects of design thinking, i.e. the broadening exploration of problem and solution space as a basic step of product development. They explain this interest in so far as this aspect is addressed only rudimentarily in their ordinary working background. Reasons for that lie in particularly strong tendencies towards converging activities due to established engineering-based problem solving patterns as well as common corporate pressure on coming up with results very quickly. Third, it was a striking insight that albeit most interviewees showed strong personal interest in design thinking methods, very few were able to apply it in their daily work routines. We rather gained much information about how an organization can hinder the application of design thinking. In sum, we learned that translating design thinking into action from a didactic perspective can work well on an individual or group level through a learning-by-doing approach, but it may come up against limiting factors when applying it within an organizational context.

4.2 The Organizational Perspective: Design Thinking as a Front-End Technique or as an Integrated Development Philosophy?

When it comes to the organizational perspective, we are confronted with two typical approaches: first, implementing design thinking at the very front-end of a development process, as a methodology to support the development of concepts for future products or the definition phase of a development project, and second, implementing design thinking as a comprehensive development philosophy with strong implications for organizational processes and structures. However, deciding about what design thinking strategy would work better has a lot to do with the (still open) question of how to bridge the gap between a company's need for reliable control of their processes and resource flows and an open and entrepreneurial approach to new product development. Applying design thinking in an organization presupposes good answers to this question, as it stands in contradiction to common management techniques such as stage gate innovation management that rely strongly on predefined workflows and standardized quality gates, anticipating and selecting solution paths in a restrictive manner so that explorative and creative solution paths become rather constrained. Also, employees who are generally evaluated – apart from their ability of scientific reasoning – by punctual shipment and budgeted resource plans and thus work in tight and fixed time schedules with scarce resources, get in conflicts when they deal with product development approaches that entail the uncertainty of extensive divergent thinking. One core finding of our interviews is that *those employees who report to higher hierarchy levels perceive design thinking as a risk.* For them, it was more secure to plan milestone-based development processes (with a main focus on converging thinking), even if the results may be not as innovative as they could be. Against that background it is not surprising that design thinking-centered organizations have been built up first in university labs and agencies while established companies have been dealing with fundamental change management issues. When it comes to the decision to integrate design thinking within a company's internal organizational structure, it is rather likely to be regarded as a front-end technique. The intervention into the organization is in both cases rather small as design thinking workflows are either outsourced to external design agencies (such as IDEO), semi-autonomous research labs (such as the T-labs of the Deutsche Telekom), or are restricted to selected working methods which are integrated into the established organizational workflows.

Our research has led to the insight that the more design thinking is limited to fuzzy front-end matters, the easier is its implementation because there are hardly any conflicts with established development processes and the corporate reward, reporting and controlling systems. An IT development company following a waterfall approach, for instance, could apply design thinking techniques to the specification phase, and likewise, a company pursuing an agile approach can start with design thinking-inspired concept development before beginning the actual agile development process. We could find both cases in our case studies and in the latter case the question came up whether this is the ideal form of connecting design thinking with IT development because the agile logic would meet the aspect of aligning problem and solution space through strong team communication, continuous integration of user feedback and a self-organizing process roadmap.

However, we identified one problem that arose in both cases: *the risk of a fundamental disruption of the knowledge flow between front-end design thinking and subsequent development stages* due to dissimilar communication media used in design thinking and IT development. This can be traced back to conflicting usage of prototyping: Prototypes in design thinking generally are mock-ups that support the elaboration and evaluation of product concepts with the goal of finding out which ways are right or wrong. This means that they can be very experimental and consist of any material that allows achieving information about the ideas behind the concept (and not so much about its technical specifications). Consequently they have to get handed over to the development phase and must still be translated into technical specifications and task definitions. Design thinking prototypes have the main purpose of supporting learning about the underlying product concept. In contrast, software prototypes are generally made of the same material as the final product, and are – in the case of agile – continuously iterated into the final product. Hence, they focus less on learning about the general product idea but on finding a smooth way towards a final solution without running into the wrong direction for too long. As a result of that difference, there is a serious danger of misconception regarding the use of prototypes between the protagonists of the design thinking phase and the development phase, so that a design thinker, on the one hand, does not know how to transfer their acquired knowledge to later stages, and a developer, on the other hand, does not know how to continue his work with the sort of information that is passed on to him. Therefore, the central problem of locating design thinking solely at the front-end of a development process is to find a modus operandi how to transfer design knowledge to the succeeding development stages without loosing it at the interfaces.

This is one major problem to which an integrated design thinking strategy seems to have better answers. The problem, for instance, to support a better flow of knowledge throughout the process could be answered through a comprehensive one-team approach, which means that (at least) core members of the team, who represent all available disciplines, are involved throughout the development. This would support – besides an enhanced *building on diversity* – a better mutual understanding as well as a general tacit design knowledge base in all parts of the process. This again, however, would presuppose a general project-centered organization that allows its employees to concentrate on one development project at the time instead of participating in numerous projects simultaneously. Also, there would be a call for new quality and controlling measures that do not cut off divergent thinking but still deliver an effective understanding for a project's steps forward. In particular a company's middle management would have to rely on those measures, as no manager would take on the risk of getting bad evaluations when they are a structural result of spending resources on design thinking.

5 Outlook

Overall, it is yet an open question, which ways of applying design thinking to IT development, apart from specialized agencies or research labs, are promising, and which are not. There still is a lack of good practice from which we can derive reliable insights, for instance with regard to the following questions: How do appropriate combinations of design thinking with common IT development models look like? What are the didactic and organizational implications? In which areas in IT development would design thinking be congruous? In our second year's research we will elaborate concepts responding to those questions, building on our accomplished and future case study research.

References

Beck, K.: Extreme Programming – Das Manifest. Munich, Addison-Wesley, 2003
Boehm, B.W.: A Spiral Model of Software Development and Enhancement. IEEE Computer, 21(5) May (1988) 61–72
Brown, T.: Design Thinking. Harvard Business Review June (2008) 84–92

Buxton, W.: Sketching User Experiences – Getting the Design Right and the Right Design. San Francisco, Morgan Kaufmann, 2007

Davis, A.M.; Bersoff, E.H.; Comer, E.R.: A Strategy for Comparing Alternative Software Development Life Cycle Models. IEEE Transactions On Software Engineering 14(10) October (1988) 1453–1461

Dewey, J.: How We Think. Mineola, Dover Publications, 1997

Dix, A.; Finlay, J; Abowd, G.D.; Beale, R.: Human-Computer Interaction. Harlow, Prentice Hall, 2003

Dunne, D.; Martin, R.: Design Thinking and How It Will Change Management Education: An Interview and Discussion. Academy of Management Learning and Education 5(4) (2006) 512–523

Höhn, R.; Höppner, S.: Das V-Modell XT – Grundlagen, Methodik und Anwendungen. Berlin Heidelberg New York (Springer), 2008

Krippendorf, K.: The Semantic Turn – a New Foundation for Design. Boca Raton, Routledge Chapman & Hall, 2006

Lawson, B.: How Designers Think. Oxford, Architectural Press, 2006

Lindberg, T.; Noweski, C.; Meinel, C.: Design Thinking: Zur Entwicklung eines explorativen Forschungsansatzes zu einem überprofessionellen Modell. Neuwerk, Zeitschrift für Designwissenschaft (2009) 47–54

Mandel, T.: Elements of User Interface Design. Hoboken, John Wiley & Sons, 2009

Martin, R.: The Design of Business. Boston, 2009

Newell, A; Shaw, J.C.; Simon, H.A.: The Process of Creative Thinking. In: Gruber, H.; Terrel, G.; Wertheimer, M. (eds): Contemporary Approaches to Creative Thinking. New York (1967) 63–119

Pichler, R.: Scrum – Agiles Projektmanagement erfolgreich einsetzen. Heidelberg, d.Punkt Verlag, 2007

Plattner, H.; Meinel, C.; Weinberg, U.: Design Thinking. Munich, mi-wirtschaftsbuch, 2009

Royce, W.: Managing the Development of Large Software Systems. Proc. of IEEE WESCON 26, (1970)

Rittel, H.W. J.: On the Planning Crisis – Systems Analysis of the First and Second Generation. Bedrifsökonomen 8 (1972) 390–396.

Vredenburg, K.; Isensee, S.; Righi, C.: User-Centered Design – An Integrated Approach. Upper Saddle River, Prentice Hall, 2002

A Unified Innovation Process Model for Engineering Designers and Managers

Philipp Skogstad and Larry Leifer[*]

Abstract An innovation process model, which includes the tasks of engineering designers and managers, is presented based on evidence collected from research in an engineering design curriculum. This research shows that engineering designers develop innovative breakthroughs in an evolutionary manner through insights gained during experimentation, and that these insights cannot be predicted. However, managers, experts, or other reviewers often prevent experimentation for fear of resource waste and demand predictability. This leads to conflict and can preclude progress in the worst case. The proposed model shows how the two groups interact and succeed and recommendations are provided for engineering designers and mangers.

1 Introduction

Innovation is the basis for economic growth and is therefore to be maximized. The manifesto for BusinessWeek's "Inside Innovation" section reads "we dedicate ourselves to the proposition that making innovation work is the single most important business challenge of our era". Similarly, Friedman (2005) argues that in today's "flat world", the ability to innovate successfully decides the survival of companies, communities and nations. Leadership in industry identifies innovation as the most important driver of competitiveness as well as their number one job priority (Palmisano 2006).

At the same time, 35% of CEOs call an "unsupportive culture and climate" a critical roadblock to innovation (Chapman 2006). Nussbaum, BusinessWeek's

P. Skogstad (✉) and L. Leifer
Center for Design Research, Stanford University, Building 560, 424 Panama Mall, Stanford, CA 94305, USA
e-mail: skogstad@cdr.stanford.edu; leifer@cdr.stanford.edu

[*] Principal Investigator

H. Plattner et al. (eds.), *Design Thinking: Understand – Improve – Apply*, Understanding Innovation, DOI 10.1007/978-3-642-13757-0_2, © Springer-Verlag Berlin Heidelberg 2011 former editor-in-chief, described the situation in a speech at the Royal College of Art (RCA) in London (2007) as follows:

> "There are two great barriers to innovation and design in the world today. Ignorant CEOs and ignorant designers. Both groups are well-intentioned and well-dressed – in their own ways – but both can be pretty dangerous characters."

Designers create innovations by generating new ideas, demonstrating their feasibility and then developing them to full functionality, ready for production. Managers steer the design process by allocating resources based on their judgment of the merits of each idea. They also have to ensure that value is created for shareholders. The two groups have different approaches to succeeding at their tasks and often do not understand each other's actions and decisions. This has a negative impact on the ability of each group to do its job.

It was the aim of this research to further the understanding of **how innovation is accomplished and how the achievement of innovation can be hindered or supported by managers and designers**. The results can guide both groups on how, when and where they can become helpful characters that foster innovation.

Research in the context of an engineering design curriculum was performed in order to develop this understanding. Case studies of how designers arrived at their solutions revealed that significant insights, which allowed advancement of the designs, were typically gained while building and testing a possible approach, rather than while planning it, and that these insights were often unexpected. This suggests that in order to create new concepts, designers must go beyond the theoretical phase and implement their ideas so they can learn from their experiments to create new ideas and advance the design. The fact that many of the important insights were unexpected suggests that designers have limited ability to plan for insight discovery. Therefore, it can be challenging for designers to justify their actions and use of resources, before they actually build and test.

In several instances, the designers gained important insights while they built and tested ideas despite advice from their teachers (i.e. managers) or experts not to build or test (based on the preconception that the outcome was known a priori, and therefore such activity would be wasteful). Hence, if managers are not convinced by the merits of an idea, and successfully prevent designers from building and testing it, they block bar the designers from gaining insights necessary to advance the design. In such cases, managers block the use of resources for fear of wasting time and money. Indirectly, however, they block innovation and accomplish the opposite of what they intend.

Following the methodology suggested for building theory from case study research (Eisenhardt 1989), a unified innovation process model was devised. This model provides a theoretical explanation for the hypotheses generated through case study research and interviews. Unlike other models from innovation management or engineering design, it incorporates the actions of both designers and managers. The model is therefore expected to help each side to better understand the other side's behavior, which should make both managers and designers less ignorant.

2 Unified Innovation Process Model for Engineering Designers and Managers

The unified innovation process model for engineering designers and managers (henceforth 'model') shown in Fig. 1 was developed. It depicts the design process and explains how its participants' actions affect it. The model represents the kernel of the design process and shows where reviewers interrupt its flow and can be used as a communication tool by designers and managers, and as an instrumentation map by design researchers.

At the core of the model are three activity functions: 'Plan', 'Execute', and 'Synthesize'. All phases of the design process, and the activities they entail, can be abstracted to these three activities. The entire string represents the design process from start to finish – going from a 'Wish' (some form of prompt, need, or problem) to a 'Solution'.

At the micro level, the three activity functions, Plan, Execute, and Synthesize occur repetitively during every phase of the design process. Table 1 demonstrates their applicability in the needfinding, brainstorming, prototyping and testing phases.

At the macro (project) level, planning is associated with needfinding, idea generation, brainstorming, and the plotting of an approach. Going into this stage, designers have a rough idea of what they want, and coming out of it, they have a plan to tackle the problem with their know-how. The plan usually consists of one or more concrete ideas, a division of labor, and sometimes includes contingency planning in case of failure. Once armed with a plan, and management consent if needed, designers begin to execute. As its name implies, execution is where the work gets done. Drawings are crafted, and prototypes are built, modeled, machined, sculpted or coded. 'Getting real' is the central theme for the execution function; this is where designers channel their ideas from their heads into their hands, birthing them into the world and making them testable. Last in the design process chain is the synthesis activity. Synthesis is the gathering of the fruits from execution to form the output solution. Synthesis occurs in many different ways and typically includes assembly of the parts into a whole system and testing.

The three-activity string (Plan, Execute, Synthesize) is a universal kernel of the design process. Design activity during all phases can be abstracted to these three

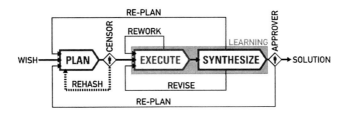

Fig. 1 'Unified Innovation Process Model for Engineering Designers and Managers' depicting the kernel of the design process and where reviewers interrupt its flow

Table 1 Examples of actions performed during each activity at the micro (phase) level to show the universal applicability of the model at this level

Phase	PLAN	EXECUTE	SYNTHESIZE
NEED FIND & BENCHMARK	Who to observe? What to observe?	Observe and collect data	Develop PoV & define need or problem
BRAINSTORM	What is a possible solution?	Articulate idea	Synthesize own ideas with ideas of others
PROTOTYPE	How to manufacture? What tools to use?	Manufacture	Assemble with other parts
TEST	What to test? How to test?	Perform test	Analyze result & determine if wish is satisfied

fundamental steps. The examples also show that activity strings are actually nested within one another; for every activity at one level, there is one or more entire activity string included at lower levels in a recursive pattern. The time constant of one traversal through the entire activity string can therefore range from a few seconds for the generation of an idea during brainstorming to multiple years in the case of designing and building a new aircraft.

Designers create new concepts through consideration of new knowledge or new combinations of existing knowledge. However, to reach past the known or obvious, designers need at least one new useful insight. Designers must therefore maximize the probability of gaining the necessary insight(s), to maximize the probability for success. Insights are new knowledge that is gained through study or experience, and adapted to advance the design. The case and interview data presented later show that most insights are discovered while designers try an idea rather than debate it. This occurs during the execute and synthesize activities rather than during the plan activity.

2.1 Designer-Initiated Feedback Pathways

Iteration and feedback are important because they allow designers to apply their insights to advance the design. Hence, the model is further enhanced to express the circular nature of design by means of feedback pathways.

Largest of the three feedback pathways, the 're-plan' pathway extends from the synthesis stage to the input of the planning phase. Re-planning signifies the action taken by designers when the results gained during synthesis are so different from what was expected that designers must return to planning to change their approach. This pathway is engaged when the problems in synthesis are large in scope and require a reconsideration of 'everything'. An example for this at the macro level is when the project aim changes mid-development-cycle. Similarly, this happens at the micro level, when for example a 'wild' idea, such as relying on gravity and friction as a fastening method, was followed but then failed in synthesis, and no contingency plans had been made beforehand. In these cases, new knowledge is brought back to the planning phase and the design process restarts.

The 'revise' pathway, like the 're-plan' pathway, reads from the synthesis stage. Instead of feeding into the planning phase, however, it modifies the execution activity. Revision occurs when the results of synthesis are not sufficient to qualify as a solution, but they are not so far off that the overall approach must be changed.

Examples for this can be found at the macro level: if a 'wild' idea has failed, but a contingency plan was made, the execution and synthesis simply need to be repeated using the alternative approach. In a similar fashion, this happens at the micro level if, for example, during prototyping, the adhesive used to fasten two components heats up and dissolves during normal operation of the system. In this case, the specifications for the adhesive are amended, but the overall plan does not need to change. The execution must simply be repeated with a different adhesive that is designed for higher operating temperatures.

Most frequently engaged is the 'rework' pathway, which serves as a feedback mechanism to the execution activity only. Reworking is the process of re-executing until the output is satisfactory enough to advance to synthesis. This feedback pathway is the most frequently traveled due to the highly unpredictable nature of activities that occur inside the execution activity.

2.2 Reviewer-Initiated Feedback Pathways and Gates

Reviewers intercept the design process at two gate points: after the plan activity, when they give permission to execute the proposed approach, and at the end of the design process, when they either accept the proposed design as the solution to their wish or require a redesign. These reviewers are external to the design team. They are managers, advisors, experts, coaches, teachers, and clients. At these two gate points, any of them can initiate two additional feedback pathways.

The largest reviewer-initiated feedback pathway is that created by the approver. The approver judges whether the output of the design process satisfies the original wish. If the approver is satisfied by the proposed solution, then the design process is finished and the proposed solution becomes the solution. However, if the approver is not satisfied with the solution, then the 'Re-Plan' feedback pathway is activated and the designers have to return to the plan activity and reconsider their approach. Regardless of the amount of feedback the approver provides when sending the designers back to the plan activity, the designers return to the plan activity with more experience. The traversal of the execute and synthesize activities allowed them to gain insights, which they can apply in their redesign efforts.

On the other hand, designers are deprived of the opportunity to gain insights when the 'Rehash' feedback pathway is activated by a 'Censor'. Censors are people with the authority or influence to prevent the design team from moving certain ideas to execution. They make decisions and recommendations based on their judgment of the proposed plan. Undoubtedly, these censors want to help the designers by ensuring that resources are only spent on economically or technologically feasible ideas. However, they restrict the ability of the designers to test novel ideas and to make the discoveries that lead to the necessary insights. When an idea is censored, the designers will rehash the plan activity. In this case, the designers will go through the planning process again but without significant new information. It is therefore unlikely that the new plan will be significantly better.

Censors can only avoid this problem if they provide the designers with detailed feedback and information, which will result in a significantly improved plan. However, reviewers can also err. In particular, if they fail to recognize that an idea falls outside the bounds of their own limited experience and expertise, or do not see that their expertise acts as a constraining mental set, then they risk killing potentially viable ideas before they can be proven. In the worst case, censors hold designers hostage in a planning loop by forcing them to rehash the plan activity without allowing for the development of new insights. They stifle the possibility for discovery, insight, project progress and innovation. In the process, they can also damage designer morale.

The censor gate and rehash feedback pathway are the final piece of the model. Even though self-censorship by designers certainly occurs and is an important issue, it is not generally externally observable. The only way to overcome self-censorship is by making designers understand that they must transition to the execute activity to gain insights and by encouraging this transition.

3 Research Methodology

Stanford University's 'Mechanical Engineering 310 – Project-Based Engineering Design, Innovation & Development' (henceforth '310'), a graduate level project-based curriculum, served as a living laboratory for this research. Over fifty design teams participating in the curriculum were studied from multiple perspectives.

Multiple research methods and data streams were combined for the investigation. The nature of the projects and the structure of the teams closely resemble the working mode of start-ups and "tiger teams" (Wheelwright and Clark 1992) in industry. Like many Silicon Valley initiatives, design teams start with a vague idea of an area that allows for the creation of innovation. The problem briefs are purposely phrased broadly to challenge the students to determine, isolate, and pursue a particular opportunity for innovation. Student teams tackle the industry-posed problems over the course of 7 months, and develop fully functional product prototypes of their solutions. Several milestones, intermediate prototype reviews with a teaching team and presentations to industry help structure the project and ensure that results fulfill expectations.

In this research, the design process interactions were studied from the points of view of a student/designer, teaching assistant/project manager, instructor/manager or partner, and remote executive. There are few opportunities to live all of these roles as an embedded researcher. In this case, the researcher was able to spend at least one year performing each role with full responsibility. This experience provided inside knowledge of actions, perceptions, and situations that would be inaccessible to an outside observer. The combination of insights from this multitude of perspectives is a distinguishing characteristic of this research. The multi-perspective protocol suits the dual goal of understanding the design activity as design synthesis and as management analysis. It allows the researcher to see the entire 'gestalt' of a process that often depends on unobserved subtleties or unspoken perceptions, which only an insider can access.

The ultimate goal of this research is to increase innovative performance. Proper measurement of performance is therefore important. Unfortunately, objective performance measurement is particularly difficult to achieve in a design context. Definition and measurement of design performance is subjective, analogous to the adage, 'beauty is in the eye of the beholder'; solutions that might seem trivial to one person could appear profound to another. To further complicate matters, performance relates not only to the outcome of the design process, but also to the process itself. It can look drastically different from the perspective of a team member vis-à-vis that of a manager. To address this challenge, multiple indicators of performance were tracked. In accordance with the goals of this research, performance is measured from the perspectives of different stakeholders. The different performance indicators are:

1. Outcome performance measurement by external judges (independent assessment of result)
2. Outcome performance measurement by designers who created design (self-reported assessment of result)
3. Design process performance measurement by designers using Team Diagnostic survey (self-reported assessment of process, adapted from Wageman et al. 2005)
4. Combined outcome and process performance measurement by reviewers based on course grades (manager's combined assessment of process and result)

These four different methods for measuring design performance can be expected to reveal which factors are important for each stakeholder and how they relate to the design process variables observed in this study.

The research began without preconceived hypotheses. Based on the observations and interviews gathered, the research question of 'how do designers create new concepts and how can managers support or hinder the design process' was formulated. To answer this question, four cases of top-performance were selected for detailed analysis using the documentation created by the designers. Data from semi-structured interviews with designers and observations by an embedded research complement the data. As suggested by Eisenhardt (1989), the analysis was performed within and across cases. This process adds a general validity to the findings, which is necessary for credible theory building. The cases were first analyzed internally and then examined for common patterns across cases.

4   Designers Gain Necessary Insights by Experimenting

The following analysis of project cases indicates that designers create new concepts by assembling insights. It was found that they gain key insights efficiently through learning by doing (or executing) rather than through theoretical pondering (or planning) of the merits of an idea. Based on the analysis, it is hypothesized that designers who move from planning to execution most frequently and adaptively will perform best in generating new concepts.

4.1   Case A: Paper Bike

The 310 course begins with a 2 week-long design challenge that requires students to design, build, and race a vehicle constructed from paper or cardboard. The rules of the design challenge change every year while the scoring remains essentially the same – as a combination of the vehicle's weight and the race completion time. The design challenge includes two reviews by the teaching team: one review at the end of the first week and a second review the day before the race. This case takes a close look at the design process of the team that won the competition in 2003/2004.

Initially, the team began with a theoretical approach using morphological analysis and Pugh charts as design tools.

> "The results showed that the 'toboggan' style bike was the best design, primarily because it was the most reliable (least number of parts), was simple to operate for the driver, was lightweight, and could be built the fastest. However a quick test revealed that there was no way to pull a cardboard toboggan around the Quad, so that design was eliminated."

Based on the finding from the test, the team took a more experimental approach to the problem and performed tests with simple prototypes derived from existing products.

"Benchmarking for the frame design primarily consisted of evaluating the proof of concept wheelchair design that was supplied by the teaching team. The team spent several hours walking around the Quad, evaluating push versus pull approaches. The passenger driver interface and protocol were also evaluated for strengths and weaknesses. This effort resulted in three conclusions:

- It was more comfortable to have something in front when blind
- The passenger could see best when in front (pushed)
- It is difficult to feel tactile instructions with the hands if they are busy pushing the bike

The team thus focused its efforts on a jogger stroller style bike and quickly began building a bike. Moving parts and friction, as encountered at the wheel axle interface, represented a particularly difficult engineering challenge. The problem was tackled as follows:

"The initial wheel design was created after a very short, informal brainstorming session. No formal concept selection tools were used. After examining the available materials, an excellent axle/hub pair were selected that provided minimal running clearance between the hub and axle. The overall goal of the design was to reduce weight, so a seemingly ingenious design of a small diameter solid wheel was selected."

"The initial prototype wheels were tested on the prototype frame. While the test was essentially a 'failure', the test results brought to light several key points..."

"The wheel redesign effort proceeded in a structured manner, with a brainstorming session generating several different wheel designs. The relative weight of each of these designs was calculated to select the best design. Five basic wheel designs were developed. The lightest weight wheel was determined to be the laminated spoke design with weight reducing holes."

"[However,] the team had concerns relative to the structural robustness of the cored wheel designs. The concern was whether the weight reducing holes would cause the wheels to fail during either testing or the actual race. To reduce the perceived risk of this design, the team fabricated enough laminations for three complete sets of wheels: It was agreed that the final wheel selection would occur after the entire bike was tested."

"The wheel testing also revealed that the cardboard/cardboard interface was perfectly acceptable for the race conditions. The hub/axle interface was inspected prior and post two complete practice runs of the entire racecourse [sic] at race speed. No change to the interface was discernable, so the final wheel configuration did not include any tape or added lubricants."

The above account of the team's process shows that the designers relied on testing their ideas in practice, and that by doing so, they gained important insights, which would not have been possible with a theoretical approach. Through building and testing, the team discovered structural weaknesses and learned that the actual weight of the built vehicle was higher than the designed weight. Since the team had worked with hardware early in the process, these insights were gained in time to make major revisions before the day of the race. This decision to test early, and thus have time for revisions, provided the winning team with an important competitive advantage.

In the report, the team describes its philosophy as follows:

"Team Telestroller operated under one simple guiding principle: 'I haven't built a paper bike before. Have you? Crap-it-type-it and let's see if it works.' It was concluded early on that no one on the team had expert knowledge in the realm of paper bike design and fabrication. So, instead of spending hours debating the merits of different design ideas, the team would quickly mock up crude prototypes and test them. A lot of insight was gained from these crap-it-type exercises, which greatly enhanced the final design resulting in the construction of a 100% paper bike (driver/passenger interface not included)."

Following this philosophy, the team designed and fabricated a vehicle during week one of the project and was able to test it five days after the project started. This put the team ahead of other teams who put their effort into the detailed design, CAD work and careful manufacturing of components rather than simply assembling a prototype vehicle.

4.2   Case B: Convertible Experience

One industry project challenged the students to redesign the convertible automobile experience by eliminating the wind screen behind the front seats because it disturbs the aesthetics, blocks access to the rear seats and is tedious to handle. Even though the resulting design is not (yet) in production, the carmaker, which brought the challenge, has invested in patenting to protect it. In addition, the team received the highest grade in the class for that year.

The designers began by testing a number of obvious solutions while discarding a revolutionary idea as silly. When they actually tested the 'silly' idea, they found that it was a solution that exceeded all expectations.

"The team performed a plethora of tests designed to improve the convertible experience on the path towards their final solution [using a team member's personal convertible]. These tests included numerous iterations of Blowers, Flaps, Wings, Redirectors, Scoops, Tubing, Noise Cancellation, Vortex Generators, Nose Flow Dampers, and Reactive Concepts."

"In short, none of these tests provided remarkable results when tested on the [ABC]. [...] However, the tests revealed important lessons in convertible airflow. Namely:

- It is virtually impossible to change the general flow over the entire car with small structures
- Any flow-inducing blower system must be very powerful
- Small flaps do very little to produce consistent changes
- Head loss drastically reduces the effectiveness of proactive ducting concepts
- Current adaptive filtering technology is unable to cancel wind noise
- Vortex generators produce no noticeable effect
- Air can be redirected with much of its original energy
- User feel can be substantially improved with shielding around the head"

One member of the design team had previously suggested during a brainstorm that they should simply get rid of the windshield. However, this idea was discarded

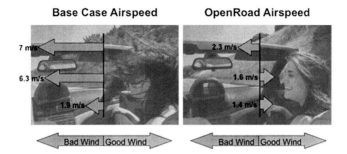

Fig. 2 Comparison of final design with base case

as silly. Under pressure, because none of the ideas tested up to that point had led to the desired effect, and having acquired an understanding of airflow and its perception by the occupants of the vehicle, the team decided to reconsider this idea carefully. Said designer convinced the design team to puncture a hole in the middle of the windshield of a water tunnel model after all other tests were completed and the model was no longer needed.

> "The water channel tests yielded an important discovery. This was the first indication that placing a vent or hole in the windshield could possibly combat recirculation into the front of the cabin."

Encouraged by the insights gained from this simple experiment, the designers decided to further test the idea by cutting a hole into the windshield of a brand-new (126 miles on odometer) luxury (more than $45,000) convertible car. Road tests with initially crude prototypes confirmed the expectations created in the water tunnel and the hole in the windshield was refined into a roadworthy solution that could be sold to customers (Fig. 2).

This case shows that even a 'silly' idea should not necessarily be discarded without at first testing it in a simple and quick manner. Initially, the idea seemed too crazy even to the designers themselves. However, when they actually tested a prototype based on this unconventional idea, the result exceeded all expectations. The designers write in their design report:

> "The key to [...] development is duct tape and a tool-chest. The team kept at least a few rolls of tape and a complete toolkit in the vehicle at all times, allowing for most any sort of rapid roadside prototyping that was necessary. Furthermore, the team kept a small stock of raw materials, such as felt, foam core, metal, and acrylic scraps, in the vehicle to handle any unanticipated needs that may arise during testing. Roadside prototyping is an important part of the development process because many of the best ideas or changes are likely to be realized in the middle of the testing itself, and so should be prototyped as immediately as possible before they are forgotten."

This account underlines the importance of experimentation to gain insights and the fact that many insights cannot be planned for.

4.3 Case C: Task Management Software

In 2005/2006, the 310 curriculum was cloned at the University of St. Gallen, Switzerland (Skogstad et al. 2008). The students in this course were tasked with designing a software system to manage tasks in an enterprise environment. The following case describes how the designers gained key insights while building and testing prototypes and were inspired while experimenting with Lego™ pieces. The resulting solution exceeded all expectations of the company that provided the design challenge and shows how experimentation with seemingly unrelated tools can provide key insights.

The designers started with extensive literature searches, user surveys, and benchmarking of existing technologies. While benchmarking, they encountered 30boxes, a social calendar tool, which provided the inspiration for the first part of their solution, the so-called the BlinxBar.

While creating the input mask, the designers discovered that appointments and tasks have many similarities. These similarities could be used to simplify the management of tasks and appointments drastically. Furthermore, when the designers performed tests, they gained additional key insights.

> "We invited five students for our user test. We first explained them the principles of 30boxes. Then we gave them a list of activities that these students had to put into their agenda. Some of these were tasks and some were appointments as defined in Outlook. For comparative reasons, we wanted the test users to also write down tasks in the tagging system with pen and paper as well as to use Microsoft Outlook to record tasks and appointments. [...] Blinx! then asked the users, what were their reactions after working on Outlook vs. paper and pen. Our test results and findings were astounding:

- Quality of data recorded with MS outlook was lower than with other methods; user often chose the wrong functions (calendar, task manager, e-mail) and explained "I wanna try like this".
- Many of the users had little experience with MS Outlook and were confident with the tagging method more quickly.
- When recording tasks with MS Outlook, users seldom differentiated between the two separate Outlook functions calendar and task manager.
- Users had different priority judgment for the wedding date: no priority for men, highest priority for women."

The results of the user tests made the designers reconsider tasks and appointments as activities, which paved the way to the proposed enterprise task management system solution.

> "The BlinxBar and the Calendar Module provided a solution for a personal task management system, whereby mainly simple activities are handled. Therefore, two questions were raised:
>
> How can more complex activities be handled? [...]
>
> How can team collaboration be supported?"
>
> "During the development of the BlinxBar, there was an intense discussion about workflow integration for more complex standard activities. However, since the focus of the project lies

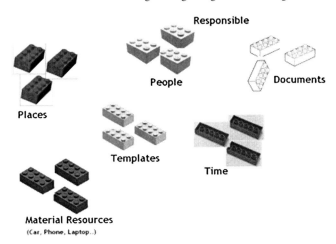

Fig. 3 Lego™ pieces were used to simulate the attributes of complex tasks. The different colors stand for different kinds of attributes (such as place, time, resources, documents, etc.). This visualization provided the inspiration for a task management interface, which assembles tasks from interchangeable and reusable activities. Each block can be fit with any other block and is interchangeable so that tasks may be modified for reuse without the need for recreating it. For example, a weekly meeting preparation task may be updated for each week by modifying specific documents that are needed and the time of the meeting without the need to modify the other attributes such as place and responsible persons

on unstructured tasks this would have been insufficient, the user could only handle standard, and therefore structured tasks. Through the idea of a personal workflow management tool, we finally developed our BlinxBuffet based on activity patterns."

"Why are they called activity pattern? The target is to provide flexible and not fixed patterns of activities. It is a pattern, which can be reused and adapted to similar situations. It was not meant to get unstructured tasks into a fix structured form as provided by predefined workflows, but rather to keep an activity pattern flexible for any changes within the lifecycle. Furthermore, since one unstructured task is never identical to the last one (otherwise it would be a structured task), it allows the user to adapt a similar activity pattern, which someone else has already created, to his or her current needs."

"By first creating a Lego prototype, we visualized our ideas to discuss them in detail."

"At this point, we found our idea." (Fig. 3)

Even though the team was working on the design of a software interface that did not involve any hardware, the students used hardware to physically represent and manipulate the attributes of activities. The interaction with the Lego™ pieces inspired the design of the final interface and the assembly of tasks from interchangeable attributes (Fig. 4).

In this case, the designers gained important insights during user testing and from having tried a new toolset. The work with presumably unrelated tools – software versus physical Lego™ pieces – provided the inspiration for a simple and effective representation. The designers would not likely have come up with this idea if they

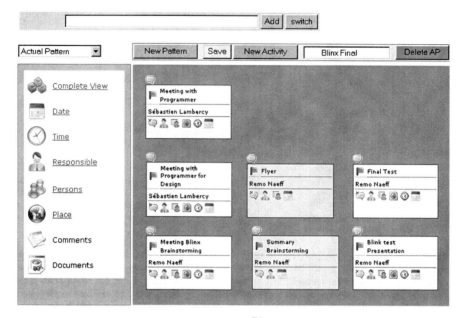

Fig. 4 Task Management Interface inspired by Lego™ pieces that represent attributes, which are interchangeable and can be assembled into a task

had stuck to using the tools that they were taught and expected to use. The interface and visualization the team developed is now being considered for implementation as a component in enterprise software.

4.4 Cross-case Analysis Reveals Pattern

These and other cases that were looked at have in common that the designers had their breakthrough after they learned something new. The insights were often unexpected and were gained through prototyping and testing ideas rather than through pondering the theoretical merits of ideas. The designers would likely not have created such innovative outcomes if they had not switched modes from thinking about ideas to prototyping and testing them.

A designer who worked on the task management software project said in an interview:

> I still remember, when we did the first survey at the university up on the hill. It was amazing that nobody was able to recognize a text multiple times in the same way with the same pattern. Instead, everyone treats information differently. I believe that we found many results in this test, which were unpredictable. And we thus took a different path. That was important. For sure.

Similarly, the idea of cutting a hole in a complete car to fix a problem (Case B) defies traditional wisdom or even common sense. However, to create new concepts it is necessary to reach beyond what was considered possible and made sense in the past. Although conventional wisdom is often right, in some instances, it is wrong or incorrectly applied. Unfortunately, it is not possible to know this without testing and therefore crazy ideas must be tested to avoid stagnation.

Critics may argue that prototyping and testing many ideas results in many failures. This is not, however, a waste of time and resources. Case C shows that failures are also learning opportunities and therefore help pave the path to success. Thomas Edison, unarguably one of the most creative inventors of all times, is attributed the quotes:

> "Results? Why, man, I have gotten lots of results! If I find 10,000 ways something won't work, I haven't failed. I am not discouraged, because every wrong attempt discarded is often a step forward. ..."
>
> "Just because something doesn't do what you planned it to do in the first place doesn't mean it's useless. ..."

Simonton (1999) found that the greatest historical artists, scientists, and composers did not have any lower failure rates than their contemporaries but they simply did more. This means that the probability of one success increases as more ideas are tested. Venture capitalists and financial investors rely on this simple fact to diversify their risk.

Drucker, who described seven sources of innovation, writes that innovation is "conceptual and perceptual" and that "would-be innovators must also go out and look, ask, and listen" to gain the insights that will lead to new ideas (1998). Hargadon and Sutton (2000) explain that new ideas are typically old ideas, which are applied in new contexts or new ways. Based on their study of innovation powerhouses, they concluded that the most successful innovators are "knowledge brokers" who transfer existing ideas to new contexts. They also found that testing ideas "teaches brokers valuable lessons, even when an idea is a complete flop". They quote Thomas Edison as having said: "The real measure of success is the number of experiments that can be crowded into 24 h." This suggests that designers excel when they are able to gather and test ideas rapidly.

If Edison is right, management should encourage designers to experiment as much and as often as possible. However, every prototype and test, whether the outcome aligns with predictions or not, is only useful if the results lead to an insight, which is adapted to advance the design. This is highlighted in the "Theory of Adaptive Design Expertise" (Neeley 2007).

4.5   Execution Hypothesis

The four cases demonstrate that the design process is a process of creating opportunities to gain new insights, and of advancing the design by adapting these insights. Those insights are gained through learning by experimenting. Therefore, if designers can increase their learning rate, they will have more insights at their disposal, which they can then assemble into new concepts.

The case analyses revealed that most insights were gained during prototyping and testing rather than theoretical deliberations. This finding suggests that it is important for designers to move from debating (or planning) to doing (or executing) in order to maximize learning and discovery.

The resulting Execution Hypothesis is:

Designers who move from planning to execution most frequently and adaptively will perform best in new concept generation.

5 Reviewers Often Discourage Experimenting

Reviewers such as managers or experts often discourage execution, thereby potentially preventing innovation, as shown by the following review of the cases described before.

5.1 Case A: Paper Bike

The design team that constructed the winning paper bike in 2003/2004 discovered during testing that the interface between the axle and the wheel hub provides opportunities for major improvement. In order to reduce the weight penalty due to non-paper weight, the designers considered eliminating lubricants and traditional bearings in favor of a simple cardboard-cardboard interface. Even though some members of the design team were initially skeptical about this, the designers tested this prior to the race, and found the design to be sufficiently strong for the stresses expected during the race.

However, during the review session on the day before the race, the teaching team expressed strong concerns regarding the reliability of the design. One member of the teaching team even urged the designers to redesign the interface before the race, predicting that the design would fail. Although the designers considered this, they trusted their test results and finished the race victoriously with their novel design. In the epilogue of their report, the designers write:

"Lastly, I wish there was a meaningful way to have the design review after the race instead of before. While I understand the need to have a milestone prior to the race to preclude procrastination, there were several concerns expressed about the design and skepticism about whether it would survive the race. Our team specifically worked to push the design envelope with a non-traditional design. We chose not to use bearings or lubricants, but only after several testing the concept. We eliminated much of the frame tubing to reduce the weight, and had tested the design to ensure it was strong enough. Yet several of the "wishes" from the design review would have pushed us back to a more traditional design, based on the fear of failures during the race. It was pointed out that race conditions were very difficult to duplicate or simulate in testing, so in essence our testing did not prove that the design would work. In the end our bike performed perfectly during the race, even surviving an unplanned "Lawrence Lap". Presenting the design after the race would have given us test results from the race to validate that our design was adequate and sufficient to meet the requirements of the race. Unfortunately it is a "chicken and the egg" scenario, so I do not know if there is a simple way to resolve this."

Had the designers not tested the design before the review, it is likely that the critique by the teaching team, whose members are considered experts and authorities, would have killed this new concept. The associated lost learning opportunity would have impacted not just this team, but many future teams as well, as the majority of design teams used the same design during the following years.

5.2 Case B: Convertible Experience

The design team that worked on the convertible experience project initially received great help from the carmaker's engineers, who ran several simulations for the team on their CFD computers. Each of these simulations takes about one day to complete. However, when the designers asked the company's engineers to run a simulation on a 'hole in the windshield', they were refused the help because the idea was too outlandish. Only after the designers had successfully shown the merit of their concept in reality, was the concept given time on the CFD computer. After the final presentation, one engineer from the company stated that "We couldn't have done this", referring to the fact that the organizational make up of the company precludes such a 'crazy' idea from being implemented or even tested. This indicates that at the company, reviewers and experts would likely have prevented the idea from being validated based on limited conventional wisdom or for fear of embarrassment if it failed.

Similarly, when the designers wanted to cut a hole into the windshield of the car, they consulted with various experts for help with the cut. The designers write:

> "The team had researched with countless experts the process of cutting windshield glass, and had been told that it simply wouldn't work. Nonetheless, the team recognized that removal of the windshield would be destructive regardless, so they took the opportunity to attempt a cut. Using a diamond coated cutting disc at 6,000 rpm in a Dremel tool, cooled by flowing water from a small pump over the windshield, this imperfect process yielded an entirely usable and clean hole with only a few cracks propagating from the corners of the cut."

This shows that even experts may err in knowledge and judgment, and advise against a course of action because they do not understand the goal behind it. Wiley (1998) writes that "novices may outperform experts in conditions in which experts cannot make use of their domain knowledge". She continues saying that "experts can be outperformed by novices when a new task or context runs counter to highly proceduralized behaviors. Experts perform worse than novices when a shift from standard means of representation is required or when a standard response is inappropriate." In experiments, Wiley found also that "domain knowledge can indeed act as a mental set and promote fixation [...] on the incorrect solutions, preventing a broad search of the solution space" (1998). This suggests that experts can inadvertently prevent viable ideas from being tested based on their limited and sometimes erroneous preconceptions. In doing so, they prematurely lay to rest potentially successful new concepts and prevent designers from gaining necessary insights.

5.3 Reviewers Can Encourage Experimenting as Exemplified by Case C: Task Management Software

The interface for the task management software system designed by the team of management students in case C was inspired by Lego^{TM} pieces. It is unlikely that software engineers would use a hardware toy to prototype an interface or that managers would consider representing attributes of a business task with toy pieces. However, in this case, the designers were encouraged to venture out into uncharted territory and to try unproven ideas with atypical tools in order to create new concepts.

The following excerpts from interviews with student designers show the importance of being allowed the freedom to try, and even more importantly, to be encouraged to try.

> Student: Also that the environment allowed for all the "crazy ideas". We were told: "Yes, just do it", especially "the dark horse", "Just do something even if it is not useful". I believe that therefore you are not under the pressure that "You have to do it this way from the beginning" and that one is given the room for one's own ideas."
>
> Interviewer: So you would say that the possibility to make mistakes has helped?
>
> Student: Yes. Yes, it is so unusual for university. Here you always have to memorize everything and understand and always do it right – otherwise you have to leave. And this was finally a course where you can really do what you want to. Of course, there was a goal given, but that did not mean that we worked too goal focused. We at first simply just did something…
>
> Interviewer: This just doing something… Would you say that this "just doing something" had an impact on trying?
>
> Student: Yes, for sure. Crafting and when we had an idea, we went to the crafts stores right away and bought something and then we put it together and saw it (for example) did not work.

Another student alluded to this as follows:

> We did not have the fixed target given from the top down as in "you do this and that". No. It was the uniqueness of the project that we could develop on our own. That ideas come from everywhere and had to be filtered. It was important that we had the freedom to do what we wanted to without fear. And this [freedom] was important.

The importance of the reviewers' openness to new ideas and the ability of designers to trust them were described by a third student designer:

> The relationship of the teaching team to the students [was important], because through it, it was clearly communicated that you can come round at any time. There is a communication, which gets across relatively clearly that you can come by at any time. For example walk

into Barbara's [Note: a member of the teaching team] office. The teaching team allows you to present solutions for a problem, which have not been thought through yet. [...] Everyone always says "there are no dumb questions". But the [trust and openness] really create the environment where you are finally willing to let out the dumb. Elsewhere, you don't do it.

These comments suggest that the designers would not have been as successful if they had operated in the regular framework: under close supervision by reviewers and experts who rely on traditional tools, are constrained by conventional wisdom, and maintain the authority to kill an idea before it is tested. However, they also show that reviewers can have a positive effect by encouraging experimentation and empowering the designers to venture into new territory.

5.4 Cross-Case Analysis Reveals Pattern

In Cases A and B, the designers succeeded by pursuing approaches that experts and other reviewers had explicitly advised them not to pursue. In several instances, the teaching team and experts were limited by their knowledge and experience, which led to premature judgments, constrained the perceivable solution space, and made them wary of new and unproven concepts. The only way to convince the experts in these cases was by demonstrating the functionality in reality. This, however, may not be possible if the reviewers or experts have the authority to stop the designers from executing and testing an idea.

Furthermore, even though reviewers and experts may already know the immediate result of a proposed idea, they cannot imagine the indirect lessons, which can be learned from testing an idea. Therefore, they may have to let designers go down the 'wrong' path for some time to gain the insights that allow for the creation of new concepts. On the other hand, reviewers can help designers by encouraging and empowering them to experiment. The interviews from Case C show that the reviewers had encouraged experimentation and deferred judgment until test results were known. Here, the designers succeeded when they went beyond their traditional toolset and tried something unusual. Thus, reviewers and experts must recognize that designers will only create more standard results if they use only standard tools and practices. Reviewers and managers must also acknowledge that experimentation with new ideas comes with a lot of failure and that failure should not be perceived as negative. The students at the University of St. Gallen especially emphasized this. One student said:

Student: The individual prototypes and papers, which we did were often only attempts. We had that freedom that things could go wrong sometimes. I believe that is very important. Ok, maybe did not accomplish everything but one learns from it.

Interviewer: Fail early and fail often – and succeed sooner?

Student: Exactly. I cannot let that happen in other courses. In other courses, in a paper, I am afraid that it is directly reflected in the grade.

In several interviews, the students declared that being given a second chance allowed them to take risks, which they were unable to take in other classes. They argued that in other classes, they have one submission deadline with no feedback beforehand and whatever they turn in seals the grade. Therefore, they play things safe and simply regurgitate what they were told while taking as little risk as possible. In this class, on the other hand, they realized that they would have another chance to make things right and thus could try out ideas, which they were unsure about. The students also commented on the positive attitude of the teaching team towards failure. They explained that in other courses, failures were turned into "burn marks" whereas in this class they were almost celebrated. Here, a failure counted like a success if it was carefully analyzed and lessons were learned and insights gained from it. They also felt that the teaching team understood that failures were a necessary part of operating at the cutting edge of new discovery and not the result of a lack of planning or thinking. It is therefore important that reviewers appreciate failures as possibly helpful to the advancement of the design, and that they communicate this to the designers.

Finally, reviewers must consider the motivational impact of their feedback on designers in addition to its effect on the ability to execute. One student responded to the question about significant events as follows in two separate questionnaires:

> "We get excited when we get ideas. Then they get shot down and we lose motivation for a week."

> "Getting bashed by the TTeam 3–4 weeks in a row was bad for team morale. Then it was just trying to get along after that."

These comments demonstrate that by killing ideas, reviewers not only prevent designers from gaining insights but also risk the motivation of the designers. Scott and Bruce (1994) found that leadership's expectations and the quality of their exchange significantly impacts innovative behavior in the workplace. Instead of "shooting down concepts by constantly saying 'this will not sell'", managers should encourage designers to "propose, experiment, and learn from the results, until [they] arrive at a satisfactory result" (Dorst 2003). Kim and Wilemon (2002) argue that it is critical to hire staff with "knowledge and passion (motivation)" in addition to the relevant skills. This suggests that the role of managers goes beyond decision making to filter ideas and that managers must create a culture and climate that is supportive of innovation. Parnas and Weiss (1985) recommend that reviewers should "make positive assertions about the design rather than simply [...] point out defects" and that "the designers pose the questions to the reviewers, rather than vice versa". In their studies of design research reviews at the Navy, they have found that "Reviewers are often asked to examine issues beyond their competence. They may be specialists in one aspect of the system, but they are asked to review the entire system." This happened in several instances in the cases described and resulted in erroneous judgments by the reviewers. The focus on review of the system rather than a specific section occurred by choice of the reviewers and by the way the review was arranged. Parnas and Weiss also found that "Often the wrong people are present. People who are mainly interested in learning about the status of the project, or who are interested in learning about the purpose of the system and may turn the review into a tutorial."

Observations indicate that this problem also occurs regularly during design reviews in 310 (especially during reviews of high performing design teams who work on exciting projects).

5.5 *Censorship Hypothesis*

Managers, experts and reviewers should encourage the shift from planning to execution, if designers gain most insights that advance the design through experimenting. However, in academia and industry alike, regularly scheduled review sessions, gates and milestones are designed to keep projects on schedule, feasible and within budget, not to gate learning. At these points, the project ideas and concepts are scrutinized and many unproven ideas, which are risky in the eye of the reviewer, are killed. Therefore, instead of accelerating the design process, reviewers impede it by acting as censors. They bar the designer from creating learning opportunities that hold the potential for discovery and insight.

Wheelwright and Clark (1992) have shown that "autonomous or tiger teams" are the most effective vehicle for developing new concepts. They suggest that motivation through ownership is an important reason for the superior performance of these teams. The lack of involvement from outside reviewers in those teams may be another important reason. These teams can simply try out ideas and learn as they wish without requiring approval before shifting from planning to execution.

This is stated in the Censorship Hypothesis as follows:

Designers who can move freely from planning to execution will outperform those who must pass through approval gates.

6 Discussion

The methodology for analyzing the cases and generating the hypotheses closely followed established practice (Eisenhardt 1989) by using within-case and cross-case analyses and enfolding the current literature. The simultaneous rather than successive development of theory and data analysis, however, bears the danger of selection bias and a premature focus on specific aspects. Therefore, based on the qualitative data analysis, no claim can be made towards the magnitude of the issues discovered but only to their existence.

The unified innovation process model is shown as a flow diagram. This representation combines elements familiar to both engineering designers and managers. It also illustrates that the design process consists of both continuous and discrete elements, with labels for each block that are part of the daily vocabulary of designers and managers. On the one hand, this ensures that both sides can quickly relate to and grasp the model. On the other hand, the use of common terminology can lead to ambiguity because everyone has a unique preformed understanding of the meaning of each label. An ontology, which explicitly specifies every block and every function, was created to eliminate this ambiguity.

All quantitative and qualitative data used in this study is from open-ended long-term projects. The data describes the design process from original need for innovation to functional proof-of-concept prototype. This allows for a more realistic investigation than data gathered from 2-h laboratory experiments would. However, this also reduces the comparability of the data because every project is unique, and because only a limited number of factors can be measured and controlled for. At this time, when the interaction between designers and managers is barely understood, this kind of field research is appropriate to uncover factors and relationships, which must be verified and quantified in controlled experiments in the future.

The research described was performed in the context of an engineering curriculum rather than in an industrial setting. Naturally, this questions the validity of the results outside of education. The 'Unified Innovation Process Model for Engineering Designers and Managers' was presented to practitioners at the product consultancy IDEO and prompted the following comments:

> "Prior to IDEO, I experienced censorship constantly. In fact, it's part of the reason why I left that company. On any given day, I'd find myself spending 30 to 40% of my time creating PowerPoints in order to justify work that I should have been doing anyway as part of innovation strategy. I had to create the decks so that my boss could take it to his boss who would take it to his boss, and so on through various levels of senior management, so that they could take the PowerPoint, and...censor it.

> "At the corporation where I worked prior to IDEO, the notion of small experiments or prototyping was not part of the ethic. It was frustrating for those of us who worked in innovation. I didn't think of myself as a designer back then but I certainly wanted to get stuff done, so I was interested in doing more than talking."

> Holly Kretschmar, Practice Lead at IDEO

> "I think it is just important to point this out. The censorship as a key; as you said, it's a gate switch or it's something that most organizations don't let people actually get in the execution mode and they spend a lot of energy on the censorship part and you see so many work-arounds."

> Diego Rodriguez, Partner at IDEO

These comments indicate that the model is applicable to industry and resonates with both designers and managers. It can therefore serve as a tool that fosters communication and understanding between the two sides. The breadth of the investigation, using multiple locations and cultures, also suggests that the findings are relevant to individuals and organizations outside of Silicon Valley, and are not restricted locally by culture or other circumstances. The results are also expected to be applicable to innovation outside of engineering design. In all areas of innovation, whether it is technology, business model or social innovation, important insights can be gained during execution. Innovators in all areas and disciplines should therefore consider prototyping and testing ideas rather than censoring them after only theoretical deliberation.

At the same time, it is important to point out that the recommendations are limited to new concept development. Managers and designers must be careful to understand when and where new solutions are desirable and when they can be dangerous.

For example, software would become unusable if interface programmers created a unique design for each screen based on what they think is the best user interface for the application they are working on. In this situation, censorship, templates and rules are needed so that users who are familiar with one screen can easily navigate other screens.

It is therefore important that designers and managers know where they want innovation and where they do not, and that this is clearly communicated and agreed on. The 'Unified Innovation Process Model' should help them understand the importance of aligning their expectations.

7 Conclusion

The unified innovation process model synthesizes the perspectives and tasks of designers and managers. It provides a map of the new concept development process that clarifies the roles of engineering designers and managers relative to each other and their respective influences on the innovation process. The resulting recommendations for designers and managers can be summarized as follows:

1. Designers should maximize the probability of gaining insights by experimenting with many ideas (i.e. executing) using simple prototypes rather than contemplating (i.e. planning) the possible merits of ideas in the abstraction of words.
2. Managers and other reviewers should let designers experiment instead of censoring untested ideas, which forces engineering designers to rehash their planning effort without new knowledge (Fig. 5).

The model provides an explanation for the success of practices employed by three renowned innovation icons: 3M, Google, and Genentech. These companies are in unrelated industries (manufacturing, information technology, and pharmaceuticals respectively) and have historical track records ranging from more than 100 years to only ten years. What all three companies have in common is the practice of embracing independent projects, also known as pet-projects. In these projects, employees are given the opportunity to work on their own visions without management

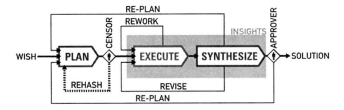

Fig. 5 Unified Innovation Process Model for Engineering Designers and Managers depicting the kernel of the design process. It shows where designers gain the insights to advance a design and where reviewers intercept the design process at the censor and approver gates

intervention. This allows employees to execute and test their ideas before a reviewer can act as a censor. Key innovations have resulted from these independent projects in each company.

The mantra of successful brainstorming (idea generation) is to "defer judgment" and to "encourage wild ideas" (Kelley and Littman 2001). Continuing this line of thought, when innovation is a priority, judgment must be deferred and any idea is worthy of being tested. Since the necessary insights are gleaned mostly during execution and synthesis, managers and reviewers must let designers move to execution and resist censoring ideas before they are tested.

Of course, this does not mean that all ideas should be taken to development for production. Successful managers let designers create simple prototypes and then decide on the next steps at the approver gate, based on the proposed solution and considerations of the business at large. Steve Jobs, the CEO of Apple, another innovation icon, said that if the company had created another PDA when everyone wanted it, "we wouldn't have had the resources to do the iPod. We probably wouldn't have seen it coming." (Morris 2008). This is an example of killing an idea to make room for others. On the other hand, Jobs also said the following about the birth of the iPhone: "We had a big debate inside the company whether we could do that or not. And that was one where I had to adjudicate it and just say, 'We're going to do it. Let's try'." Here, he embraced a 'just try it' approach thereby encouraging the designers to experiment with novel and unproven ideas. These examples show that organizational culture and leadership style can enable and facilitate or discourage and prevent innovation. However, there is no standard recipe for creating successful new concepts.

References

Chapman, M. (2006). Building an innovative organization: consistent business and technology integration. *Strategy and Leadership, 34*(4), 32.

Dorst, K. (2003). *Understanding design*. Amsterdam: BIS.

Drucker, P. F. (1998). The discipline of innovation. *Harvard Business Review*, (Nov–Dec), 149–157.

Eisenhardt, K. (1989). Building theory from case study research. *Academy of Management Review, 14*(4), 532–550.

Friedman, T. L. (2005). *The world is flat: a brief history of the twenty-first century* (1 ed.). New York, NY: Farrar, Straus and Giroux.

Hargadon, A., & Sutton, R. (2000). Building an innovation factory. *Harvard Business Review, 78*(3), 157–166.

Kelley, T., & Littman, J. (2001). *The art of innovation: lessons in creativity from IDEO, America's leading design firm*. New York, NY: Doubleday.

Kim, J., & Wilemon, D. (2002). Strategic issues in managing innovation's fuzzy front-end. *European Journal of Innovation Management, 5*(1), 27–39.

Morris, B. (2008). America's most admired companies: Steve jobs speaks out. *Fortune*. Retrieved from http://money.cnn.com/galleries/2008/fortune/0803/gallery.jobsqna.fortune/index.html

Neeley, W. L. J. (2007). *Adaptive design expertise: a theory of design thinking and innovation*. Stanford, CA: Stanford University.

Nussbaum, B. (2007, February 12, 2009). CEOs must be designers, not just hire them. Think Steve jobs and iPhone. http://www.businessweek.com/innovate/NussbaumOnDesign/archives/2007/06/ceos{_}must{_}be{_}de.html.

Palmisano, S. (2006). *Expanding the innovation horizon: the global CEO study 2006*. Somers, NY: IBM Global Business Services.

Parnas, D., & Weiss, D. (1985). *Active design reviews: principles and practices*. Los Alamitos, CA: IEEE Computer Society Press

Scott, S., & Bruce, R. (1994). Determinants of innovative behavior: a path model of individual innovation in the workplace. *Academy of Management Journal, 37*, 580–580.

Simonton, D. (1999). *Origins of genius: Darwinian perspectives on creativity*. New York, NY: Oxford University Press.

Skogstad, P. L., Currano, R. M., & Leifer, L. J. (2008). An experiment in design pedagogy transfer across cultures and disciplines. *International Journal of Engineering Education, 24*, 367–376.

Wageman, R., Hackman, J., & Lehman, E. (2005). Team diagnostic survey: Development of an instrument. *The Journal of Applied Behavioral Science, 41*(4), 373.

Wheelwright, S., & Clark, K. (1992). *Revolutionizing product development: quantum leaps in speed, efficiency, and quality*: New York: Free Press.

Wiley, J. (1998). Expertise as mental set: the effects of domain knowledge in creative problem solving. *Memory and Cognition, 26*(4), 716–730.

Product Differentiation by Aesthetic and Creative Design: A Psychological and Neural Framework of Design Thinking

Martin Reimann and Oliver Schilke

Abstract As firms increasingly use design to successfully differentiate their products from competitors, the concept of design thinking has lately received raised attention among practitioners. Many consider design thinking to fundamentally change the way firms will strive to innovate. Design thinking can be thought of as a methodology for innovation that systematically integrates human, business, and technical factors in problem-forming, problem-solving, and design. As initiatives for design thinking grow significantly, we need to better understand how design thinking helps to foster creativity of designers and product managers and how it supports firms' goal of creating aesthetically appealing products. Despite the relevance of the concept of design thinking, its underlying mechanisms have been poorly understood. The purpose of this chapter is to shed light on the processes of design thinking by integrating extant literature from psychology and neuroscience. In particular, this research focuses on aesthetics and creativity as crucial processes of design thinking. Subsequently, a definition of design thinking is offered, which is accompanied by a psychological and neural framework of design thinking.

1 Introduction

In business environments, where core product attributes have become homogenous across competitors, it is increasingly important for firms to understand how to successfully set their products apart from other market participants by creating additional value for customers (Reimann et al. 2010a, b). Following this line of thought, design has been argued to add a substantial amount of value to core product attributes (Reimann et al. 2010c). In particular, Verganti (2008b) observes

M. Reimann (✉) and O. Schilke
University of Southern California, Department of Psychology/Brain & Creativity Institute,
Los Angeles, CA 90089, USA
e-mail: mreimann@usc.edu; schilke@ucla.edu

Principal Investigator: Brian Knutson

H. Plattner et al. (eds.), *Design Thinking: Understand – Improve – Apply*,
Understanding Innovation, DOI 10.1007/978-3-642-13757-0_3,
© Springer-Verlag Berlin Heidelberg 2011

several firms using design to innovate product meaning and, therefore, increase the emotional and symbolic value of their products. Moreover, Brunner et al. (2009) calls design one of the last great product differentiators for firms to use. As such, the design of products can be seen as a critical component of business competitiveness, to the extent that major firms such as Apple, Procter & Gamble, and Sony have committed themselves to becoming design leaders in their industries (Dunne and Martin 2006). Overall, firms are increasingly devoting to design and engaging design specialists in their innovation processes (Nussbaum et al. 2005).

Despite design becoming a key strategy of differentiation for many firms, its underlying mechanisms remain poorly understood. Particularly, two questions, which are crucial for a better understanding of innovation processes based on design, are in need of answering. First, *what constitutes "good" design from the perspectives of the individual designer?* In trying to answer this question, we will review the extant literature from psychology and neuroscience and argue that good design must be aesthetically appealing to its viewer. Verganti (2008a) posits that "if engineers use technology to make products function, then designers use form to make things beautiful" (p. 23). In line with this argument, our research will provide insights into the affective and cognitive processes at play while experiencing aesthetic design. Second, based on the notion that design is a creative activity (Maldonado 1991), *which methodologies can firms leverage to increase the creativity of their designers and product managers?* Here, the concept of design thinking has emerged as a powerful methodology for integrating human, business, and technical factors in problem-forming, problem-solving, and design (Martin 2009; Plattner et al. 2009). As firms increasingly engage in design thinking, there is a need for a better comprehension of how design thinking helps to foster creativity. While several principles of design thinking are well-established and anchored in a long history of social science research (e.g., the brainstorming literature), other design thinking aspects are unique and novel. Prior research on design thinking, however, has largely been restricted to practitioner-oriented publications. Thus, there is a lack of systematic knowledge of what the design thinking concept has to offer and how it distinguishes itself from other problem solving approaches. Therefore, to arrive at potential answers to the second question, we will integrate literature on creativity from both psychology and neuroscience to shed more light on the mechanisms at play during creative design thinking. As a result, we will define design thinking and present a conceptual framework, derived from the psychological and neural foundations of aesthetics and creativity.

The objective of this research is to establish a model of design thinking by integrating previous psychological and neuroscientific research on aesthetics and creativity. Moreover, providing answers to the aforementioned questions will support firms in their quest for better product design and successful differentiation from competitors.

The remainder of this chapter is organized as follows. Next, we lay out the theoretical background of aesthetics and creativity – two concepts, which we argue are critical for a better understanding of design thinking and, consequently, product differentiation by design. Subsequently, we will define design thinking and derive a conceptual framework of its psychological and neural properties.

2 Aesthetics and Creativity as Design Thinking Mechanisms

In design research, the "first generation" of design theories and methods predominantly leveraged the fields of operations research for its optimization techniques and cybernetics for its systems thinking approaches (Beckman and Barry 2007; Rittel 1972, 1984). However, these purely mechanistic approaches to the design process frustrated followers who were unable to reconcile the methods of the "first generation" with the complexities of real design problems, especially once values of social equity and pluralism were considered (Beckman and Barry 2007). Therefore, the "second generation" of design theories and methods was initiated, focusing on design as a social process (Bucciarelli 1988; Rittel 1972, 1984). Among those design approaches, the increasingly popular concept of design thinking is considered to fundamentally change the way companies nowadays strive to innovate (Nussbaum 2004). Design thinking can be thought of as a methodology for innovation, placing the interaction environment that promotes creative design on the center stage (Plattner et al. 2009).

As initiatives for design thinking in industry and academia grow, we need to better understand how the aspects distinguishing design thinking from other problem solving approaches help foster creativity and aesthetically appealing product design. Prior research on design thinking has often been restricted to practitioner-oriented case studies (e.g., Brown 2008), reflecting its early stage. As such, there has been little research aimed at exploring the psychological processes while a person is engaging in creative design thinking or experiencing aesthetically appealing design. Thus, our research aims at providing further insight into the mechanisms that underlie design thinking, while focusing on prior research on aesthetics and creativity. Besides investigating important psychological properties, this research also integrates recent evidence from neuroscience. To isolate relevant mechanisms, we aim at capturing specific affective and cognitive processes involved when people are engaged in design thinking.

2.1 Psychological and Neural Bases of Aesthetics

The word *aesthetics* was coined by Baumgarten (1735), based on the Greek word *aisthēsis* (i.e., perception from the senses, feeling, hearing, and seeing), and subsequently defined as "perfection of sensate cognition" (Osborne 1979). In this section, we review aesthetics research in the context of psychology and neuroscience, focusing on relevant affective and cognitive processes while experiencing aesthetic objects, including product design, artwork, and beautiful faces (e.g., Aharon et al. 2001; Kampe et al. 2001; O'Doherty et al. 2003; Senior 2003; Vartanian and Goel 2004).

2.1.1   Psychology of Aesthetics

Numerous views on aesthetics have developed within psychology research. These perspectives include empirical aesthetics (e.g., Berlyne 1971, 1974; Fechner 1871; Martindale et al. 1990; Seifert 1992), Gestalt theory (e.g., Arnheim 1943; Eysenck 1942), and psychoanalysis (e.g., Hanly 1986; Segal 1952), among others. Within these streams of research, aesthetics and associated terms of aesthetic appreciation, experience, judgment, perception, and preference have been related to arousal (Berlyne 1971, 1974), prototypicality (Martindale 1988; Martindale and Moore 1988; Martindale et al. 1990), and appraisals (Silvia 2005). Recently, Leder et al. (2004) proposed a psychological model of aesthetic experience, comprising of a five-stage process, which includes the perceptual analyses of the object of aesthetic interest, implicit memory integration, explicit classification, cognitive mastering, and evaluation. This process results in aesthetic judgment and aesthetic emotion. While aesthetic judgment (i.e., the cognitive element) is argued to be a result of understanding ambiguity in the object, Leder et al. (2004) further posited that aesthetic emotion (i.e., the affective element) may be seen as an outcome of continuous and satisfactory affective evaluation while processing the five process stages. Moreover, in the tradition of these affective-cognitive models, Hagtvedt et al. (2008) have developed measurement scales for affective and cognitive components perception of aesthetic objects. On the basis of these insights into potentially underlying affective and cognitive mechanisms, we would propose increased affective and cognitive processing for viewers confronted with aesthetic product design.

An effective measure of affective and cognitive processing is reaction time (Bruner and Postman 1947; Sternberg 2004). We expect greater attention and more intense emotional responses (Chatterjee 2004; Leder et al. 2004) and, therefore, longer reaction times, for design that is aesthetic (Reimann et al. 2010c). The notion of longer reaction times in response to aesthetic design may be based on prior research in psychology; for example, Madsen et al. (1993) found longer reaction times in the aesthetic experience to music. As such, aesthetic product designs elicits longer reaction times to arrive at choice than standardized packaging, resulting from increased affect (e.g., increased emotional responses) and cognition (e.g., increased attention) (Reimann et al. 2010c).

2.1.2   Neuroscience of Aesthetics

Recent studies in neuroscience have tried to draw neural frameworks of aesthetics (Chatterjee 2004; Nadal et al. 2008). Chatterjee (2004) developed a conceptual model of visual aesthetics, which was adapted from the cognitive neuroscience of vision. After the viewer is confronted with the visual stimulus, the model proposes a phase of early vision (i.e., a processing of color, luminance, shape, motion and location), followed by a phase of intermediate vision (i.e., grouping of theses features). These phases are coupled with attention and a representational domain (e.g., places or faces) and subsequently followed by an emotional response (i.e., liking versus wanting), and then the decision.

In a follow-up study, Nadal et al. (2008) laid empirical results over Chatterjee's (2004) conceptual framework by comparing it to three different neuroimaging studies (i.e., Cela-Conde et al. 2004; Kawabata and Zeki 2004; Vartanian and Goel 2004). Three components of Chatterjee's (2004) model were identified in the data of the reviewed neuroimaging studies: the process of early vision, the emotional response, and the decision.

Early visual processing was found in the *occipital cortex*, the most prominent brain area for vision (Vartanian and Goel 2004). Emotional responses became evident in the representation of reward value and the awareness of the emotional state (Kawabata and Zeki 2004; Vartanian and Goel 2004). Specifically, Nadal et al. (2008) argued that the cortical component of reward value of the aesthetically judged stimuli corresponds to activity in the *medial orbitofrontal cortex*. That is, visual stimuli rated as beautiful were associated with a higher reward value in participants' brains than those rated as ugly (Kawabata and Zeki 2004). Further, the subcortical component of reward value was identified in the *caudate nucleus* by Vartanian and Goel (2004). Nadal et al. (2008) further proposed that increased activation in the *motor cortex* could represent reward magnitude of ugly stimuli or the motor readiness elicited by them (Kawabata and Zeki 2004). Further, the subjective emotional experience associated with aesthetically preferred stimuli was identified in the *anterior cingulate cortex* by Vartanian and Goel (2004) and the decision component of Chatterjee's (2004) framework was identified in Cela-Conde's (2004) work. Yet, Nadal et al. (2008) admitted that it is not possible to determine whether the identified brain activity in the *left dorsolateral prefrontal cortex* reflects decisions based on perceptual information or on information regarding reward value or on both.

In summary, Nadal et al.'s (2008) review of Chatterjee's (2004) model provides a comprehensive overview of potential mechanisms at play while being confronted with aesthetic stimuli. In another empirical neuroimaging study, Jacobsen et al. (2006) showed specific brain activations for aesthetic judgments in comparison to decisions on symmetric objects. As such, while the results of the three former neuroimaging studies refer specifically to neural correlates of judging stimuli as aesthetic versus ugly, Jacobsen et al. (2006) identified neural correlates of judging the beauty of images compared to judging their symmetry, referring to the neural correlates of the judgment process itself.

Although the insights into the visual and decision-making processes in the brain are interesting, the findings on emotional responses seem to be most promising for the present research. These findings suggest that reward (i.e., wanting the aesthetic product) is what may trigger aesthetic preference, judgment, and subsequently decision (Leder et al. 2004; Zeki 1999). In their neural theory of aesthetic experiences, Ramachandran and Hirstein (1999) claimed that experiencing aesthetics is by itself rewarding. This claim is supported by several other empirical neuroimaging studies.

Specifically, Aharon et al. (2001) found that viewing beautiful faces activate the reward circuitry, particularly the *nucleus accumbens*. Additionally, Kampe et al. (2001) identified increased activation in the *ventral striatum* when an attractive faces looks directly at the viewer instead of when eye gaze is directed away, also indicating that the reward system is engaged. Further, O'Doherty et al. (2003) showed that smiling, beautiful faces produce activation of *medial orbitofrontal cortex*, a brain area which is argued to be involved in representing stimulus-reward value. These findings are in line with the studies reviewed earlier, who also found activation in the *medial orbitofrontal cortex* (Kawabata and Zeki 2004) as well as the *caudate nucleus* (Vartanian and Goel 2004), which is an area of the *striatum*.

In summary, while experiencing aesthetic product design (i.e., after early vision, when emotional responses are elicited), we key areas of the brain's reward system are significantly greater activated for aesthetic design (Reimann et al. 2010c). These brain areas incorporate the *striatum* (which includes the *caudate nucleus* and the *nucleus accumbens*) as well as the *prefrontal cortex*. We expect that increased activation in these areas arises at the point in time when viewer experience (i.e., emotionally respond to) the aesthetic design.

2.2 Psychological and Neural Bases of Creativity

Creativity underlies most of the performance assessments in the design thinking literature (e.g., Brown 2008; Paulus and Brown 2003). But what is a creative idea? The common definition that creativity involves both novelty (i.e., something that is original and unexpected) and usefulness (i.e., something that is appropriate and adaptive regarding the task constraints) (Amabile et al. 1996; Shalley et al. 2004) works for understanding why the *outcome* of a product design process may be judged as creative (Litchfield 2008). This outcome, however, is influenced by a multitude of factors, including available resources to promote product design and opportunities for innovation in the marketplace. Yet, to improve our understanding of how firms can intervene to improve creative *idea generation* of designers, it seems useful to measure creativity at an earlier stage, focusing on factors that can be attributed to the humans involved in the product design process. In the following sections, we will discuss creativity from the perspectives of psychology and neuroscience and focus on the processes while people are being creative.

2.2.1 Psychology of Creativity

In psychology, the subject matter of creativity did not substantially develop until after Guilford's (1950) call for more research on this topic (Simonton 2000). Since then, a number of theories have been proposed, including social, developmental, cognitive, and biological perspectives (e.g., Amabile 1983; Eysenck 1993; Martindale 1995, 1999).

Simonton (2000) summarizes that most research progress has been made in four areas of creativity: first, the cognitive processes involved in the creative act; second, the distinctive individual characteristics of the creative person; third, the development and manifestation of creativity across the life span; and fourth, the social surroundings that are associated with creativity. In particular, the *cognitive processes* related to creativity span from the process of insight (e.g., Sternberg and Davidson 1995) to the creative cognition approach (i.e., creativity as a combination of ordinary cognitive processes; e.g., Ward et al. 1997). Moreover, relevant *individual characteristics* of creativity have been said to include intelligence (e.g., Gardner 1993) and personality traits such as being independent, nonconformist, or unconventional (e.g., Dellas and Gaier 1970; Martindale 1989; Simonton 1999). Yet another topic of research on creativity is its *developmental dimension*. Here, research has investigated acquisition and actualization of creative potential, suggesting, for example, that exceptional creativity does not at all times emerge from creatively nurturing environments (e.g., Eisenstadt 1978). Finally, after earlier research on creativity focused mainly on the cognitive, individual, and developmental perspective (i.e., creativity was viewed as a process taking place in the mind of a single individual, e.g., see Simonton 2000), research became interested in the *social impact* on creativity (e.g., Amabile 1983). For example, prior research investigated the interpersonal environment of creativity, especially how reward or surveillance impact a person that is engaging in a creative task (Amabile 1996), or how brainstorming improves the level of creativity of an outcome (Osborn 1957).

In summary, psychological research offers a broad spectrum of insight into the cognitive, individual, developmental, and social aspects of creativity. Especially, research findings on the cognitive and social aspects of creativity seem to be valuable to the study of design thinking. For example, based on the notion that creativity is a combination of specific cognitive processes that interact (Ward et al. 1997), we propose that design thinking also recruits a unique set of interacting mechanisms. For example, these processes include attention pertaining to the design problem as well as acquisition and integration of memory, leading to a new, creative design idea.

2.2.2 Neuroscience of Creativity

The subject of creativity has recently also been approached with neuroscientific methodology. A topical literature review by Fink et al. (2007) reveals that electroencephalography (EEG) – a technique that allows the recording of electrical activity in the brain's cortex – is the most commonly used method for the study of creative thinking. Besides other methods, functional magnetic resonance imaging (fMRI) comes second to EEG in the number of existing creativity studies (Fink et al. 2007). FMRI measures changes in blood flow in the brain, which is highly correlated with brain activity (Logothetis and Wandell 2004). Compared to EEG, fMRI reveals brain activity not only in the cortex but also in subcortical brain areas (i.e., regions related to affective responses). Experimental designs in prior studies comprise a range of facets of creativity, including mentally composing a drawing (Bhattacharya and Petsche 2005), generating creative stories by using given words (Howard-Jones et al. 2005), and creating uses for real objects (Folley and Park 2005), among others.

In particular, prior neuroscientific research indicates that creativity is related to several regions in the brain. For example, Folley and Park (2005) report that their divergent thinking task (i.e., creating uses for real objects) is associated with activation in the prefrontal cortex (PFC) in both hemispheres of the brain. Furthermore, in a fMRI experiment, Jung-Beeman et al. (2004) found increased activity in the anterior superior temporal gyrus for creative insight (i.e., an "Aha!" moment) relative to noninsight solutions. Moreover, Howard-Jones et al. (2005) report activation increases in the right medial frontal gyrus as well as the cingulate gyrus for creative versus uncreative stories.

In summary, extant neuroscientific research suggests that multiple regions of the brain are involved. While it is too early to make conclusions of the unique neural network that lies beneath creativity, prior research using neuroimaging methodology such as fMRI indicate that affect and cognition play an important role in the process of creativity.

3   A Definition and Framework of Design Thinking

Prior research considers design thinking as a methodology for innovation that systematically integrates human, business, and technical factors in problem-forming, problem-solving, and design (Plattner et al. 2009). This chapter focuses on the human factor by considering aesthetics and creativity as crucial dimensions of design thinking. In line with previous research on aesthetics and creativity, we propose that creative design thinking comprises of increased affect and cognition. In particular, design thinking may require increased attention, memory acquisition, and learning, followed by an aesthetically appealing design as an outcome, which in turn results in increased attention (e.g., slower reaction times while viewing it) as well as an emotional response (e.g., wanting). Specifically component of the emotional response to the aesthetically appealing design is linked to the reward system in the brain (Reimann et al. 2010c). Besides these individual-level factors of creative design thinking and its consequence – an aesthetically appealing design – a number of social-level factors are at the core of the design thinking concept and, therefore, may distinguish design thinking from other problem solving approaches. Drawing from the fragmented business literature on design thinking and related concepts, four factors can be highlighted as being central characteristics of design thinking in product design.

Inspiration Before Ideation According to Brown (2008), product development projects following a design thinking approach pass through three broad phases: inspiration (i.e., motivating the search for solutions), ideation (i.e., generating and developing ideas), and finally implementation (i.e., bringing the product to the market). In this process, it is considered fundamental that inspiration precedes ideation.

User-Centricity Design thinking is a methodology that imbues the full spectrum of innovation activities with a user-centered design ethos (Brown 2008; Gerber 2006). As such, innovation activities are driven by focusing on what people want and need in their lives and what they like or dislike about the way particular products are made, packaged, marketed, sold, and supported.

Prototyping Design thinking is heavily dependent upon socially constructed, physical objects (Brereton and McGarry 2000). With a rudimentary prototype in hand, product designers have a more precise idea about what the ultimate design should accomplish. Prototypes also help to learn about the strengths and weaknesses of the idea and to identify new directions that product improvements might take.

Avoiding Criticism Social interaction in exploring the intersection of different points of view is at the heart of the design thinking approach (Gerber 2006). Embracing concepts from brainstorming research (Osborn 1957), design thinking involves a commitment of participants and facilitators to discouraging criticism in product development interaction (Litchfield 2008; Sutton and Hargadon 1996). Deferring adverse judgments has been argued to fundamentally help improve creativity in idea generation processes (Paulus and Brown 2003).

In summary, design thinking consists of specific individual-level and social-level factors that determine the design outcome and its level of aesthetic appeal. Figure 1 illustrates the framework of design thinking. Based on this framework, we offer the following definition of design thinking:

> Design thinking is a creative, individual-level process influenced by social-level factors (that is, high inspiration by others, high user-centricity, high prototyping, and low criticism by other), which includes attention, memory, and learning and leads to an aesthetically appealing object.

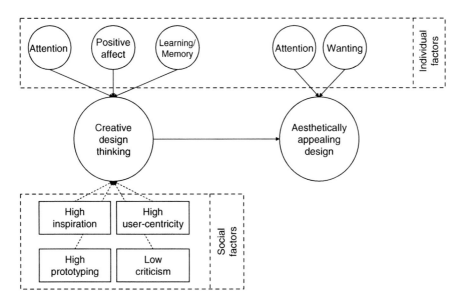

Fig. 1 Framework of design thinking

4 Conclusion

The prospect for research on the psychological and neural bases of design thinking is promising. Adapting ideas from the extant literature on aesthetics and creativity may help guide the testing of hypotheses about the affective and cognitive aspects of design thinking, leading to a better understanding of differentiation by design. The purpose of this chapter is to shed light on aesthetics and creativity, two important processes at play during design thinking. Our conceptual framework now underscores the need for empirical research in seeking to understand the mechanisms underlying design thinking and aesthetically appealing designs. We hope that further studies will conduct experimental work both in the field as well as in controlled settings, using psychometric, behavioral, and neuroimaging methodology.

Acknowledgments The authors thank the Hasso Plattner Foundation for a generous grant to conduct research on the psychological and neural basis of design thinking. The authors are also thankful for helpful comments from Ingo Balderjahn, Brian Knutson, Roderick M. Kramer, Larry Leifer, Bryce Merritt, Mark Schar, Barbara Tversky, and the participants of several workshops of the Hasso Plattner Design Thinking Research Program held at Stanford University and the University of Potsdam. This research was conducted at Stanford University.

References

Aharon, I., Etcoff, N., Ariely, D., Chabris, C. F., O'Connor, E., & Breiter, H. C. (2001). Beautiful faces have variable reward value fMRI and behavioral evidence. *Neuron, 32*(3), 537–551.

Amabile, T. M. (1983). The social psychology of creativity: A componential conceptualization. *Journal of Personality and Social Psychology, 45*(2), 357–376.

Amabile, T. M. (1996). *Creativity in context*. Boulder, CO: Westview.

Amabile, T. M., Conti, R., Coon, H., Lazenby, J., & Herron, M. (1996). Assessing the work environment for creativity. *Academy of Management Journal, 39*(5), 1154–1184.

Arnheim, R. (1943). Gestalt and art. *Journal of Aesthetics and Art Criticism, 2*(8), 71–75.

Baumgarten, A. G. (1735). *Meditationes philosophicae de nonnullis ad poema pertinentibus*, dissertation, University of Halle.

Beckman, S. L., & Barry, M. (2007). Innovation as a learning process: Embedding design thinking. *California Management Review, 50*(1), 25.

Berlyne, D. E. (1971). *Aesthetics and psychobiology*. New York, NY: Appleton-Century-Crofts.

Berlyne, D. E. (1974). *Studies in the new experimental aesthetics: Steps toward an objective psychology of aesthetic appreciation*. Washington, DC: Hemisphere.

Bhattacharya, J., & Petsche, H. (2005). Drawing on mind's canvas: Differences in cortical integration patterns between artists and non-artists. *Human Brain Mapping, 26*(1), 1–14.

Brereton, M., & McGarry, B. (2000). An observational study of how objects support engineering design thinking and communication: Implications for the design of tangible media, *CHI 2000*, 217–224.

Brown, T. (2008). Design thinking. *Harvard Business Review, 86*(6), 84–92.

Bruner, J. S., & Postman, L. (1947). Emotional selectivity in perception and reaction. *Journal of Personality, 16*(1), 69–77.

Brunner, R., Emery, S., & Hall, R. (2009). *Do you matter? How great design will make people love you company*. Upper Saddle River, NJ: FT Press.

Bucciarelli, L. L. (1988). An ethnographic perspective on engineering design. *Design Studies, 9*(3), 159–168.

Cela-Conde, C. J., Marty, G., Maestú, F., Ortiz, T., Munar, E., Fernández, A., et al. (2004). Activation of the prefrontal cortex in the human visual aesthetic perception. *Proceedings of the National Academy of Sciences of the United States of America, 101*(16), 6321.

Chatterjee, A. (2004). Prospects for a cognitive neuroscience of visual aesthetics. *Bulletin of Psychology and the Arts, 4*(2), 56–60.

Dellas, M., & Gaier, E. L. (1970). Identification of creativity: The individual. *Psychological Bulletin, 73*(1), 55–73.

Dunne, D., & Martin, R. (2006). Design thinking and how it will change management education: An interview and discussion. *Academy of Management Learning and Education, 5*(4), 512–523.

Eisenstadt, J. M. (1978). Parental loss and genius. *American Psychologist, 33*(3), 211–223.

Eysenck, H. J. (1942). The experimental study of the "good gestalt" – a new approach. *Psychological Review, 49*(4), 344–364.

Eysenck, H. J. (1993). Creativity and personality: Suggestions for a theory. *Psychological Inquiry, 4*(3), 147–178.

Fechner, G. T. (1871). *Zur experimentalen Aesthetik*. Leipzig: Hirzel.

Fink, A., Benedek, M., Grabner, R. H., Staudt, B., & Neubauer, A. C. (2007). Creativity meets neuroscience: Experimental tasks for the neuroscientific study of creative thinking. *Methods, 42*(1), 68–76.

Folley, B. S., & Park, S. (2005). Verbal creativity and schizotypal personality in relation to prefrontal hemispheric laterality: A behavioral and near-infrared optical imaging study. *Schizophrenia Research, 80*(2–3), 271–282.

Gardner, H. (1993). *Creating minds: An anatomy of creativity seen through the lives of Freud, Einstein, Picasso, Stravinsky, Eliot, Graham, and Gandhi*. New York, NY: Basic Books.

Gerber, E. M. (2006). Relations in design thinking: A case study of a social network. *Academy of Management Proceedings, 2006,* T1–T6.

Guilford, J. P. (1950). Creativity. *American Psychologist, 5*(9), 444–454.

Hagtvedt, H., Hagtvedt, R., & Patrick, V. M. (2008). The perception and evaluation of visual art. *Empirical Studies of the Arts, 26*(2), 197–218.

Hanly, C. M. T. (1986). Psychoanalytic aesthetics: A defense and an elaboration. *Psychoanalytic Quarterly, 55*(1), 1–22.

Howard-Jones, P. A., Blakemore, S. J., Samuel, E. A., Summers, I. R., & Claxton, G. (2005). Semantic divergence and creative story generation: An fMRI investigation. *Cognitive Brain Research, 25*(1), 240–250.

Jacobsen, T., Schubotz, R. I., Höfel, L., & Cramon, D. Y. (2006). Brain correlates of aesthetic judgment of beauty. *Neuroimage, 29*(1), 276–285.

Jung-Beeman, M., Bowden, E. M., Haberman, J., Frymiare, J. L., Arambel-Liu, S., Greenblatt, R., et al. (2004). Neural activity when people solve verbal problems with insight. *PLoS Biology, 2*(4), 500–510.

Kampe, K. K., Frith, C. D., Dolan, R. J., & Frith, U. (2001). Reward value of attractiveness and gaze. *Nature, 413*(6856), 589.

Kawabata, H., & Zeki, S. (2004). Neural correlates of beauty. *Journal of Neurophysiology, 91*(4), 1699.

Leder, H., Belke, B., Oeberst, A., & Augustin, D. (2004). A model of aesthetic appreciation and aesthetic judgments. *British Journal of Psychology, 95*(4), 489–508.

Litchfield, R. C. (2008). Brainstorming reconsidered: A goal-based view. *Academy of Management Review, 33*(3), 649–668.

Logothetis, N. K., & Wandell, B. A. (2004). Interpreting the bold signal. *Annual Review of Physiology, 66*(1), 735–769.

Madsen, C. K., Brittin, R. V., & Capperella-Sheldon, D. A. (1993). An empirical method for measuring the aesthetic experience to music. *Journal of Research in Music Education, 41*(1), 57.

Maldonado, T. (1991). The idea of comfort. *Design Issues, 8*(1), 35–43.

Martin, R. (2009). *Design of business: Why design thinking is the next competitive advantage.* Boston, MA: Harvard Business Press.

Martindale, C. (1988). Aesthetics, psychobiology, and cognition. In F. Farley & R. Neperud (Eds.), *The foundations of aesthetics, art, and art education* (pp. 7–42). New York, NY: Praeger.

Martindale, C. (1989). Personality, situation, and creativity. In E. P. Torrance, J. A. Glover, R. R. Ronning & C. R. Reynolds (Eds.), *Handbook of creativity* (pp. 211–232). New York, NY: Plenum Press.

Martindale, C. (1995). Creativity and connectionism. In S. M. Smith, T. B. Ward & R. A. Finke (Eds.), *The creative cognition approach* (pp. 249–268). Boston, MA: MIT Press.

Martindale, C. (1999). The biological basis of creativity. In R. J. Sternberg (Ed.), *Handbook of creativity* (pp. 137–152). Cambridge, MA: Cambridge University Press.

Martindale, C., & Moore, K. (1988). Priming, prototypicality, and preference. *Journal of Experimental Psychology: Human Perception and Performance, 14*(4), 661–670.

Martindale, C., Moore, K., & Borkum, J. (1990). Aesthetic preference: Anomalous findings for berlyne's psychobiological theory. *American Journal of Psychology, 103*, 53–80.

Nadal, M., Munar, E., Capo, M. A., Rossello, J., & Cela-Conde, C. J. (2008). Towards a framework for the study of the neural correlates of aesthetic preference. *Spatial Vision, 21*(3–5), 379–396.

Nussbaum, B. (2004). The power of design. *Business Week,* 68–75, *May 17.*

Nussbaum, B., Berner, R., & Brady, D. (2005). Get creative. *Business Week,* 60–68, *August 1.*

O'Doherty, J., Winston, J., Critchley, H., Perrett, D., Burt, D. M., & Dolan, R. J. (2003). Beauty in a smile: The role of medial orbitofrontal cortex in facial attractiveness. *Neuropsychologia, 41*(2), 147–155.

Osborn, A. F. (1957). *Applied imagination.* New York, NY: Scribner.

Osborne, H. (1979). Some theories of aesthetic judgment. *Journal of Aesthetics and Art Criticism, 38*(2), 135–144.

Paulus, P. B., & Brown, V. R. (2003). Enhancing ideational creativity in groups: Lessons from research on brainstorming. In P. B. Paulus & B. A. Nijstad (Eds.), *Group creativity: Innovation through collaboration* (pp. 110–136). New York, NY: Oxford University Press.

Plattner, H., Meinel, C., & Weinberg, U. (2009). *Design thinking.* Munich: mi-Wirtschaftsbuch.

Ramachandran, V. S., & Hirstein, W. (1999). The science of art: A neurological theory of aesthetic experience. *Journal of Consciousness Studies, 6*(7), 15–51.

Reimann, M., Schilke, O., & Thomas, J. S. (2010a). Customer relationship management and firm performance: The mediating role of business strategy. *Journal of the Academy of Marketing Science, 38*(3), 326–346.

Reimann, M., Schilke, O., & Thomas, J. S. (2010b). Toward an understanding of industry commoditization: Its nature and role in evolving marketing competition. *International Journal of Research in Marketing, 27*(2), 188–197.

Reimann, M., Zaichkowsky, J., Neuhaus, C., Bender, T., & Weber, B. (2010c). Aesthetic package design: A behavioral, neural, and psychological investigation. *Journal of Consumer Psychology, 20*(4), 431–441.

Rittel, H. (1972). On the planning crisis: Systems analysis of the "first and second generations". *Bedrifts Okonomen, 8*, 390–396.

Rittel, H. (1984). Second-generation design methods. In N. Cross (Ed.), *Developments in design methodology* (pp. 317–327). New York, NY: Wiley.

Segal, H. (1952). *The work of Hanna Segal: A Kleinian approach to clinical practice.* New York, NY: Jason Aronson.

Seifert, L. S. (1992). Experimental aesthetics: Implications for aesthetic education of naive art observers. *Journal of Psychology, 126*(1), 73–78.

Senior, C. (2003). Beauty in the brain of the beholder. *Neuron, 38*(4), 525–528.

Shalley, C. E., Zhou, J., & Oldham, G. R. (2004). The effects of personal and contextual characteristics on creativity: Where should we go from here? *Journal of Management, 30*(6), 933.

Silvia, P. J. (2005). Cognitive appraisals and interest in visual art: Exploring an appraisal theory of aesthetic emotions. *Empirical Studies of the Arts, 23*(2), 119–133.

Simonton, D. K. (1999). *Origins of genius: Darwinian perspectives on creativity.* Cambridge, MA: Oxford University Press.

Simonton, D. K. (2000). Creativity: Cognitive, personal, developmental, and social aspects. *American Psychologist, 55*(1), 151–158.

Sternberg, R. J., & Davidson, J. E. (1995). *The nature of insight.* Cambridge, MA: MIT Press.

Sternberg, S. (2004). Memory-scanning: Mental processes revealed by reaction-time experiments. In D. A. Balota & E. J. Marsh (Eds.), *Cognitive psychology: Key readings* (pp. 48). New York, NY: Psychology Press.

Sutton, R. I., & Hargadon, A. (1996). Brainstorming groups in context: Effectiveness in a product design firm. *Administrative Science Quarterly, 41*(4), 685–718.

Vartanian, O., & Goel, V. (2004). Neuroanatomical correlates of aesthetic preference for paintings. *Neuroreport, 15*(5), 893.

Verganti, R. (2008a). Design driven innovation: Boston, MA: Harvard Business Press.

Verganti, R. (2008b). Design, meanings, and radical innovation: A metamodel and a research agenda. *Journal of Product Innovation Management, 25*(5), 436–456.

Ward, T. B., Smith, S. M., & Vaid, J. (1997). *Creative thought: An investigation of conceptual structures and processes.* Washington, DC: American Psychological Association.

Zeki, S. (1999). *Inner vision.* Oxford: Oxford University Press.

Part II
Understanding Design Thinking

Re-representation: Affordances of Shared Models in Team-Based Design

Jonathan Edelman and Rebecca Currano

Abstract The use of media within the process of designing new products has not been directed by rigorous research findings. In this chapter a media-model framework is discussed, which categorizes media according to levels of resolution and abstraction. This framework can be used to assess characteristics of various models and as a general guide for discerning differences between media types. Designers can utilize the media-model framework to make informed judgments about appropriate prototyping and modeling approaches within various stages of the design process. New research in the application of media-models to Business Process Modeling (BPM), which traditionally employs electronic media (in the form of complex computer-generated flow-charts) aids in the generation of Business Process Models. This research has resulted in the development of an innovative modeling tool, called Tangible Business Process Modeling, or TBPM.

Keywords Media models · Media cascades · Prototyping · Tangible media · Business process modeling

1 Introduction

Our research investigates the unexamined assumptions that underlie the use of media in current design practice. The object of this type of investigation is to ether debunk best practices or to find a scientific basis for them. Can we find rigorous frameworks in order to make informed choices in the course of product or service development?

The hypothesis that we have examined this year concerns the use of rough prototypes in early product development cycles and has two parts (Frederick 2007; Buxton 2007):

J. Edelman (✉) and R. Currano
Center for Design Research, Stanford University, Building 560, 424 Panama Mall,
Stanford, CA 94305, USA
e-mail: edelman2@cdr.stanford.edu; bcurrano@stanford.edu

Principal Investigator: Larry Leifer

H. Plattner et al. (eds.), *Design Thinking: Understand – Improve – Apply*,
Understanding Innovation, DOI 10.1007/978-3-642-13757-0_4,
© Springer-Verlag Berlin Heidelberg 2011

Rough sketches and prototypes yield **paradigmatic** changes in a model and high-resolution renderings and models yield **parametric** changes in a model.

If we can establish these postulates as true, the next step is to develop an instructional framework which can inform intelligent design and implementation of prototyping strategies to improve product and service development.

Our research led us to explore several domains, including cognitive science, design theory and methodology, science and technologies studies, economics, and information technology. We have been fortunate to have the opportunity to work closely over the past year with business process modeling researchers at the Hasso-Plattner-Institute in Potsdam. This partnership enabled us to collaboratively design a tool to assist designers and business managers in applying the framework we developed, and to test it in both Stanford and Potsdam to see if our assumptions were correct. This collaboration was particularly helpful in assisting the transfer of mechanical engineering design practices into the domain of business process modeling. This in turn, deepened our understanding of how shared models work and led us to make adjustments to improve our framework.

2   Media Models and Media Cascades

During the initial phase of our investigation, we looked at the properties of the media that design engineers use during product development. Specifically, we examined the resolution of shared models and the kinds of conversations practitioners reported during development meetings. Observations in the field led us to posit that, while *resolution* was a critical factor in unpacking shared models, another factor was at work, which we identified as ***abstraction***.

2.1   Resolution

By *resolution* we mean the level of *refinement* or *granularity* that can be observed in the fit and finish of a shared representation.

Figure 1 shows two shared representations used in the development of a test car at a major university in the United States. The sketch of the car on the left exhibits lower resolution than the CAD model on the right.

2.2   Abstraction

By ***abstraction*** we mean ***amplification through simplification***, or pulling specific characteristics out of context. This includes the notion of deliberately translating

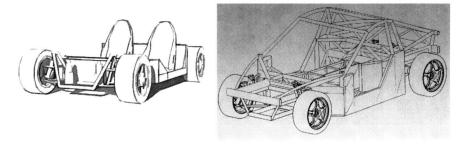

Fig. 1 Low- and high-resolution depictions of an experimental vehicle

Fig. 2 High and low material abstraction in research vehicle

something that is familiar into something *un*familiar. We have observed four classes of abstraction:

1. Material, e.g., material construction
2. Formal, i.e., shape or appearance
3. Functional, e.g., "works-like"
4. Mathematical, e.g., dimensions, optimization

Figure 2 presents an example of two levels of abstraction. The wooden car on the left is more abstract than the steel car on the right. The explicit rationale that went into choosing wood as a material to prototype the car was so designers wouldn't fall into the trap of thinking about how cars are typically designed. The team supervisor, a well seasoned design engineer, felt that using steel would limit choices. This is an example of how abstraction can make the familiar *un*familiar.

2.3 Media Cascades

Hundreds if not thousands of representations are enlisted in the development of new products. We have coined the term ***media-model*** to refer to a ***single representation***

Fig. 3 A media cascade from a student project

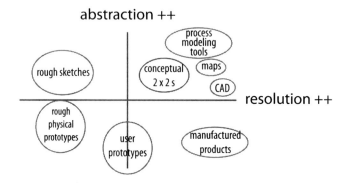

Fig. 4 Media-models framework

in the arc of new product development. Media-models are characterized by the dimensions of resolution and abstraction. We have appropriated Bruno Latour's notion of "cascades of media" to describe the ***sequence of representations*** though which projects develop and unfold in different media during the course of a development cycle, and which we refer to as a ***media-cascade***.

Figure 3 depicts some highlights of a media cascade from a student project, a binding for a snowboard. Shown here are product briefs, rough sketches, rough prototypes, CAD models, functional prototypes, and an actual working model. Rather than seeing these representations as examples of different classes, we see them as different examples of the same class, media models, and we examine how they differ in respect to abstraction and resolution.

2.4   The Media-Models Framework

Figure 4 shows the framework for media models as a conceptual 2×2 matrix. CAD models are both highly abstract and highly resolved. In CAD rendering, specific and actual physical things are reduced to geometric boundaries, or lines, which have no specific material existence. CAD models refer to an entire class of objects, not one real object. In this respect they are highly abstract. CAD models are highly resolved in that they clearly define features and tolerances. There is little or no ambiguity in a CAD model. Instead, design engineers enlist CAD to reduce uncertainty.

Rough sketches and prototypes exhibit low resolution and varying levels of abstraction, depending on the context in which they are used. For example, we consider a sketch to be more abstract than a physical model in the context of designing a physical object. The rationale here is that the three dimensions of the physical object are reduced to two dimensions in the sketch. In the case of the wooden car prototype, the material itself is leveraged as an abstraction to pull out specific design constraints that are invoked by steel.

Note that we consider manufactured products to be highly resolved and not at all abstract. We assume here that the product development has undergone numeric optimization before manufacture. We say that manufactured products are not abstract because they are the actual things.

2.4.1 Completion

Media-models only present a slice of an actual or finished project, and therefore present a *profile of incompleteness*. A media-model's profile of incompleteness allows design engineers to fill in the presented gaps. Thus, media-models encourage different levels of *completion* in order to frame discussion.

Media-models may be classified into three categories - **ambiguous media, mathematized media**, and **hybrid media**. Each class encourages a different kind of completion.

2.4.2 Ambiguous Media

Ambiguous media, such as rough sketches and rough physical prototypes, serve as a scaffold for engineers to fill in the gaps, and are completed as engineers posit many possible formulations of the problem. They are pluri-potential objects, and may express as variants depending on the experience and knowledge of each design engineer who works with them. They encourage *divergent conversations* (Fig. 5).

The objects say: I am not the real thing. I am an ephemeral notion.

Fig. 5 Ambiguous media prototype for a communication device

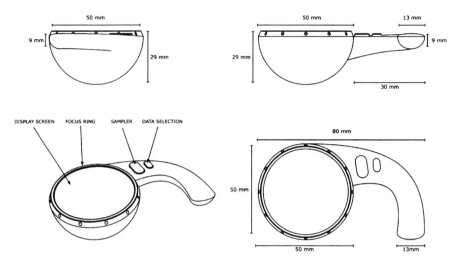

Fig. 6 Mathematized media, CAD model of a device for analyzing material

2.4.3 Mathematized Media

Mathematized media, maps, and highly realistic images are completed through refinement of what is presented. Thus they encourage **convergent conversations**. These media-models present themselves as sacrosanct, and seem to resist substantial changes (Fig. 6).

The objects say: I am the real thing. I am the underlying, unchanging truth of the thing.

2.4.4 Hybrid Media

Hybrid media allow several kinds of operations and discussions. Media-models in this category are in the sweet spot for design engineers. They often involve using physical interfaces in conjunction with high-level frameworks. This has proven to allow a flexible exploration of how different elements relate to one another. Design engineers are able to move elements to see how they fit into frameworks, as well as change frameworks to see how they describe phenomena. Hybrid models often involve combinations of different media, such as photographs, drawings, and text. The type of media enlisted in hybrid media has an effect of how the model is completed. Mathematized elements tend not to get changed, while ambiguous elements invite change of the element (Fig. 7).

The objects say: I am about provisional relationships among things.

To summarize:

Ambiguous media-models afford **paradigmatic** shifts.
Mathematized media-models afford **parametric** adjustment.
Hybrid media-models afford **understanding** and changes in **relationships**.

Fig. 7 Hybrid media, physical objects with text narrative on a 2 × 2

We have observed that successful design projects employ many kinds of media-models, or have a *broad bandwidth* of media-models. This is because the varying kinds of media-models engender different kinds of thinking and different kinds of exploration. It is through the translation form one kind of media-model to another that insight is gained, and the project is moved forward.

On the other hand, some media-cascades are characterized by a *limited bandwidth* of media-models. Design engineers may make *more judgments* with six CAD models than with one, but they are making the **same kind of judgment**, and are engaged in the same kind of thinking. This can also be said of media-cascades constituted of a *single, homogeneous material*, such as white foam core.

3 Cognitive Strategies

It is through the agency of media-models, which serve as c*ognitive prostheses*, that various kinds of thinking occur. Insight is gained by the *translation of concepts* into media that embody different levels of resolution and abstraction. Successful product development is dependent on the ability of a design team to employ different *cognitive strategies*.

The underlying assumption here is that by moving the choice of representation around the media-models framework, design engineers can benefit from different kinds of thinking. As mentioned, highly resolved, abstract media is associated with parametric adjustment. Media that exhibits low levels of resolution and high levels of abstraction is associated with paradigmatic shifts. In order to understand these phenomena, we turn to contemporary findings in cognitive science and to an experiment of our own.

Andy Clark has pointed to research that indicates that certain kinds of thinking cannot occur unless subjects' hands actually move (Clark 2008). Clark asserts that much of what we consider to be thinking happens in the hands as well as the mind. Clark's research suggests that thinking doesn't happen only in our heads but that "certain forms of human cognizing include inextricable tangles of feedback, feed-forward and feed-around loops: loops that promiscuously criss-cross the boundaries of brain, body and world" (cf. Clark 2008, p. 129f). In other words, the media itself has an effect on how and what design engineers can think.

Cognitive scientist Barbara Tversky has observed that when presented with rough sketches, experimental subjects engaged in what Tversky calls sketchy thinking (Tversky et al. 2003, 2006), or the ability to think conditionally, or roughly. Other work in cognitive science has investigated the fitness of representations. According to the Cognitive Fit theory, the way the problem is re-presented determines the thinking model applied (Agarwal et al. 1996; Vessey and Galletta 1991). All of this research supports the notion that the kind of media and the characteristics of the media with which people engage have a profound effect on how they think and consequently on the nature of their conversations.

4   Experimental Data

We performed an experiment in order to test some of the assumptions that underlie the media-models framework. We videotaped four teams of three members in two redesign tasks using two different stimuli. One stimulus was a CAD model of a device intended to analyze the properties of material (Fig. 8). The other stimulus was a rough physical prototype of a device intended to project a voice to a specific user (Fig. 9). Instructions were deliberately left vague, in order to see what effects the stimuli would have.

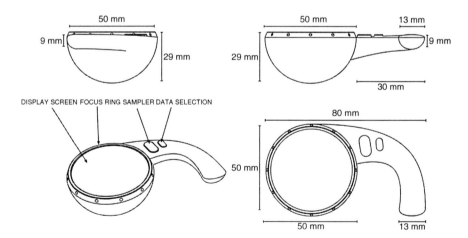

Fig. 8 Experimental stimulus, CAD model

Fig. 9 Experimental
stimulus, rough physical
prototype

Our instructions for the CAD model were, "Do whatever is necessary to take the model forward. This product enables you to analyze *and identify the material composition of objects*."

Our instructions for the rough prototype were, "Do whatever is necessary to take the model forward. This product enables you to project your voice to a specific target."

4.1 Results

The results were for the most part what we expected. The CAD model generally led to convergent conversations, meaning only parametric changes in the model, or the addition of features. Discussions pertaining to the rough prototype generally led to divergent conversations, which suggested big changes in the model, including adding functionality, as well as frequent additions of features. However, when teams deviated from the norm, we got a close look at how teams innovate and how media supports innovation.

When teams suggested paradigmatic changes in the presence of the CAD model they made lots of rough sketches and prototypes. In a very real way, they covered the CAD rendering with rough sketches. This had the effect of giving the CAD model a cognitive vote, but not a veto. This reinforced our assumptions about the effect of objects on conversations.

4.2 New Insights

We also noted several behaviors that were unique to these teams:

1. Statement of **intention**
2. Asking **process questions**
3. Envisioning **user scenarios**

4. **Enacting** user scenarios
5. Combining metaphors (**It's like X + Y**)
6. Experiencing eureka moments (**"Ahhh!"**)

4.2.1 Statement of Intention

When teams were able to deviate from the norm of convergent conversations while engaging with a CAD model, they explicitly agreed that they intended to change the model completely. Other teams either never agreed on what they intended to do, or agreed to improve the existing idea. An example of strongly stated intention is, "…[Let's] throw out this design all together."

4.2.2 Asking Process Questions

We noted a significant increase in the number of process-oriented questions in the conversations of the teams who deviated from the norm. Process questions refer to how the team will approach the problem, rather than focusing on the problem itself. An example of this is, "Do we want to make assumptions about whether this is used in the field or in the lab?"

4.2.3 Envisioning User Scenarios

User scenarios differ from *use cases* in that the latter are generic assumptions about a class of users and don't take into account specific circumstances of engagement. An example of a use case would be, "archeologists could use this." The conversations of all teams with both stimuli contained numerous examples of use case. The conversations of teams who deviated from the norm also included numerous depictions of *user scenarios*. User scenarios tend to concern an actual user in a specific situation, often described with rich sensate detail. An example of a user scenario is, "This is so cool that people will want to use it doing anything. They'll use it all the time. They'll be going home and they'll steal it from work…What's in my counter top…"

This insight led us to postulate a mechanism for how radical change to a model occurs. We refer to these changes as "K–C Transits", that is "Knowledge to Concept Transits", invoking Hatchuel and Weil's work on C–K Theory (Hatchuel and Weil 2002) (Fig. 10).

The Cad model may be considered to be an anchor object when it is the single reference point that influences the conversation. When teams generate several user scenarios, they loosen the authority of the anchor object, and the user scenarios themselves become new anchor objects, affording new perspectives that allow the team to make changes in the CAD model, which is now a mutable object.

Fig. 10 Mechanism for K–C Transit

4.2.4 Enacting User Scenarios

Enactment is a phenomenon related to user scenarios, and often occurred in the course of describing a user scenario. Enactment can be observed when team members *act out* the use of an object. This can occur by either pantomiming the action or using a proxy object like a water bottle or a cell phone to represent the object while enacting a scene in which the object is being used. Here again, we found numerous examples of enactment in teams that made paradigmatic shifts with CAD models.

4.2.5 Combining Metaphors (It's Like X + Y)

It's like X + Y involves combining two example metaphors, and seemed to occur in conjunction with enactment. When teams used single instances of metaphor to describe how a stimulus was thought to work, we observed that functional changes would be made to the model. However, when two metaphors were combined, we found that paradigmatic changes in the model occurred. For example, one team combined the metaphor of a scanner with the metaphor of a glove during an enactment and came up with a new notion that was a radical departure from the form of the device in the CAD rendering.

4.2.6 Experiencing Eureka Moments (Ahhh!)

In teams that achieved their explicit intention to change the model, a moment of excitement and recognition occurred. The teams seemed to have co-crafted a new, shared vision. Outbursts of "Oh yeah!" and "Ahhh!" were recorded, and these teams set about hammering out the details of the vision.

5 Tangible Business Process Modeling

The development of **Tangible Business Process Modeling (TBPM)** began in response to information deficits in process elicitation. A year ago, our colleagues at the Hasso-Plattner-Institute approached us in order to collaborate on solving the problem of how to get meaningful information about processes from end users. Software implementations are only as good as the blue prints (process models) upon which they are based, and theirs depend on solid, nuanced end user input. Current elicitation practices rely heavily on end-user interviews, which have yielded less than satisfactory results (see Grosskopf and Veske, Sect. 2): when confronted with a formal business process model and a narrative, which embodied a distillation of the interview, most end users found themselves at a loss. Hundreds of thousands of dollars are typically spent on software implementations of the knowledge contained in process models based on interviews, only to find that important information was missed.

5.1 The Media of BPM

When we examined the media (Fig. 11) that was in use during the process model development, we noted that BPM media-cascades are overwhelmingly weighted toward highly abstract and highly resolved media-models (Fig. 12). We were anxious to see if adding media-models with a different profile of abstraction and resolution would help solve the problem. IT was new ground for us, as we had been accustomed to dealing with physical products and services, and not used to translating user input into process models.

In working with business process model researchers, our driving question was, "How can we engender better conversations among the stakeholders (domain experts and process experts) by consciously shifting the BPM media-models around our framework?" We felt that working in a new area was a perfect way to test our framework in a real world arena. In the course of addressing this question, we made unexpected discoveries about media-models and how they worked.

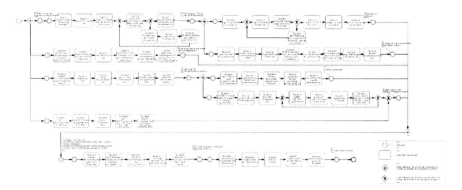

Fig. 11 BPMN process model

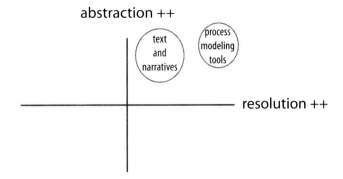

Fig. 12 BPMN media-models

5.2 Intermediary Objects

A second, related question we tackled concerned a close relation to the media-model framework. (Eric Blanco has found that representations serve as intermediary objects Blanco et al. 2007; Boujut and Blanco 2003), which act and are acted upon in the network of design practices and which permit distributed cognition. According to Blanco, shared models may be considered as enlistment devices, either allowing or barring access to collaborative participation. Media that allows collaboration is *open* and media that restricts collaboration is *closed*.

Often, the modeling that is done with software can be considered *closed*, as it keeps control of the model and possible changes in the model in the hands of a few people that are experts with the software tool. Another characteristic of closed models is that they contain little or no explicit affordance inviting change from stakeholders.

The media of BPM has little affordance for direct user involvement. Process experts own and drive the model. As a result, domain experts are left to watch. This means that they have difficulty accessing the kinds of thinking that hands-on work fosters. Thus, our second question became, "How can we create an *open* media in order to give direct involvement to BPM end users?"

5.3 Development of TBPM

We went through several iterations of prototyping strategies in the course of developing Tangible Business Process Modeling, or TBPM (Fig. 13).

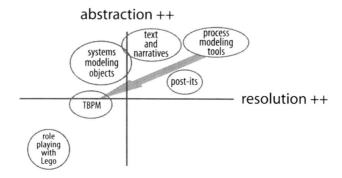

Fig. 13 Media-models used in the development of TBPM

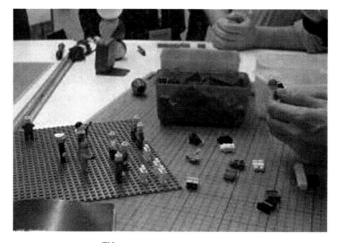

Fig. 14 Role-playing with Legos[TM]

5.3.1 Role-Playing with Legos[TM]

Our early explorations into changing the media of BPM centered around the notion of getting process experts and domain experts to engage in role playing using Lego[TM] blocks to represent stakeholders and their places of work (Fig. 14). In respect to the media-models framework, this is a move away from high abstraction and high resolution (Fig. 13). While not as concrete as actual enactments, these mediated simulations encouraged players to gain empathy and insight with other players. We also found that the simulation was often cumbersome, encouraging a level of process detail that seemed unnecessary.

Fig. 15 Interview using Post-It® Notes

5.3.2 Post-It® Notes

In another experiment, we enlisted a favorite media of design thinking practitioners, Post-It® Notes (Fig. 15). We found that Post-It® Notes served as an excellent memory aid for domain experts in recalling the steps of their processes. This type of media also provided an object that both the domain expert and the process expert could point to for clarification. One significant shortcoming to Post-It® Notes, we found, was that it failed to frame the elicited process in terms of BPM. This meant that domain experts failed to develop insight into BPM structures, insights which we believe would be central to breaking down the barrier to informed involvement in later stages of process modeling.

Even though Post-It® Notes are easily moveable and rearrangeable, they did not seem to encourage domain experts to express their processes in terms of parallelism or alternatives. Post-It® Notes allowed domain experts to quickly enumerate the steps of their process, but did not lead to greater depth in their understanding. When domain experts were asked if there was anything else they would like to share about their processes as laid out in Post-It® Notes, few if any changes were made.

In respect to the media-models framework, Post-It® Notes are less abstract and less resolved than traditional BPM media (Fig. 13). Our observations of domain experts and their conversations when using Post-It® Notes support our laboratory findings about media and conversations in design teams.

5.3.3 Systems Modeling Objects

In our next iteration, we made a set of acrylic blocks based on Systems Modeling Language (Odum 2004; Meadows 2008). Domain experts and process experts could use dry erase markers and write directly on the acrylic blocks (Fig. 16). Users

Fig. 16 Interview using systems modeling objects

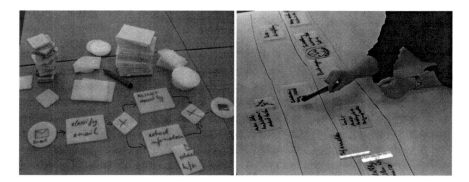

Fig. 17 TBPM elements and interview with TBPM

reported that the pieces were gratifying to handle, and that it was easy to make changes in their renditions of their processes by sliding the pieces around the table. With respect to the media-models framework, tangible systems modeling objects constitute a move towards less resolution and less abstraction than traditional BPM media (Fig. 13).

We found systems modeling rubric to be somewhat arbitrary in respect to BPM. Why not try a tangible set based on BPM Notation? While this may seem obvious in retrospect, it was not a clear choice to begin with.

5.3.4 Tangible Business Process Modeling (TBPM)

In our current instantiation of BPM media, TBPM, we translated four basic BPMN shapes into tangible acrylic pieces (Fig. 17). Virtually all other BPMN shapes could be made form these four basic shapes by writing on them with dry erase marker. With TBPM, the table itself becomes an explicit player, upon which BPM swim lanes are drawn, along with lines connecting activities.

Experimental subjects who had used TBPM elements had the benefits of a memory aid. However, they were able to frame their experience not simply as steps, as with Post-It® Notes, but as a process, which included an understanding of parallelism and alternatives, achieved by placing TBPM elements above one another. The final question, "Is there anything else you would like to add?" led to numerous adjustments and changes, including exceptions to the process they had not yet reported.

When we observed interactions between domain experts and process experts, we found the heightened level of involvement of both parties striking. Domain experts easily grasped fundamental BPM concepts, noting parallelism and alternatives in their processes. At the end of modeling sessions, when asked if there was anything else they would like to share, domain experts dug more deeply into their processes, noting details, exceptions, and making changes.

We were also surprised to learn that interviewers exhibited a higher level of engagement with the domain expert than they did in standard interviews or interviews conducted with Post-It® Notes. We speculate that this was due to two factors: using a shared physical object, and using a domain specific representation.

Interviewers were able to focus on the unfolding of the process without attempting to hold all the disparate pieces in their memory or having to concentrate on writing down responses to questions. Furthermore, because TBPM is domain specific, the burden of interpreting data was lifted, since much of the work of interpretation happened on the table. It seems that our bias toward the end user in user-centered design obscured the fact that there was more than one kind of user in the equation. We realized that the interviewer, or process expert, is a user as well.

In respect to the media-models framework, TBPM is an example of hybrid media, tangible elements on a loosely rendered timeline. While more abstract and more resolved than our first attempt, role-playing with Lego™, TBPM is less resolved and less abstract than traditional BPM media (Fig. 13).

One of the most enjoyable outcomes of our work with HPI was the unexpected learning we gained. The biggest insight showed us the importance of domain-specific instantiations of media-models. Having worked almost entirely in mechanical engineering design, we took for granted that the media-models we used should be situated in that practice. It took some time to realize that we had to create media-models that were specific to BPM. Through framing the *media of TBPM* as a process model, we found that end users could frame their *experience* also as a process with very little training. This made it much easier for them to understand and give meaningful feedback when they were presented with formal process models.

The comparison of TBPM and Post-It® Notes told us that simply having movable objects did not make for meaningful interviews. In order to be effective, shared media needs to be tuned to the domain in which it is situated.

6 Conclusion

While our research is still in the early stages, the media-models framework has been a successful guide to navigating the landscape of shared media. Through the empirical investigation of shared objects, we have brought a modicum of research-based rigor to the perceived best practices of the engineering design community.

The media-models framework has been particularly useful in identifying the "missing media" in BPM practice. As detailed in this paper, traditional BPM relies heavily on highly abstract and highly resolved media, such as flow charts and well-formed narrative. Media of this sort has been shown not to support paradigmatic shifts in the shared model, a necessary component of innovative design thinking. Furthermore, the media of traditional BPM has been "owned" by process experts, which has the effect of barring domain experts from participating in uncovering their implicit processes.

In response to our first question, "How can we engender better conversations among the stakeholders (domain experts and process experts) by consciously moving the BPM media-models around the media-models framework?" we have found that by translating traditional BPM media into media characterized by lower resolution and lower abstraction, we have made a more flexible media that supports exploration and negotiation amongst stakeholders.

As for the second question, "How can we create an *open* media in order to give direct involvement to BPM end users?" TBPM explicitly delivers control of the model into the hands of all participants at the table, allowing the ability to "think with their hands" as they work out what the nature of their implicit process is. TBPM affords moving, rearranging, adding, and putting aside its elements.

7 Future Work

More work remains in the development of a robust TPMN toolkit and methodology. Process improvement is a facet of BPM that is particularly interesting to us. We believe that TBPM will prove to be a strong tool for process improvement among existing stakeholders. However, a broader perspective may serve process improvement. To that end, we are exploring Customer Value Chain Analysis (Donaldson et al. 2006) with the TBPM toolkit. It is our desire to develop media and methodologies which support a *generative* approach to modeling the Customer Value Chain (CVC) in contrast to an *analytic* approach. Though physical embodiment of relations, time, and effort we hope to uncover pain-points for stakeholders. This in turn will allow designers to explore alternatives to the current CVC. The insights gleaned from this approach can be channeled back to TBPM as a framework for making global improvements to process models.

References

Agarwal, R., Sinha, A., Tanniru, M.: Cognitive fit in requirements modeling: A study of object and process methodologies. Journal of Management Information Systems 13(2) (1996) 137–162

Blanco, E., Grebici, K., Rieu, D.: A unified framework to manage information maturity in design process. International Journal of Product Development 4(3) (2007) 255–279

Boujut, J., Blanco, E.: Intermediary objects as a means to foster co-operation in engineering design. Computer Supported Cooperative Work (CSCW) 12(2) (2003) 205–219

Buxton, W.: *Sketching User Experiences: Getting the Design Right and the Right Design*, 2007, Morgan Kaufmann, San Francisco, CA

Clark, A.: *Supersizing the Mind*, 2008, Oxford University Press, Oxford, UK

Donaldson, K.M., Ishii, K., Sheppard, S.: Customer Value Chain Analysis, in Research in Design, 2006, 16: 174–183, London

Edelman, J.A., Leifer, L., Banerjee, B., Jung, M., Sonalkar, N., Lande, M.: Hidden in Plain Sight: Affordances of Shared Models in Team-Based Design, International Conference on Engineering Design, ICED'09, Aug 24–27, Stanford, CA, USA

Frederick, M.: *101 Things I Learned in Architecture School*, 2007 MIT, Cambridge, MA

Hatchuel, A., Weil, B.: "C-K Theory: Notions and Applications of a Unified Design Theory", 2002 Proceedings of the Herbert Simon International Conference on Design Sciences

Odum, H.T.: *Ecological and General Systems: An Introduction to Systems Ecology*, 1994, University Press of Colorado, Niwot, CO

Meadows, D. H.: *Thinking in Systems*, 2008, Chelsea Green Publishing Company, White River Junction, Vermont

Tversky, B.: "What Does Drawing Reveal About Thinking?", 2006 Lecture for *Visualizing Knowledge Seminar*, Stanford University

Tversky, B., Suwa, M., Agrawala M., Heiser J., Stolte C., Hanrahan, P., Phan D., Klingner, J., Daniel, M.-P., Lee, P., Haymaker, J.: Sketches for Design and Design of Sketches, 2003, Stanford University, Stanford

Vessey, I., Galletta, D. Cognitive fit: An empirical study of information acquisition, Information Systems Research 2(1) (1991) 63

The Co-evolution of Theory and Practice in Design Thinking – or – "Mind the Oddness Trap!"

Julia von Thienen, Christine Noweski, Christoph Meinel*, and Ingo Rauth

Abstract In Design Thinking, theory and practice are closely interconnected. The theory serves as a blueprint, guiding companies in general and design teams in particular through the design process. Given such a close interrelation of theory and practice, we argue that Design Thinking research needs to be set up in a particular way too. This setup ties in with Design Thinking process models: To attain ever more befitting design solutions, prototypes are supposed to be tested and refined. Correspondingly, Design Thinking research should help to test and refine theory elements of Design Thinking. Researchers may serve as "dialogue facilitators," aiding the community of Design Thinkers to intensify their "dialogue" with empirical reality.

To provide reliable data on issues of central concern, we have tested experimentally two widely held convictions in the field of Design Thinking: (1) Multidisciplinary teams produce more innovate design solutions than monodisciplinary teams. (2) Teams trained in Design Thinking (by the D-School) produce more innovative solutions than untrained teams. In addition, degrees of communication problems were assessed. While both "multidisciplinarity" and "D-School training" have been associated with more unusual design solutions, with respect to utility a different picture emerged. Thus, hotspots have been identified that may stimulate some productive refinements of Design Thinking theory.

1 From Design Thinking to Design Thinking Research

How should teams approach design challenges? What do students need to learn to tackle design challenges successfully? With increasing frequency, *Design Thinking* is called upon to help answer these questions. Used by multiple big companies such as SAP, P&G, IDEO or GE Healthcare, accompanied by a lot of media attention and

J. von Thienen (✉), C. Noweski, C. Meinel, and I. Rauth
Hasso-Plattner-Institute, Campus Griebnitzsee, P.O. Box 900460, 14440 Potsdam, Germany
e-mail: e.valuate@hpi.uni-potsdam.de; meinel@hpi.uni-potsdam.de

* Principal Investigator

H. Plattner et al. (eds.), *Design Thinking: Understand – Improve – Apply*,
Understanding Innovation, DOI 10.1007/978-3-642-13757-0_5,
© Springer-Verlag Berlin Heidelberg 2011

propelled by an increasing number of training institutions, Design Thinking seems on its way to become the state-of-the-art innovation method. And yet, we understand only little about what really matters for it to be successful.

In the armchair we may think about these issues, but many crucial questions will remain unanswered. Those who truly wish to know will have to confront the real world: Careful empirical analyses are in place! With this thought in mind, we decided to make a real job of it – and put fundamental assumptions of Design Thinking to an experimental test.

Naturally, in the booming, buzzing field of Design Thinking there are innumerable aspects that warrant careful scientific investigations. Of course, one might just cherry-pick some questions, selecting the issues according to personal interests. Yet, the research ought to take into account the interests of people working in the field as well, or shouldnt it? So, we made it our first empirical research task to scan in a somewhat broader fashion the interests, hopes and worries of experts in the field. But sure enough, there was some trouble ahead: While the term "Design Thinking" seems to allude to a common set of practices and a common theoretical matrix, the experts held ready an astonishing variety of understandings. What does that imply for the task of testing empirically central assumptions of Design Thinking theory? Our answer will be an outlook on research endeavours particularly designed to match the characteristic relation of theory and practice in Design Thinking. It will be the basis we start from and return to in our experimental work.

2   Experts Revealing What They Think About Design Thinking

In the winter of 2009, we had the opportunity to speak to a number of Design Thinking experts and conducted a series of guideline interviews of about $1\frac{1}{2}$ h each. In this context, we wish to thank once more members of IDEO, the Design Services Team of SAP, design consultants from Procter & Gamble and Palm as well as members of the staff and teachers of the Design Schools in Potsdam and Stanford. The interviews focussed on three major issues:

1. The definition and understanding of Design Thinking (the process and its methods) as well as prototypical conflicts in Design Thinking projects
2. needs regarding the work environment and tools
3. successful team orchestration and its specific needs

Key insights were synthesized using storytelling and clustering techniques within the project team. Papers have, or will be published on each of the topics. Here, we shall briefly review those issues that helped to shape our further approach within the *HPI* research program.

What stroke us as most momentous for the whole enterprise of Design Thinking research was the grand variety of understandings across experts in the field: The interviewees did not convey a common understanding of Design Thinking. They specified differing process models and named differing methods as crucial elements of the design process.

We found, for example, opposite beliefs regarding the question whether design work should be outsourced or not. According to some experts, design teams need to work outside of common business contexts to avoid being "captured" in their routines. These experts argue that creative freedom needs to be maximized. Ideally, the development of new design ideas should therefore be outsourced. Other leading experts prefer integrative approaches where managers set up teams by bringing together employees from different departments. This way, a single team may attend a project from the earliest up to the latest stages. While different departments are responsible for different steps in the design process (e.g., idea generation versus final implementation), representatives of all departments are joined in the responsible design team right from the start.

To mention another point of divergence, some experts highlight the pivotal importance of individual genius. Others believe, however, that individual genius is comparably unimportant when it comes to predicting the success of a design project. Instead, they say, teams need to be assembled according to sophisticated theories so as to combine particularly "matching" characters and competences.

Interestingly, the experts did not only differ in the concrete approaches they preferred. They explained their understanding of Design Thinking on different scales and reflected upon differing academic discourses. Obviously, there is no common set of beliefs (yet) associated with Design Thinking. Rather, there are differing lines of debate as well as differing practices. To what extent we should strive to bring them together is an interesting question by itself.

Apart from considerable differences in the general understanding of Design Thinking, there were – fortunately! – a number of important commonalities too. Without any such visible connecting factors it would be hard to see how Design Thinking could be studied as a collective enterprise.

A strong focus on **user needs** is considered essential across the board and the aim of true **innovation** is a shared concern. Design teams should not just head for quantitative improvements (such as devising a memory stick with yet more storage capacity, applying well known technologies). They should also be able to bring about qualitative improvements (e.g., by devising new technologies that are more potent or by developing solutions that make memory sticks superfluous altogether). That is, design teams should reconsider initial design challenges ("reframing"): They should try to understand what the users' true needs are. Then, they should consider a whole variety of approaches, including (and quite essentially so) uncommon ones, the so called "wild ideas." In a continuous dialogue with the users, a solution shall finally be worked out that suits the users' needs particularly well.

Another aspect that many Design Thinkers view as central is the academic diversity of design teams. Commonly, **multidisciplinarity** is considered a good choice. Teams are supposed to be academically diverse so that they may integrate impulses from many different domains. It is assumed that multidisciplinarity is particularly well-suited to foster true innovation.

Next to multidisciplinarity, other factors are thought of as crucial for team performance too. In particular, many interviewees stressed the importance of a positive **communication culture**.

In sum, the experts named a number of common concerns. But, strikingly, they did not sketch out a common theoretical matrix associated with the term "Design Thinking." This is a finding that should occupy us! Given the cloudy theory structure of Design Thinking, what are we to expect of Design Thinking *research*?

3 Telling Differences, Illuminating Parallels

Traditionally, theories are considered to be systems of axioms: There are a couple of fundamental propositions from which everything about the field of interest may be deduced. When a scientist refers to "the theory," he refers to its set of axioms. Correspondingly, accepting a theory means to accept "the axioms." With this classical picture in mind, there seems to be something quite worrisome about Design Thinking. If it is a theory – or builds on a theory – where are its axioms? As became all too clear in the expert interviews, there is no common set of propositions that Design Thinkers accept in virtue of their expertise. There are *some* shared convictions that may be understood as guiding theoretical ideas. But, they certainly do not cover the whole domain of interest. Apart from that, rather than there being fundamental assumptions, there are shared *centres of concern*: Usability, multidisciplinarity, unusualness ("go for the wild"), reframing of original tasks – to name some in a random order. Experts occasionally disagree as to how important each issue is in differing project phases. But they routinely monitor and discuss them. Now, what does the lack of a classical theory-structure mean for Design Thinking? Is it nonprofessional after all? Is it in such an early stage of its development that it has not even managed to produce a meagre axiomatic system?

We, in contrast, believe the "axiomatic system" is a misguided ideal for Design Thinking. There are good reasons for the open theory-structures that characterize Design Thinking today. These open structures are sensible, but nonetheless they may – of course – be improved. To see how the structures make sense and what likely aims there may be for improvements, it seems a good idea to scan the academic field for domains with similar challenges.

Musicology, for instance, does have some interesting parallels to Design Thinking. First of all, its subject is something *productive* and *creative*: Musicologists study pieces of music and their composition just like academic Design Thinkers study design solutions and their coming about.

When looking at – say – pop songs, music theory serves a dual function. On the one hand, it *describes* songs. On the other hand, by working out and comparing song patterns the theory provides a *blueprint* how songs may be composed (successfully). For example, there typically is an intro, then strophes and the chorus alternate, there are bridges, breaks and, finally, an ending. Longer instrumental interludes are typically placed in the second half of a song, not the first.

Yet, such a scheme is not enough for a song. Individual musicians have to fill in the blanks. Novices in particular may profit from following strictly the blueprint they are given. But experts (or: visionaries) may produce masterpieces by breaking the rules. Some of the time, they thus establish new patterns that other musicians will use fruitfully in the future.

In Design Thinking, things are not all that different. Design Thinking theory serves a dual function as well. It helps to describe and analyse design projects (e.g., does reframing happen at some point? What does the team do and when to ensure usability?). Design process models convey standards as to which phases there are and in which order they be put. They also encompass methods that may be invoked.

When a design team orchestrates its own project, it may well profit from given schemes. But sure enough there are blanks to fill in. (For instance, "Here we are in the research phase. We have methods A through H at our hands. Which shall we pick? How exactly shall we proceed?")

As Design Thinkers grow more and more experienced, they may identify circumstances in which unconventional procedures seem more promising than standard ones. Out they move of common schemes. They break the rules! If this happens, it is an interesting case for Design Thinking theory. Such a "breaking of rules" should not be generally damned. It is a precious test case. Maybe it fails. But if it doesn't, Design Thinking theory hits on an alternative whose potential is yet to be explored.

The parallels between musicology and Design Thinking illuminate two important issues that we need to keep in mind to avoid working towards an inadequate theoretical ideal.

The co-evolution of theory and practice. According to the classical understanding, a theory is true if it describes the empirical world correctly. An unbridgeable gap separates theory and world. Changing the theory will not change the world.

In the case of Design Thinking, as in the case of musicology, the gap is being crossed all the time. Since the theory provides blueprints to practitioners, a change in the theory is likely to change the empirical world itself. Theory and practice co-evolve. In consequence, the question of whether or not Design Thinking theory is true does not "function" in a conventional way. In many respects, Design Thinking theory may be true for trivial reasons: Because it serves as a scheme according to which practitioners proceed. Truth is cheep to have for Design Thinking theory in these regards. And truth does not suffice.

Consider the two claims:

(a) The theory is true.   True or false?
(b) The theory is (most) useful. True or false?

Conventionally, scientists ask whether claim (a) is maintainable. In the case of Design Thinking, claim (b) seems to be the more fundamental, the more demanding. It is the one whose correctness calls for rigorous empirical investigations.

Since theory and practice *are meant* to co-evolve, empirical evidence for a lack of utility will not (and should not) lead to the rejection of claim (b). Instead, careful analyses need to follow. Design Thinking theory – in particular: aspects of its process model – may have to be modified to become ever more useful.

The researcher as a dialogue facilitator. What is the second issue we may – and should – learn from the parallels between musicology and Design Thinking? In our understanding, one more point is particularly important for a proper setting of goals. The example of musicology teaches us how fruitful it can be to have both at the same time: An overall-open theory structure that may seem cloudy – yet a rigorous precision in analytic conceptions.

On the one hand, it is clear that there are many ways to produce felicitous pieces of music; and there are different music styles that may be just as appealing. In this sense, it would be detrimental if musicology would specify one single theoretical matrix according to which music ought to be produced. Musicological theory needs to be open; it needs to be able to handle plurality and to incorporate new developments that the future will (hopefully) bring. This openness in theory structure does not, however, imply that it is necessary or helpful to work with cloudy concepts and claims. For example, think of notes and rhythms that do a marvellous job in documenting and structuring something as elusive as played music! (Do you think you could come up with just *two concepts* such that whole design projects could be reconstructed on their basis? If you have some spare time, maybe sitting in a bus or plain, why not give it a try?)

The aim of potent and precise analytic conceptions – despite of an overall open theory structure – is, we think, an excellent target for Design Thinking as well. While it is clear that Design Thinking theory needs to remain open to allow for new developments, we should still strive to refine our analytical conceptions so that they be ever more potent systematizing factors. We should also try to learn more about our individual versus collective claims – and how well they are substantiated.

With this background understanding, we feel that some rather peculiar role befits us, the researchers. We wish to serve as dialogue facilitators: We wish to help Design Thinkers enter in an intense dialogue with empirical reality. What concepts, what assumptions work well, which do not work all that well yet? The research ought to put Design Thinkers in a position to sharpen their vocabulary and their fundamental beliefs in a way that makes them ever-more adapt to reality, ever more fruitful.

4   Preparing a Look Behind the Curtain: Specifying Hypotheses

As there is no written out axiomatic system in Design Thinking that specifies crucial assumptions one after the other, it is the researchers' first job to pin down crucial beliefs in the field. Our take in the last year was this: In general, it is assumed that Design Thinking fosters innovation. After all, Design Thinking is supposed to be an innovation method (or even: *the* state-of-the art innovation method). So, people who have been trained in Design Thinking should produce more innovative solutions than people who have not been thus trained.

Of course, there are multiple institutes who offer Design Thinking education. As the *Design Thinking Research Program* in Potsdam and Stanford enjoys a close cooperation with the D-Schools in Potsdam and Stanford, the Design Thinking education we shall look at will be a D-School training. Our starting hypothesis may thus be formulated more specifically: It is assumed that D-School trained teams produce more innovative solutions than teams without this training. Additionally, to consider one rather confined factor, we shall test the widespread belief that multidisciplinarity enhances innovation. If the belief is correct, multidisciplinary teams produce more innovative solutions than monodisciplinary ones on average.

While the two hypotheses concerning D-School training and multidisciplinarity are viable starting points, they need to be further refined. In particular, "innovation" is such an abstract notion that it is too remote from potential measurement operations. In such a case, it is usually a good idea to break the abstract concept down into disparate factors that may be assessed more easily. This is our take:

A design solution S_1 is considered more innovative than a solution S_2 if S_1 is more unusual as well as more useful than S_2.

Given this clarification of what "innovative" means, both of the starting hypotheses split into two more specific claims. These are the assumptions regarding D-School education:

1. D-School trained teams produce *more unusual* solutions than teams without this training.
2. D-School trained teams produce *more useful* solutions than teams without this training.

Accordingly, two hypotheses may be formulated concerning multidisciplinarity:

3. Multidisciplinary teams produce *more unusual* solutions than monodisciplinary teams.
4. Multidisciplinary teams produce *more useful* solutions than monodisciplinary teams.

While there are ample reasons to believe that multidisciplinary teams will indeed produce more innovative solutions than monodisciplinary ones on average, there is at least one notable reason to believe the opposite – and it may be fruitful to consider these reasons distinctly.

Experts who have been trained in the very same way of analyzing and approaching a subject matter are likely to invoke the strategies they are all used to when working on a new problem. Whatever work strategies are being used, by and large they pave the way for some particular type of result while detracting from other options. For example, imagine a team of chemists and a team of classical philologists who are to analyze a painting. While the chemists might take tiny samples of the paint and find out which material components have been used, the philologists might identify a scene from Greek mythology and reason backwards to the exact literary sources the painter had been exposed to. Given the specialized knowledge and training of the experts, there seems no way that the philologists could hit on the work results that chemists get and vice versa. Limiting oneself to a fixed set of (common) work strategies usually means limiting oneself to particular types of (common) results. In multidisciplinary teams, however, the approaches that team members are familiar with are likely to differ. Thus, there will be no immediate way of setting about the task. Rather, team members will have to (re-)consider the approaches they find convenient. In bargaining how to move on, they will have to detach themselves from common practices – melding, merging, blending the strategies they know in a way that seems appropriate in the context of their current challenge. The broader the domain of strategies experts are willing to consider, the broader is the domain of results that their team may obtain. Insofar as new approaches are tried, the odds increase that something rather unusual results. Thus, it seems likely that multidisciplinary teams produce more unusual results than monodisciplinary teams.

Regarding the second facet of innovation – usefulness – multidisciplinarity may be all the more advantageous. After all, the development of useful solutions depends upon knowledge, e.g., knowledge concerning the situation of users or knowledge about technical options for realizing some particular idea. Imagine experts who are equally well trained. Clearly, if they are all trained in the very same domain, the knowledge their team disposes of is rather limited compared to the knowledge of a team whose members differ in their fields of expertise. Thus, multidisciplinary teams seem better equipped for developing useful solutions.

Yet, at the same time, there is a reason to believe that, on average, multidisciplinary teams will produce less innovative solutions than monodisciplinary ones. Why that? Even if multidisciplinary teams have a greater potential for innovation, communication problems might hinder them. It seems reasonable to expect that communication will be more challenging in multidisciplinary than in monodisciplinary teams. Just as people with differing academic backgrounds have been trained to use different strategies when approaching a problem, they have also been trained to use different concepts. The words they use may differ, the categories by which they sort things in the world may differ and the implications associated with one or the other categorization may differ as well. If design teams are unable to work out a common conceptual ground, they may not be able to make good use of the wide-ranging expertise of their team members. Thus, we decided to consider a fifth hypothesis that may shed some light on important team processes in the design process:

5. Multidisciplinary teams experience more communication problems than monodisciplinary teams.

At the same time, D-School training might well make a difference with respect to communication success. D-School trained team members might – or rather: they should – be able to handle potential communication problems, whether or not working multidisciplinarily. After all, it is assumed that they are particularly apt for design work. Thus, they must not be thwarted or halted by potential communication obstacles. A sixth and final hypothesis is therefore:

6. D-School trained teams experience less communication problems than teams without this training.

5 Why Experiments Matter

As preliminary considerations have been formulated, a choice needs to be made as to how the subject matter shall be tackled empirically. In principle, two alternatives are available. Investigations can be experimental or non-experimental. Both approaches have their advantages as well as their disadvantages. The experimental method has been devised to fade out or "oppress" all the factors potentially relevant to an outcome except for those factors whose influences are to be investigated (as specified by the hypotheses). Thereby, the relationship between the factors that one takes interest in becomes maximally clear. But, naturally, one doesn't find out anything about the other factors (not addressed by the hypotheses) that one is at such pains to fade out in the experimental setting. In non-experimental studies, on the other hand, one may explore all the facets of real-life situations in their full booming buzzing mix-up. Thus, you may come to consider aspects you would never have thought about in your office armchair, extrapolating from the data hypotheses as to how they *might* be interrelated. Yet, whether these putative causal relations truly exist, one cannot really tell.

In our case, factors have been selected that are of primary interest. The crucial question is whether or not they are causally related. If D-School training and multidisciplinary actually do enhance innovation (as is hypothesized), a hook-up question may be how strong their effect is. These are questions to which experiments alone provide thoroughly compelling answers.

6 The Challenge

In every experiment, the setup requires thorough considerations as it sets the upper limit of what can be found out. In our case, a challenge needs to be formulated concerning a topic that all participants are about equally familiar or unfamiliar with. Otherwise, some teams might dispose over a lot of knowledge regarding the subject matter right from the start as some members would be experts, while other teams would have laypersons only. Regardless of whether one believes that teams profit from an expert (due to their knowledge) or whether one considers experts as a threat to innovation (because they might act as rigorous sensors), the teams with versus without experts would not be working under comparable conditions. Let's assume that, in the end, the presented solutions actually differ in their quality. These differences could not be clearly attributed to the factors of multidisciplinarity versus monodisciplinarity or D-School training versus no such training if the teams had differed in other respects as well, such as expert knowledge versus no such knowledge.

In addition, the scope of the challenge should be somewhat grand, or at least not minute. It should be "open" enough so that it would be possible to come up with a technical or a social solution or an artistic or political or yet other type of solution. A related demand is that there should be the possibility of using knowledge from diverse fields. If, on the other hand, only people with one particular academic training could complete the task (e.g., implement a certain computer algorithm), this would probably forestall successful Design Thinking right from the start.

The challenge that was chosen to meet these needs was this: Come up with something that helps traumatized people to manage their everyday lives!

Indeed, the participants of our experiment (40 students) indicated that their pre-experience with the subject matter, trauma, was basically negligible. For example, no one had ever been a practitioner in the field or had had a considerable training in the domain. Only one student had ever encountered the subject matter in her university studies.

7 Operationalization or: Let's Be Concrete!

Now that a challenge has been specified the question of how to asses, how to "measure" the attributes of interest needs to be considered. Each team will present its suggestion for how to help traumatized people. What is to be done so that reliable measures result, i.e. estimates of the unusualness of each solution?

When invoking numbers in every day life, we often ask questions about concrete things. For example, how many eggs are left in the fridge? In cases like these, we may start counting right away. In our study, on the other hand, the factors of interest are quite abstract. This does make a difference for the procedure of assessing or "measuring" those factors. How is one to count the unusualness of a design solution, for instance? Obviously, some further steps need to be taken.

In order to assess abstract factors they need to be *operationalized*. The question to be pondered is this: Given the context of your particular study, what could you observe straightforwardly to find out about the factor(s) of interest? Your task is to find concrete entities that one can look at to arrive at reasonable statements about the abstract notions of interest.

In the setup of an experiment, the operationalization is a crucial step. If one's operationalization is unconvincing, one's data will fail to bear on the issue that one sets out to investigate! Thus, in the case of our experiment as well as in general, we want to invite you to take a very careful look at the operationalizations: What do people (we) actually observe when they (we) make claims about highly abstract matters? Is the step they (we) take from observed entities to theoretical entities actually warranted? In our case, on the level of theory there are five factors of interest: (1) D-School training, (2) academic diversity, (3) the unusualness of design solutions, (4) the usefulness of design solutions and (5) communication problems.

While the factors (3)–(5) truly call for discussion, for reasons of completeness we shall mention the first two as well. There was a very convenient way of assessing the academic background of participants: We basically asked them. In the case of Design Thinking experience we consulted official lists of D-School trainees and alumni.

What is "unusual"? While the "unusualness of a design solution" is too abstract to be looked at and counted directly, we may ask people questions and attain concrete answers, counting how many times particular replies are given. To arrive at a pertinent question, the following consideration seems reasonable: In the context of our experiment, a group presents an unusual solution if the other teams (who have worked on the same challenge, after all) failed to consider that particular possibility when discussing options for helping.

In the course of the experiment, every team has to present its solution. All the participants need to fill out a questionnaire including the following question – regarding each single presentation (of the other groups):

Item 1 Has the presented solution been discussed in your group as well?

    ☐ Yes, exactly in this form (1)
    ☐ Yes, in about that way (2)
    ☐ More or less (3)
    ☐ No, but that may have been a coincidence (4)
    ☐ No, we would never have hit on it (5)

The brackets show our coding. Thus, the statistical values obtained range from 1 to 5. Greater values indicate a greater degree of unusualness.

Of course, the participants of our study are not the only people to ever think about how one could help in the case of traumatisation. There are experts in the field, trauma therapists in particular, whose job it is to help traumatized people. In addition, there are people who have suffered a traumatisation, of course. They too may have thought about options for improving their situation. Accordingly, these experts shall be contacted, introduced to one design solution after the other and asked a question quite similar to *item 1*:

Item 2 Have you ever considered this option for helping before?

    ☐ Yes, exactly in this form (1)
    ☐ Yes, in about that way (2)
    ☐ More or less (3)
    ☐ No, but that may have been a coincidence (4)
    ☐ No, I would never have hit on it (5)

Again, values range from 1 to 5. Greater values indicate a greater degree of unusualness.

What is "useful"? While the design teams may contribute information regarding the unusualness of a design solution, they are hardly in a position to specify utility. Of course, members of design teams can say something about *what they think* how useful their solution is (and we did ask them this question). Yet, whether or not a tool is actually helpful is not decided by the developers but by the users. In our context, the users are traumatized people or therapists who work with traumatized people. (Many teams actually developed tools that would aid the therapists in helping their clients.)

To attain judgements of how useful each solution is experts have been asked the following question:

Item 3 What do you think, how helpful is this approach for the target group?

    ☐ Very helpful (5)
    ☐ Quite helpful (4)
    ☐ Somewhat helpful (3)
    ☐ Barely helpful (2)
    ☐ Not helpful (1)

Again, values range from 1 to 5. Greater values indicate a greater degree of usefulness.

When working with operationalizations, disposing over a second estimate for each factor of interest is commonly quite advantageous. It helps you check whether the numbers you attain actually represent what they are supposed to. If two different indicators of the very same factor point in the same direction this gives you some (further) evidence for their working properly. If, on the other hand, indicators for the same subject matter point in different directions, this is ample evidence for there being something wrong with your assessment procedure(s). Thus, a second item was formulated that ought to cap onto the factor "usefulness."

Item 4 Which approaches should be realized by all means?

Please mark up to five approaches!

Marked (1)
Not marked (0)

Again, the brackets show our coding. Values range from 0 to 1. Greater values indicate a greater degree of usefulness.

How to assess "communication problems"? Communication problems, of course, would have to be estimated by the team members and not by the experts (who were contacted after the experiment). At the end of the workshop, the participants were asked to fill out a questionnaire containing three items to assess potential communication problems.

Item 5 Was it easy or difficult for your group to reach an agreement?
    ☐ Very easy (1)
    ☐ Easy (2)
    ☐ Neither nor (3)
    ☐ Difficult (4)
    ☐ Very difficult (5)

Item 6 Have there been group decisions that you felt uncomfortable with?
    ☐ Not at all (1)
    ☐ Very few (2)
    ☐ Some (3)
    ☐ Several (4)
    ☐ Plenty (5)

Item 7 Have there been communication problems in your team?
    ☐ Not ever (1)
    ☐ Rarely (2)
    ☐ Sometimes (3)
    ☐ Often (4)
    ☐ Very often (5)

Table 1 The constructs of interest and their operationalization

Level of theory	Variations (Independent variables)		Outcome (Dependent variables)		
Of interest	Team setup		Innovation		Communication
	D-School training	Academic diversity	Unusualness of solution	Usefulness of solution	Problems

Level of observation (operationalization)

Who rated			Experts and teams	Experts	Teams
Observable	Statements, list	Statements	Item 1 (team) Item 2 (experts)	Item 3 (aid) Item 4 (choice)	Item 5 (agreement) Item 6 (decisions) Item 7 (problems)

In all three cases, values range from 1 to 5. Greater values are taken to indicate more communication problems.

Table 1 summarizes the variables of interest in the experiment and how the constructs have been operationalized.

Once the blueprint has been worked out and all the necessary provisions have been made, the experiment may begin. This is what happened:

8 Looking Behind the Curtain: The Experiment

The experiment spanned over five full days. It took place at the D-School on the Potsdam campus. The participants had to be present for the whole time, beginning from 9.30 each morning; on some days there were teams still working as late as midnight.

The project had been announced both as a "workshop on trauma" as well as an "experiment." It was made clear on all placards that the project was part of an experimental research program. Thus, the activities of participants would be observed and documented. At the same time, the program to be followed throughout the five days resembled that of a workshop. Participants would be supplied with information regarding trauma and had the task of developing some helpful approach.

40 students participated in the study, 15 men and 25 women. About half of the students had a technical background (software systems engineering). The background of the other students varied widely. Majors included business studies, languages, sports and others. On average, the participants were 22.71 years old and studied in the 4.82 semester. Half of the participants had been trained by the D-School, half of them not. We randomly assigned them to the mono- versus multidisciplinary team condition, making sure that there would be the same number of teams in each condition. Ideally, there should be three teams (of four members each) in all the four conditions:

1. D-School trained, multidisciplinary
2. D-School trained, monodisciplinary

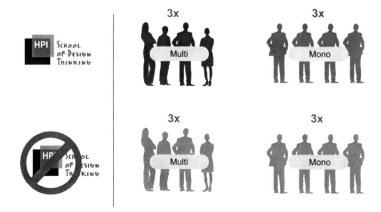

Fig. 1 The experimental setup allots three D-School trained multidisciplinary teams, three D-School trained monodisciplinary teams, three multidisciplinary teams without D-School training and three monodisciplinary teams without D-School training

3. Not-D-School trained, multidisciplinary
4. Not-D-School trained, monodisciplinary

Due to illnesses, there were some minor variations in the number of participants.

On each day of the experiment, multiple observations were made over and above those already specified. The participants filled out questionnaires regarding diverse issues such as their plan for proceeding, their satisfaction with their current standing, how they spent their time etc. A random sample of teams was filmed throughout the entire week, insofar as they were present at the D-School. Pictures were taken of all workspaces. The final presentations of all groups (approximately 10 min) were video-recorded. These video presentations as well as written summaries of the design solutions (1–2 pages) were made available online.

In the context of a lecture, the material was presented to trauma therapists and clients who had agreed to evaluate the solutions. The participants of the workshop/experiment were not present at that lecture so that personal sympathies or animosities would not bias the expert judgements (Fig. 1).

9 Design Thinkers Versus "Ordinary Students": Results

Of the two aspects of **innovation** that have been distinguished, lets consider **unusualness** first. D-School teams receive higher ratings than Non-D-School teams, as was hypothesized. The finding is consistent across experts and team members. Experts rate the unusualness of solutions by D-School teams with 2.80 on average; solutions by untrained teams 2.54. (Higher ratings indicate a greater degree of unusualness.) The participants themselves rate solutions by D-School teams 4.06 on average, solutions by other teams 3.65. The average unusualness ratings of experts

Table 2 Results regarding "usefulness" as estimated by the experts, comparing D-School trained teams with untrained teams

Question on usefulness	D-School	N	Mean	Mean diff.	p
What do you think, how helpful is this approach for the target group? (Experts, 1–5)	Trained	20	3.60	0.65	<0.05
	Untrained	24	4.25		
Which approaches should be realized absolutely? Please mark up to five approaches! (Experts, 0 or 1)	Trained	20	0.25	0.258	n.s.
	Untrained	24	0.42		

versus participants differ quite considerably in their height: Experts generally give lower ratings than participants. Thus, experts seem to have tapped the domain of potentially helpful interventions more completely than the project teams. Yet, the data consistently favors D-School teams in terms of unusualness.

Regarding the second facet of innovation, **usefulness**, all teams perform quite well. In none of the experimental conditions the average rating falls below "3," indicative of a "somewhat helpful" solution.

Just like the two measures of unusualness yield a consistent picture, the two measures of usefulness are consistent with one another too. However, the picture they suggest deviates from what had been expected. Not only does the data fail to show a significant superiority of D-School solutions. Indeed, Non-D-School teams outplay teams with D-School experience.

In Table 2, the column "N" specifies the number of ratings upon which the group averages are calculated. The column "p" specifies whether or not the difference between trained versus untrained teams is statistically significant. "N.s." means not significant, "<0.5" means significant and "<0.01" means highly significant.

Teams without D-School training receive higher ratings (4.25) on average than D-School trained teams (3.6). Higher values indicate a greater degree of usefulness; values may range between 1 and 5. The second measure of utility – whether or not a solution is chosen by the experts to be implemented "by all means" – points in the same direction. Solutions presented by teams without D-School training are selected more often (0.42) than solutions by D-School trained teams (0.25). Again, higher values indicate a greater utility; values may range between 0 and 1.

Now that we have considered trained versus untrained teams, lets take a look at the **mono-** versus **multidisciplinary** team condition.

Of all the groups, multidisciplinary D-School teams perform worst. Their average rating is close to 3 (somewhat helpful), whereas teams of all the other conditions receive an average rating above 4 (quite helpful) by the experts. Monodisciplinary teams outperform multidisciplinary teams, both in the D-School and in the Non-D-School condition.

Please note that statistical calculations for levels of significance depend not only on the size of the effect (here: the actual group difference) but also on the number of ratings. Thus, it is always a good idea to look at effect sizes over and above levels of significance. In Table 3, the average difference between mono- and multidisciplinary groups is greatest for D-School trained teams alone (first row in Table 3). It amounts to 1.083 as opposed to 0.167 for untrained teams (second row) or 0.633 for all teams

Table 3 Results regarding "usefulness" as estimated by the experts, comparing mono- versus multidisciplinary teams

	Teams	N	Mean	Mean diff.	p
D-School trained	Mono	8	4.25	1.083	0.05
	Multi	12	3.17		
Not D-School trained	Mono	12	4.33	0.167	n.s.
	Multi	12	4.17		
All teams	Mono	20	4.3	0.633	<0.05
	Multi	24	3.67		

together (third row). Yet, since the number of cases is halved when D-School teams are considered alone, the level of statistical significance is actually lower in the first row (for D-School teams only) than in the third row (where all the teams are considered).

Now, an interesting hook-up question may be whether there is some interrelation between unusualness and usefulness: Knowing that a solution is rather unusual (or usual), can you predict to some extent how useful the solution is? Or, vice versa, knowing that a solution is rather useful (or barely helpful), can you predict to some extent whether it is a rather unusual (or usual) solution?

Indeed, this is possible! The correlation between "unusualness" and "usefulness" is highly significant. It is negative: -0.547 ($p<.001$). This means, that the more unusual solutions are, the less they are helpful on average. (Correlations vary between -1 and 1. A value of zero indicates that there is no interrelation. A value of 1 indicates a perfect positive relation. A value of -1 indicates a perfect negative relation, that is: the higher the value of the first variable, the lower the value of the second and vice versa.) When only D-School teams are considered, the negative correlation between unusualness and usefulness becomes even more drastic: -0.700 ($p < 0.001$). This is an issue we will return to in the discussion.

Regarding **communication problems**, there is no statistically significant difference between mono- versus multidisciplinary teams; the effect sizes are negligible.

There is, however, a consistent difference between D-School trained teams versus untrained teams. According to all three indicators (items 5, 6 and 7), untrained teams experience more communication problems than teams with D-School training. This holds true both in the monodisciplinary as well as in the multidisciplinary team condition.

Teams without D-School training find it significantly more difficult to reach agreements (2.89 as opposed to 2.13). Members of not-trained teams report more group decisions they felt uncomfortable with (2.42 versus 1.88). Members of not-trained teams report more communication problems than members of D-School teams (2.53 as opposed to 1.88) (Table 4).

While some of the group differences fail to be statistically significant due to small N, it is noteworthy how consistent the picture is even when the mono- and multidisciplinary team condition are considered separately: All six comparisons indicate less communication problems in D-School teams (Table 5).

Table 4 Results regarding "communication problems", comparing D-School teams versus Non-D-School teams

Questions on communication problems	D-School	N	Mean	Mean diff.	p
Was it easy or difficult for your group to reach an agreement? (Item 5, teams, 1–5)	Trained	16	2.13	−0.77	<0.05
	Untrained	19	2.89		
Have there been group decisions that you felt uncomfortable with? (Item 6, teams, 1–5)	Trained	16	1.88	−0.546	n.s.
	Untrained	19	2.42		
Have there been communication problems in your team? (Item 7, teams, 1–5)	Trained	19	1.88	−0.651	<0.01
	Untrained	19	2.53		

Table 5 Results regarding "communication problems," comparing D-School teams with Non-D-School teams, multi- and monodisciplinary teams separately

		D-School	N	Mean	Mean diff.	p
Multi	Item 5	Trained	10	2.50	−0.600	n.s.
		Untrained	10	3.10		
	Item 6	Trained	10	2.00	−0.400	n.s.
		Untrained	10	2.40		
	Item 7	Trained	10	1.70	−1.00	<0.01
		Untrained	10	2.70		
Mono	Item 5	Trained	6	1.50	−1.167	<0.05
		Untrained	9	2.67		
	Item 6	Trained	6	1.67	−0.778	<0.05
		Untrained	9	2.44		
	Item 6	Trained	6	2.17	−0.167	n.s.
		Untrained	9	2.33		

10 Discussion

Regarding our two major experimental issues – **innovation** and **communication** – the second may be commented with greater ease as the findings approximate prior expectations. In terms of communication problems, no difference between mono- versus multidisciplinary teams has been found. Yet, D-School teams consistently report less difficulties than untrained teams. Does D-School training enhance communication skills so that communication obstacles may be handled more easily? Potentially. In pondering this causal claim, it needs to be considered that D-School trained team members generally knew each other in advance as they had studied together at the D-School. This familiarity yields an alternative explanation for reduced communication difficulties. Yet, quite a few of the untrained participants had known each other in advance as well. For example, most monodisciplinary teams comprised students of software systems engineering who knew each other from regular courses. Thus, there is some reason to assume that D-School training helps people to develop effective communication strategies. Whether the training does indeed have a causal effect in that regard, and what elements of the D-School experience most powerfully enhance communication skills, are issues that would have to be addressed by further studies.

More demanding, and potentially more interesting is the issue of **innovation**. Why were D-School teams, and multidisciplinary D-School teams in particular, outperformed by teams with no D-School experience?

A first reply might highlight the shortness of time available for the task. In a Design Thinking process, teams are encouraged to explore the problem space copiously before actually deciding on one particular solution. Indeed, this is what D-School teams did in the experiment. Untrained teams, on the other hand, were much quicker to decide. Quite a few of them selected their approach on the first day of the workshop. This left them with a lot more time for developing and refining a prototype. Following this line of thought, one might argue that D-School teams would have performed much better had they had a few more days to work on the project. Yet, this line of reasoning does not seem to endure careful consideration. After all, the experts did not rate the prototypes presented by the teams. These prototypes were, as a matter of fact, all rather foreshadowing than usable. What the experts did rate were the *ideas* teams had come up with. (If the suggestions were to be carried out, how helpful would they be?) D-School teams spent a lot of time selecting their idea, so the process of evaluation applied in the experiment should not work to their disadvantage. Thus, the supremacy of Non-D-School teams in our experiment calls for another explanation.

One important hint may be the strong negative correlation between **usefulness** and **unusualness**. Wild ideas are explicitly encouraged in the D-School training. While there is no need to question this outlook in general, there certainly is a danger of what may be called an **oddness trap**. When much effort is put into devising a solution that others will find surprising, solutions may be surpassed that are rather self-evident and yet highly effective. Indeed, these likely solutions may be the most effective ones in some circumstances. A "go-for-the-wild" approach might be more productive in circumstances when basically all likely solutions have already been explored and something else is wanted. In our experiment, this was obviously not the case. In all conditions, the average expert rating of "unusualness" falls between 2 and 3. That is, the experts state they have already considered the solutions presented by the teams, just not in all details precisely as the groups would have them.

In general, awareness of the oddness trap – knowing that there may be a trade-off between **unusualness** and **usefulness** – is only a first step. What we ought to strive for are means, strategies and potentially even techniques for avoiding the trap. Falling in love with funny ideas must not deflect designers from the user's true needs.

11 What We Wish to Pass Back

Having been endowed with a number of considerations by the Design Thinking community, we focused on a few recurrent believes. Now that the experimental results are in, our theory prototypes may be refined. In the dialogue between Design Thinkers and empirical reality, some hotspots have been identified that certainly span room for improvements. So, how can we sharpen our vocabulary? How can we refine our central believes so that they be ever more adapt to reality, ever more fruitful?

Regarding Design Thinking education, we might consider more explicitly what it is we wish to promote in differing circumstances. Certainly, there may be many situations in which fanciness or oddness is valuable in itself. In other cases, the users will want nothing but a working solution – whether fanciful or not. Maybe we can do a better job in systematising circumstances under which fanciness versus usefulness needs to be the ultimate standard. Maybe usefulness should always be the ultimate standard because fanciness trumps only when there is a major need for fanciness. In parallel to these theoretical issues, methodological considerations are likely as well: Should we equip students with (more) powerful methods to ensure a close(r) tie to the users' central needs? If so, ought we to provide a fixed procedure or would it suffice to make utility tests more explicit a factor in Design Thinking process models? Or, to name another possibility, should "carful utility tests" rather be taught as an overarching value/goal that students need to internalize?

Regarding the second experimental issue, we wish to turn to the advocates of multidisciplinarity in particular. Taking seriously the experimental results, some refinement in Design Thinking theory would seem helpful. This does not necessarily mean a major reorientation; some further specifications might due.

Perhaps multidisciplinarity does have a positive effect on innovation – but the effect is so small that it was easily overridden (and even "conversed") by chance variation in our experimental setting. If this is true, Design Thinking theory would surely profit from a realistic estimate of the effect size: If the effect size is small, we need to expect very limited gains with respect to innovation simply by assembling multidisciplinary instead of monodisciplinary teams. Or, to address another likely reasoning: Multidisciplinarity may have a considerable positive effect, but not in all contexts. For example, it comes to unfold its positive impact only after longer periods of time (months, not days). Another viable thought may be that multidisciplinary design teams provide more helpful prototypes than monodisciplinary ones when it comes to communicating design ideas to development divisions who work out final products. Such a handover was no subject of our experiment. Thus, there are many ways in which Design Thinking theory may be carried forwards by helpful specifications.

In sum, there is "experimental feedback" we may seek and use to refine Design Thinking theory – just as there is "user feedback" which design teams may seek and use to refine their prototypes. To be sure, this seeking and refining is a lot of hard work! And it may be a painful experience to see ones precious conceptions wobble under the pressure of an experimental test. But: We wouldnt be Design Thinkers if we were to duck out of the test, would we?

Innovation and Culture: Exploring the Work of Designers Across the Globe

Pamela Hinds* and Joachim Lyon

Abstract This chapter describes the preliminary results of a study of design practices in different regions and industries with the goal of understanding the relationship between culture, especially national culture, and the work of designers. In our ethnographic study, we have talked so far with 32 designers from Asia, Europe, and North American and observed designers as they did their work. We report initial insights about the role of the institutional context, especially client expectations, different attitudes toward what it means to be creative, different interaction norms within professions, different ways of using prototypes, and different ecologies around design education.

1 Introduction

Designers work every day in countries around the globe. They design cell phones, kitchen accessories, furniture, clothing, services, and just about everything we can imagine. How they do this and what it means to be a designer in different regions and cultures, however, is not well understood. In this research, we set out to understand and describe how design is practiced and what it means to be a designer in Asia, Europe, and the United States. Of course, this is a tall task and unlikely to be accomplished in a single year-long study. We did, however, gain insight into methods for doing such a comparative study and into a few key differences worthy of deeper exploration.

In this project, we take a broad, contextualized view of culture. Although we acknowledge that cultures are often characterized by different values (e.g. individualistic vs. collectivistic, see Hall 1963, Hofstede 1991), we focus more

P. Hinds (✉) and J. Lyon
Department of Management Science & Engineering, Stanford University, Stanford, CA 94305–4026, USA
e-mail: phinds@stanford.edu; jblyon@stanford.edu

* Principal Investigator

H. Plattner et al. (eds.), *Design Thinking: Understand – Improve – Apply*, Understanding Innovation, DOI 10.1007/978-3-642-13757-0_6,

Fig. 1 A nested view of
design thinking and practice

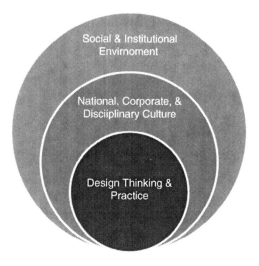

holistically on collaborative practices as situated in local and institutional contexts.
Practices, the local context, the institutional context, and peoples' values, we believe, are intertwined and inseparable. In keeping with this view, we define culture
as "a fuzzy set of attitudes, beliefs, behavioral norms, and basic assumptions and
values that are shared by a group of people, and that influence each member's
behavior and his/her interpretations of the 'meaning' of other people's behavior"
(Spencer-Oatey 2000, 4).

   We also subscribe to the point of view that culture is reflected not only in national
culture, but is a mosaic composed of cultural identities derived from a variety of
sources, including national culture, demographic features, and associations (see
Chao and Moon 2005). In this study, we focused on national culture, but incorporated company culture and disciplinary culture as intertwined cultural forces that
shape design practice. A nested view of culture considers the context in which people are embedded as instrumental in understanding behavior (see Perlow et al. 2004).
Figure 1 reflects our perspective on how design thinking and practices are embedded within their cultural context. Each layer affects and is affected by the adjacent
layers.

2   National Culture and Design Practice

In examining the related literature, we found no studies that explicitly investigated
the relationship between national culture and design practice. One of the most
relevant studies compared innovation management in Germany and China (Wang
et al. 2005). They reported that German innovation activities were more clearly divided, sequential, and scheduled while the Chinese preferred to have overlapping
activities. Khurana and Rosenthal (1998) also noted cultural differences in new

product development, suggesting formality in US firms and a holistic approach in Japan. These studies support our *a priori* belief that design practices may vary by culture. A gap, however, remains in our understanding of how national culture is manifested in the actual *practice* of designers *in context*. Further, most studies to-date focus on cultural dimensions and not the social and institutional context in which people are embedded. In a review of economic development in China, for example, Zhao et al. (2006) reported that China may have difficulty incorporating the voice of the customer because of their Confucian value for stability over change and may adhere more strictly to supervision and rules. This could directly affect how design thinking is manifested in China. A recent article published in Interactions Magazine (Chavan et al. 2009) describes the limitations of design methods in emerging countries, suggesting that there is significant opportunity to evolve design practices to be more sensitive to those cultures. Chavan describes, for example, her Bollywood method that is more suited to the Indian market because it engages users in a dramatic Bollywood-style storyline as a means of transcending Indians' reluctance to give feedback in user studies. Our study extends previous research by asking how culture and the cultural context is embodied in innovation practices.

To explore questions about the relationship between culture and design practice, we are conducting ethnographic research. Ethnographic research rests on insights that emerge during the investigation. This approach enables us to understand the *meanings* that people associate with idea generation, prototyping, sketching, and other design practices, thus providing a deeper understanding of these perspectives than is available using quantitative methods.

3 Method

Our study involved interviews with and observations of designers as they worked. We have conducted interviews with designers and design managers in North America, Europe, and Asia. Each of these interviews generally lasted about 60 minutes with a range of about 30–90 minutes. Most interviews were conducted in private offices and meeting rooms, although sometimes the situation dictated that we conduct interviews in open spaces, cafes, and over meals. The interviews were semi-structured. Although we prepared an interview protocol, our primary goal was to understand the designers, how they worked, and what it meant to be a designer from their perspective, so the interviews were driven by what they told us was important and interesting. The interview protocol also evolved over the course of the study as we learned more and identified avenues for fruitful exploration. In general, we asked questions about a current or recent project and explored with them how that project was organized, the sources of innovation, how prototypes were used, and how that project reflected (or didn't) them as a designer. All interviews (unless the interviewee requested otherwise) were recorded and transcribed. Where possible, interviews were conducted in the native language of the designer either directly or, on occasion, through an interpreter. When interviews were conducted in languages other than English, they were transcribed and then translated by a professional translator or by the interviewer him or herself. In total, we conducted approximately 32 interviews of designers in China, 8 in Korea, 12 in Europe, and 12 in North America.

In addition, we reasoned that in order to understand the work practices of designers in different regions, we need to understand how designers were trained. We therefore conducted interviews with students and faculty in design programs in the U.S., Asia (Korea), and Europe (The Netherlands). We plan to conduct additional interviews with students and faculty in China, other programs in the U.S., and in other countries in Europe.

We also observed designers at several of the firms. Our preliminary work made it clear that observations of designers were necessary to compare the nuances of how practice differed between sites. During the summer of 2009, our research team spent approximately 7 weeks in China and Korea talking with and observing designers. We will observe at additional sites as the project continues. Our observations entail watching designers as they work and keeping detailed and extensive notes of their activities, conversations, frustrations, and successes. Thus far, we have observed for 7 weeks in China and Korea and for very limited amounts of time in North America and Europe. Table 1 captures our data collection strategy, including the type of data being collected in each type of firm and in each region.[1] Although we only indicate observations when we were able to spend an extended amount of time at the field site, in all cases, when we visited the site for interviews, we conducted ad hoc observations and include these field notes in our analysis.

Our goal in this study is to understand designers from multiple regions, disciplines, companies, and countries. Our sampling strategy was therefore to study design consultancies and inhouse design firms that spanned at least two continents and operated in different design spaces (see Table 1). With the help of the Zhejiang Innovation Center, we were able to negotiate access to two Chinese design centers, one of which has a European design operation. Although SinoCo did not have design centers outside of Asia, we included them in the study because they offered

Table 1 Sample by type of company and region

	North America	Asia	Europe
SinoFashion (inhouse)		17 interviews, 7 weeks of observations	Planned
SinoCo (inhouse)		7 interviews	
Elite (design consultancy)	12 interviews	13 interviews	12 interviews
Innovat (design consultancy)	Interviews and observations planned	9 interviews, observations planned	Interviews and observations planned

[1] To maintain the confidentiality of the firms being studied, we have not specified the exact countries in which the offices are located.

useful insights into home appliance design in China and had worked extensively with design consultancies inside and outside of China and were, as a result, able to share with us their perceptions of the client-consultant relationship. We were also fortunate to gain access to two design consultancies with global operations, one of which has invited us to conduct observations of their designers in North America, Asia, and Europe.

One of the challenges of conducting cross-cultural research such as this is that the data are richer and more complete if the interviews are conducted in the designers' native language and if the observers have adequate language skills to understand the conversations that are taking place in the work setting. We therefore composed a research team in which several members had Chinese or Korean language skills and were native to or had lived for an extended time in those countries. As we continue to collect data in Europe, we will augment the team as appropriate.

4 Insights

4.1 Culture and Design

Our preliminary research has revealed several insights related to culture and design practices including the role of the institutional context, especially client expectations, different attitudes toward what it means to be creative, different interaction norms within professions, different ways of using prototypes, and different ecologies around design education.

4.1.1 Client Expectations

One of our findings was that design practices can be strongly affected by the corporate culture, but adaptations also may be required to meet the demands of the local clients. The structures of local culture, institutional context (such as client demands), and organizational culture were intertwined and mutually determined the practices of designers. Client expectations, particularly at design consultancies, were described as heavily influencing the types of prototyping, concept generation, and storytelling processes followed by designers in different regions. Our data suggest, for example, that clients have *frames* that determine their expectations for what the designers should deliver, how they should behave, and of their own role in the process. These frames then affect the way in which design is interpreted and enacted. Specifically, we found the strongest effects from frames or expectations around building relationships, process as a deliverable, whether design activity is seen as a cost or an investment, and the value of form versus function. On most of these dimensions, the client environments in North America, Asia, and Europe were quite different.

Client-consultant relationships. Building and maintaining relationships with clients was universally seen as a critical aspect of being a designer in a design consultancy. What we found interesting though was that the nature of the relationship was experienced differently in different regions. In North America, for example, the relationship with the client was described as collaborative. Clients got involved in the activities of projects, including need finding, and this was seen as a way of "bringing the client along." In Europe, the distance between the client and the designers was described as greater with some resistance on the part of the client to "reverse" the client-consultant relationship or disrupt the power relationship by "being too friendly." One designer told us, "They are in charge and in the driver's seat, and they deliver that harsher than U.S. clients." Asia was similar, if not more extreme, in their concerns that the design consultancies were "reversing the service direction" by asking clients to make choices or approve of design concepts midstream. Asian clients were described as wanting the design consultancy to work on the project and deliver a final design based on their own counsel. In addition, contracts with Asian clients tended to be more fluid and there was an expectation of getting "extras" as a show of strength in the relationship.

Differences in these perspectives on the client-consultant relationship affected how design was done in each of these locations. When the project involved more participation of the client and both parties were perceived as having more or less equal status, such as in North America, designers anticipated regular feedback from the client which they would integrate into the design process on an ongoing basis. In these cases, designers saw their role as balancing client involvement in the process and, at the same time, maintaining the integrity of their designs. A critical practice involved managing the boundaries of client involvement so that they had adequate freedom within which to innovate. In Europe and Asia, the challenge for designers was to design in the absence of regular interaction with and feedback from the client, so although they had more freedom to design, they spent a larger percentage of their time working on design briefs to sell their ideas to clients at pivotal points in the project and generally seemed more anxious about client acceptance.

Process as deliverable. With regard to process as a legitimate deliverable, Asian clients were said to not care about how the designers approached the design activities. One informant told us that "They don't care [about] the process... just show me the cool stuff." In contrast, in North America, being a partner in the process was highly valued. Clients wanted to *own* part of the process. Different attitudes toward process as a deliverable affected design practices, for example, because Asian designers were required to produce concrete and visual forms of the design much more quickly while the North American designers could remain conceptual and even deliver representations of their *processes* (as opposed to the design itself) as legitimate forms of progress. European clients seemed to occupy the middle ground, although seeing what the product was going to look like was important. As one designer put it, the client says, "You're designers, show me visuals. I want to see what this is going to look like..."

4.1.2   What It Means to Be Creative

In our conversations with designers and design directors, we found significant differences between North America and Asia in what it means to be creative. We were surprised (and intrigued) in several parts of Asia to hear that Western designers were perceived as "too creative." When we probed for the meaning of this phrase, we learned that Western designers were sometimes seen as being radical and designing products that couldn't easily be manufactured or were only appropriate for a "niche" market – they were just too "out there." In Asia, particularly when observing inhouse designers, we noticed that using existing similar products as sources of inspiration was the norm. Day after day (in multiple environments), we observed designers sketching new designs as they looked back and forth from images of similar products in magazines or on related websites. When asked about this, designers in Asia told us that their goal was to design something that fit within the stream of existing products. Although preliminary at this point, we got the sense that while the North American and perhaps the European notion of creativity is to stretch beyond what is expected or known, Asian notions of creative design valued harmony with existing products. This finding resonates with cross-cultural research on individualism and collectivism which suggests that those from the West tend to prefer to stand out, to differentiate themselves from others, whereas those from Asian cultures tend to prefer to blend in and be seen as part of the group (see Nisbett 2004). Consistent with this, in design consultancies, we were frequently told that Asian clients would ask for a design that essentially replicated an existing "hot" product on the market. These requests were puzzling for Western designers, but made sense to designers who were born and educated in Asia.

4.1.3   Interaction Norms Across Professions

Although we found that, superficially, many of the same occupations and roles existed across regions, we are beginning to see interesting differences in the way that those occupations are constituted and the interaction among professionals from different occupations. In the U.S., for example, there is a strong value placed on multi-disciplinary teams within which designers of different stripes work closely together and even learn to make contributions that go beyond their own occupational boundaries. Mechanical engineers, for example, may get involved in user studies and anthropologists might make contributions that would generally be made by industrial designers. We saw some evidence that the lines between occupations were less blurred in Asia. In our observations of fashion designers in Asia, for example, we learned that there was less cross-training between designers and pattern cutters and that it would have violated the norms for designers to cut their own patterns. In France and England, we were told, fashion designers were trained to be pattern cutters and were expected to be able to take on this role, or at least demonstrate a high level of competency when working with a specialist pattern cutter. These occupational jurisdictions had a significant effect on what work designers did (and didn't do) in different regions and how they interacted with other professions as they implemented their design ideas.

4.1.4 The Role of the Prototype

Across regions, firms, inhouse vs. design consultancies, and industries, prototypes played highly social roles as objects around which questions were asked and social interaction occurred. In all cases, designers created prototypes throughout the design process and used these as a way of understanding their own designs and getting feedback from others. We found numerous objects referred to as prototypes, including models, sketches, scenarios, CAD drawings, garment patterns, etc. The creation and use of prototypes was somewhat determined by the disciplinary training (e.g. mechanical engineering, industrial design, fashion design, etc.) of the designer as well as the local context (e.g. client expectations, speed of the design cycles, etc.). Designers, not surprisingly, relied heavily on their disciplinary training in the type of prototypes they were likely to create and the types of questions they asked through the prototypes. Although this somewhat aligned with their role in the design process, it was not a perfect match. Mechanical engineers, for example, regardless of the stage of the design, were more likely to talk about CAD drawings and physical prototypes that enabled them to see how the mechanisms were going to work. Client (internal and external) expectations also determined when and how prototypes were created and used. External clients in Asia and Europe, for example, were more responsive to prototypes that were polished and resembled the "real thing" whereas North American clients tolerated prototypes that were strung together with duct tape and bailing wire.

4.1.5 The Ecology of Design Education

From the interviews that we have conducted with design educators and students, one early insight is that the ecologies around design education vary across regions. In all cases, there are multiple constituents including students, faculty, administrators, potential employers, government bodies, and professional associations. How these constituents interact with educational institutions, the amount of influence they have, and how these interactions shape design education and the future work done by students educated at these institutions varies by region. We are continuing to collect data and analyze the interviews and observations from design programs to explore these relationships.

4.2   Methodological Insights

Although the primary goal of this study is to understand how design practices vary based on the cultural context in which designers are embedded, we also gained insight into methods for doing this type of research and summarize those here. First, we begun the study with interviews and quickly realized that observations were necessary because interviews did not yield the level of detail required to compare the nuances of how practices differed between sites. We concluded that cross-cultural comparisons of design practices require observations of the designers as they engage with ideas, objects, each other, and their clients. Second, it became clear that the most insight was available when studying the design of products whose design was not "universal," e.g. the products are likely to be used/understood differently in different cultures, since these products are more influenced by the local cultures in which they were sold and used. When studying objects such as cell phones or laptop computers, there were significantly fewer differences than when studying products such as home appliances and fashion because the design of these objects was more intertwined with the culture and context in which they were being used. Home appliances, for example, need to account for the particular culinary preferences, available ingredients, and the configuration of kitchens in a given region. Third, consistent with research in cross-cultural psychology, we found that Asia, Europe, and North America were distinct regions. Although there are, of course, cultural differences within each region, even larger differences are in evidence between these three regions. As a result, including designers from North American, Asian, and European locations enables comparisons that facilitate broader understanding. Finally, we noticed significant differences in the design practices of inhouse designers vs. those working in design consultancies. Conclusions for one may not hold for the other. Sampling strategies, therefore, need to account for these differences either by systematically including and analyzing the different types of design activity or focusing on one or the other.

5   Conclusions

In this preliminary research, we have refined methods for studying design practices in different regions around the world and have gleaned insights about how and why practices might vary. This initial foray into research on the relationship between culture and design practices reinforces our idea that there are not universal "best practices" for design and that each region, country, and culture finds its own design path that leverages the culture and context in which the designers are embedded and is sensitive to the clients for whom they are designing.

We write this chapter with great caution. First, this work is very preliminary and our insights are the result of an, as yet, superficial analysis of the data. Although we have confidence that the insights that we write about in this chapter reflect what we were told by designers, more data collection and much more analysis is necessary to make sense of all that we learned and to derive deeper and more meaningful insights. Second cross-cultural research runs the risk of using and/or perpetuating cultural stereotypes. Our goal is to identify cultural differences and to build knowledge about and respect for the importance of these differences within the cultural context in which design work is being carried out.

References

Chavan, A., Gorney, D., Brabhu, B., & Arora, S. (2009). The Washing Machine that Ate My Sari – Mistakes in Cross-Cultural Design, *Interactions Magazine*, ACM.

Chao, G., & Moon, H. (2005) The Cultural Mosaic: A Metatheory for Understanding the Complexity of Culture. *Journal of Applied Psychology* 90(6), 1128–1140.

Hall, E. T. (1963). *The Silent Language*. Greenwich, CT: Fawcett Publications.

Hofstede, G. (1991). *Cultures and Organizations*. London: McGraw-Hill.

Khurana, A., & Rosenthal, S. R. (1998) Towards Holistic "Front Ends" In New Product Development. *Journal of Product Innovation Management* 15:57–74.

Nisbett, R. (2004). *Geography of Thought*. New York: Free Press.

Perlow, L., Gitell, J., & Katz, N. (2004). Contextualizing Patterns of Work Group Interaction: Toward a Nested Theory of Structuration. *Organization Science* 15(5), 520–536.

Spencer-Oatey, H. (2000). *Culturally Speaking: Managing Rapport through Talk across Cultures*. London: Continuum.

Wang, Y. Q., Cheng, Y. J., & Jiang, Y. Z. (2005). Cross cultural innovation management - a study of automotive technology system development. *Engineering Management Conference, 2005. Proceedings. 2005 IEEE International* Volume: 2, 760–764.

Zhao, X., Flynn, B. B., & Roth, A. V. (2006). Decision Sciences Research in China: A Critical Review and Research Agenda-Foundations and Overview. *Decision Sciences* 37, 451–496.

The Efficacy of Prototyping Under Time Constraints

Steven P. Dow and Scott R. Klemmer[*]

Abstract Iterative prototyping helps designers refine their ideas and discover previously unknown issues and opportunities. However, the time constraints of production schedules can discourage iteration in favor of realization. Is this trade-off prudent? This paper investigates if – under tight time constraints – iterating multiple times provides more benefit than a single iteration. A between-subjects study manipulates participants' ability to iterate on a design task. Participants in the iteration condition outperformed those in the non-iteration condition. Participants with prior experience with the task performed better. Notably, participants in the iteration condition without prior task experience performed as well as non-iterating participants with prior task experience.

Keywords Prototyping · Iteration · Empirical studies of design

1 Introduction

Many designers evangelize the value of prototyping [3, 7–9, 31, 37, 50], encapsulated in the design adage, "Enlightened trial and error outperforms the planning of flawless intellect." Prototyping entails repeatedly trying ideas and getting feedback [31]. A canonical prototyping iteration comprises four steps: envisioning possibilities, creating a prototype to embody a possibility, getting feedback about the prototype, and reevaluating constraints [29]. However, time constraints often lead organizations and individuals to focus on realization rather than iteration [3, 50].

S.P. Dow (✉) and S.R. Klemmer
Human-Computer Interaction Group, Stanford University, Gates Computer Science Building,
353 Serra Mall, Stanford, CA 94305, USA
e-mail: spdow@stanford.edu

[*] Principal Investigator

H. Plattner et al. (eds.), *Design Thinking: Understand – Improve – Apply*,
Understanding Innovation, DOI 10.1007/978-3-642-13757-0_7,
© Springer-Verlag Berlin Heidelberg 2011

This paper investigates if, under tight time constraints, several rapid prototypes yield more valuable design insights than allocating that time to a single iteration. Twenty-eight participants were randomly assigned to one of two conditions for an individual design task. Participants in the iteration condition were encouraged to test and refine their design multiple times. Participants in the non-iteration condition spent all their design time on construction; they were prevented from testing their design. After the design period, participants set aside all prototypes and entered a build period to implement their design.

The design task for this experiment was an *egg drop exercise* where participants design a vessel from everyday materials to protect a raw egg from a fall. This task has several appealing properties: success is objectively measurable (drop height), participants need only minimal technical expertise, there are many possible valid solutions, and it can be completed in an hour-long session. Drop height was the primary dependent variable. Participants also estimated their vessel's performance before and after the design period. We gathered participant demographics and concluded each session with a semi-structured interview.

The iteration condition significantly outperformed the non-iteration condition: the iterating participants' designs reached higher drop heights before breaking an egg. Self-assessment of performance increased significantly across the design period for individuals in the iteration condition. Unsurprisingly, participants with prior egg drop experience outperformed those without prior experience. More notably, non-experienced participants in the iteration condition did as well as experienced participants in the non-iteration condition.

Prior to describing our experiment, we summarize the existing literature that sheds light on the function and value of iterative prototyping.

1.1 Oscillating Between Creation and Feedback

Prototypes can help define an idea's role, implementation, and look and feel [26]; they can build empathy for users [8]; they communicate to clients, users, and fellow designers [56]. Designers embody creative hypotheses in prototypes and then observe the outcome [31]. An iterative prototyping practice oscillates between creation and feedback: creative hypotheses lead to prototypes, leading to open questions, leading to observations of failures, leading to new ideas, and so on.

In the creation phase, designers ask the abductive question of "what might be" [43, 44]. Much of previous design research has emphasized the importance of creative idea generation [6, 34, 45, 47, 55]. Research on brainstorming [6, 45, 47, 51], synthesis [34], and framing [22, 57] techniques seeks to improve the abductive part of prototyping. Expertise literature suggests expert practitioners develop an organizational framework for retrieval and application of knowledge [17]; expert designers learn to effectively organize and act on locally contextual design information.

In the feedback phase, designers make inferences from observations [35]. Experimentation and feedback leads designers to discover unknown attributes, constraints, and opportunities that may not have been conceived of a priori. Discovery is not an automatic consequence of experimentation; the way people frame problems makes some insights salient and hides others [32].

1.2 Prototyping with Internal and External Representations

Designers can use mental imagery to envision and improve ideas [2, 18–20]. Christensen and Schun analyzed an engineering design setting where designers use mental simulation as a proxy for external prototyping, reducing "uncertainty language" within meetings [4, 10]. Similarly, Schön remarked that an expert designer possesses the ability to conduct a series of "what-if" moves with "discovered consequences, implications, appreciations, and further moves" [48]. But as Schön points out, the web of moves can become too complicated to manage in one's head – even for virtuosos – due to limitations in human memory and processing.

People leverage the physical world to overcome limitations in memory capacity [5, 46], to convert highly cognitive tasks into perceptual/motor tasks [12, 25, 27, 38], to effectively represent problems [36, 58], and to explore alternatives [33, 41, 42]. Kirsh and Maglio's study of the game Tetris found that players manipulated the pieces more than was pragmatically necessary for moving them to the right place [33, 42]. Kirsh and Maglio argue that these manipulations provide an epistemic technique for exploring alternatives. Prototypes are designer's way of trying things out.

Larkin and Simon [36] explored the representational differences between a diagram and a written description. They demonstrate two external representations may be informationally equivalent, but have significantly different computational efficiency. Designers' choice of external representations in prototyping has significant influence on how they explore a design space [9, 21, 39, 40].

Tversky and Suwa investigated how external representations promote discovery and inference. They show that by attending to visual features in sketches, designers discover ideas that were unintended when they were drawn [52, 53]. Prototypes similarly elicit information about the design context that did not previously exist in the designer's head.

1.3 Is Iterative Prototyping Undervalued?

Design is often heavily time-constrained; this can discourage designers from iterating. Many feel that organizations undervalue iteration [3, 16, 30, 49, 50]. Prototyping has an actual bottom-line cost associated with it, but this cost estimate is often inaccurate or changes over time [3]. Organizations often avoid prototyping because they believe the cost/investment will be significant and the return will be minimal. As Schrage suggests, "it is hard to persuade companies that one more iteration costs less than a flawed product," [50]. While researchers have devised economic models and performed cost-benefit analysis to argue for rapid iteration [16, 30], resource considerations remain a primary barrier to its application in industry.

On the view of prototyping as a learning process, psychological explanations of learning barriers can provide insight into why prototyping may happen too little in practice. Dweck has demonstrated that people's belief in whether intelligence is mostly fixed or mostly shaped by practice has a significant impact on whether people seek out learning opportunities [14]. Dodgson and Wood have shown that with high self-esteem, people respond less negatively to failure and focus on strengths rather than weaknesses [13]. Earnest experimentation requires risk. The educational psychology literature can inform how to structure the environment so that designers fully engage the prototyping process [1, 14].

2 Method

The design task had two conditions: individuals encouraged to conduct iterative testing (iteration) and individuals prevented from conducting iterative testing (non-iteration). We tested the following hypotheses:

- Participants in the iteration condition will outperform the non-iteration group.
- Participants in the iteration condition will report a larger increase in pre/post confidence levels (perceived ability) than the non-iteration condition.
- Participants with prior exposure to the design task will outperform participants with no exposure.
- Participants with prior general design experience will outperform participants with no design experience.

2.1 Materials and Design Task

In selecting the experimental task, we sought to achieve the following four criteria:

- Presents a clear, objective measure of design quality
- Requires minimal design or engineering expertise
- Can be completed by individuals within one hour
- Offers many paths to achieve an effective result.

We chose the *egg drop exercise*, where participants design a vessel from everyday materials to protect a raw egg from a fall. Variations of the exercise are practiced in secondary and tertiary education classrooms around the United States. This study measures performance by dropping a single egg from a one-foot marker, then two, then three, and so on until the egg cracks. Task performance is measured by the highest height (in feet) at which the egg survives a fall.

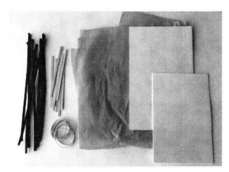

Fig. 1 *Left*: Materials constraints in the design task: pipe cleaners, popsicle sticks, rubber bands, tissue paper, poster board, and flat foam. *Right*: Experimental setup for the design exercise

Pilot studies showed that our choice of materials should be diverse enough to elicit many approaches yet challenging enough to produce a wide range of performances. We selected the following design materials: eight pipe cleaners, eight rubber bands, eight popsicle sticks, one $4'' \times 8''$ piece of poster board, one sheet of tissue paper, one $4'' \times 6''$ piece of flat foam, and 1 ft of scotch tape (Fig. 1, left). Participants worked on a table next to a drop zone area with foot markers written on the wall (Fig. 1, right). All of the supplies were on the table, including build materials, scissors, eggs, and instructions.

For their participation, subjects received either credit towards their course research participation requirement or a \$20 Amazon gift card. As additional incentive, participants were told the two best performing vessels would receive additional Amazon gift cards.

2.2 Participants

Twenty-eight students averaging 21.1 years old and representing a wide range of majors from our university participated in the study. Participants were randomly assigned to one of two conditions. The study balanced for gender, prior egg drop experience, and general design experience across the two conditions. Twelve of the participants had prior experience with the egg drop exercise. Six had either worked as product designers or participated in regular design activities.

2.3 Procedure

Participants filled out a consent form and demographics questionnaire. The experimenter verbally described the egg drop exercise and the specific rules for the assigned condition. All participants were told they would have 25 min to **design**.

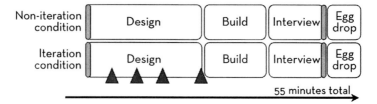

Fig. 2 Experiment procedure with time markers for requesting tests in the iteration condition (*triangles*) and for requesting task performance estimates (*vertical bars*)

They were given a set of construction materials, and were told they could get replacement materials if necessary. After the design period, the researcher cleared the workspace and provided a fresh set of the original materials (this time without replacements). Participants were given 15 min to **build** the final design, followed by a 10-min **interview**, and the egg drop **test** (Fig. 2).

During the design period, participants in the control group (no iteration) were provided one egg, which was also used in the final egg drop. Individuals in the manipulation group (iteration) were given a full carton of eggs. We encouraged iteration participants to conduct a test drop at the 5, 10, 15, and 25-min marks during the design phase. We did not limit participants to only four drops, nor did we strictly enforce all four drops. The drop zone was adjacent to the design table so participants in the iteration group could test their design ideas at any point (Fig. 1, right).

Participants were asked to estimate their perceived performance on the task (in feet), both after hearing the instructions and right before the egg drop test. We conducted a short open-ended interview at the end of the build phase, asking participants to describe their concept and their biggest concern for how the egg might break.

3 Results

This section describes the effect of iterative testing on task performance, the effect of iterative testing on task confidence, and the influence of prior task exposure on design performance.

Vessels created in the iteration condition outperformed the non-iteration condition, with an average successful egg drop height of 6.1 ft compared to an average of 3.3 ft ($t = 2.38$, $p < 0.03$) (Fig. 3).

Participants' confidence level in the iteration condition rose from an average of 4.14 to 5.93 ft from before to after the design task ($t = 2.21$, $p < 0.05$). The non-iteration condition saw no significant change in perceived ability, averaging 3.1 for both pre and post design task (Fig. 4). The pre-measure of performance slightly favors the iteration condition, although the mean self-estimates are not significantly different ($t = 1.92$, $p = 0.23$).

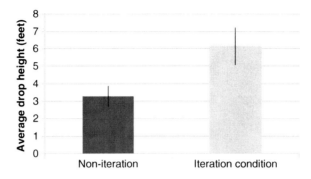

Fig. 3 Individuals in the iteration condition significantly outperformed the non-iteration condition in the egg drop mechanical design task

Fig. 4 Individuals' self estimate of performance (measured in feet) – shows a significant rise between pre- and post-task estimate, but only in the iteration condition

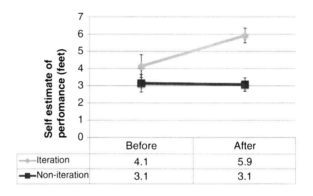

Participants in both conditions estimated their performance fairly accurately. On average, iterators estimated 5.9 ft, just underestimating their actual score of 6.1 ft, and non-iterators estimated 3.1 ft, just underestimating their actual score of 3.3 ft.

3.1 Influence of Prior Exposure to Design Tasks

Twelve of the twenty-eight participants reported previously taking part in the egg drop exercise. Prior egg droppers outperformed those without experience, 6.3 ft compared to 3.5 ft ($t = 1.98$, $p < 0.04$) (Fig. 5).

Both experienced and inexperienced participants in the iteration condition outperformed their counterparts in the non-iteration condition (Fig. 6). A two-way repeated measures analysis of variance (ANOVA) was performed, with Iteration (iteration/non-iteration) and Prior Experience (prior/no-prior) as factors and egg drop height as dependent variable. Participants with prior egg drop exposure in the iteration condition performed the best, with an average successful drop height of 8.7 ft compared to 3.8 ft for prior egg droppers in the non-iteration condition ($F(1,26) = 6.84$, $p = 0.015$). Similarly for participants with no prior egg drop

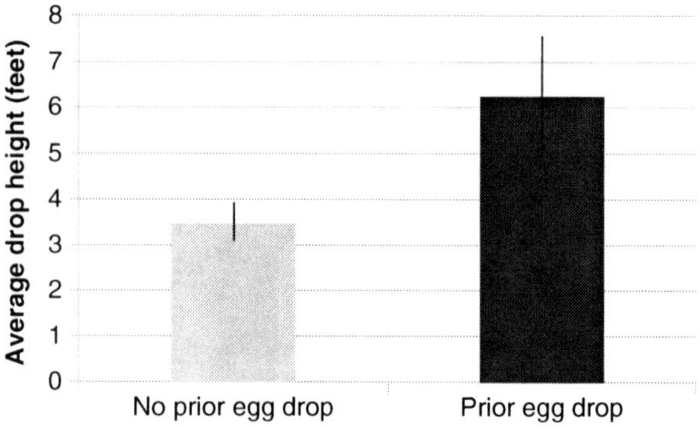

Fig. 5 Individuals with prior exposure to the egg drop task significantly outperformed those who had not done this exercise before

	No prior egg drop	Prior egg drop
◆ Iteration	4.3	8.7
■ Non-iteration	2.8	3.8

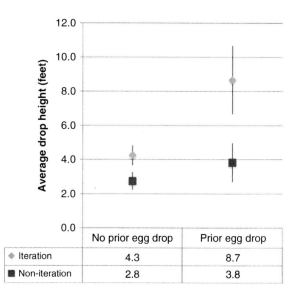

Fig. 6 Breakdown of participants with or without prior egg drop exposure and those in the iteration or non-iteration condition (chart and table numbers in feet)

exposure, the iterative testing condition outperformed the non-iteration condition, 4.3 ft compared to 2.8 ft ($F(1,26) = 5.93$, $p = 0.023$). The Iteration x Prior Experience interaction was nearly significant ($F(1,26) = 2.45$, $p = 0.130$). Iteration helped participants with no prior egg drop experience perform at the same level as non-iterators with prior egg drop exposure.

3.2 *Influence of Design Experience on Task Performance*

Six of the twenty-eight participants had prior professional product design experience or participated in regular design activities. Prior design experience had no significant effect on the outcome of design task performance ($t = 1.84$, $p < 0.17$). With only six qualifying participants, the sample size is not large enough to fully explore the effects of prior design experience.

4 Participant Creations

Participants explored a wide variety of creative design concepts including parachutes, damping stilts, tubes, boxes, suspension systems, and nests for catching the egg raw (Fig. 7). The top three performers – 15, 13, 10 ft came from the iteration condition (top of left column). Based on these participant creations, we conducted an analysis of the design space [15] and determined five key design dimensions: the amount of drag created in the air, the distance between the egg and the first point of impact, the damping upon impact, the balance of weight before and after impact, and the containment of the egg. While this analysis of the design space is informal, it sheds light on relevant design factors. The interviews provide further insight on how participants discovered important variables, and typically focused only just one or two of these factors.

5 Interviews

The interviews revealed how participants employed different prototyping strategies, learned from iteration, and used mental simulation.

5.1 Prototyping Strategies

Some participants employed their understanding of physics to build a vessel designed to absorb impact. For P22's vessel (Fig. 8, left), he coiled "the foam (into) a spring to absorb the shock." P24 said she included a "stabilizing layer" for "bigger surface area" and so "the force was a little more dispersed." As P3 explained "the part that hit the ground had the most impact, so I didn't want that part to be the egg." Her design, a self-described "spiky creation," included damping stilts protruding in many directions. According to another participant, P18, the key was to provide a "buffer," so the "impact point doesn't hit the egg directly."

Other participants approached the egg design task as bricoleurs. As P23 described, "I started with a poster board box and then lined it with the foam box, and then I tore up little pieces of foam 'cause I had extra. And then, 'cause I had 'em I threw in the pipe cleaners around the top of the egg. On the bottom there are sticks, partly because I had 'em, but also it makes it more likely to land on the bottom." P25 (Fig. 8, middle) simply wrapped the egg with as many layers of materials as possible. This approach of mashing together materials echoes the opportunistic design practices reported by Hartmann et al. [23].

Other participants drew inspiration from objects outside of the immediate design context. P11 said, "My design is a Turkish cone. This is the same thing they use to sell chestnuts… When I drop chestnuts usually they would not crack, although

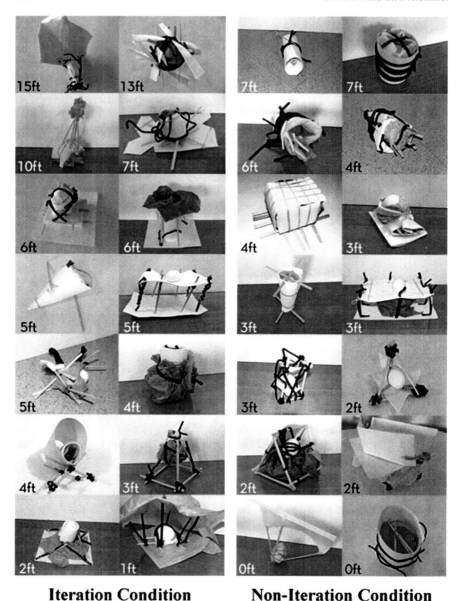

Iteration Condition   Non-Iteration Condition

Fig. 7 Twenty-eight participant creations ordered according to best performers (from top left down) and separated by study condition (iteration in left two columns; non-iteration in right two columns)

[chestnuts] are much harder" than eggs (Fig. 8, right). In a similar vein, P21 related the design task to protecting passengers in vehicles. Both participants thought of analogous situations for protecting precious objects.

Fig. 8 *Left*: Participant 22 (iteration) successfully protected the egg at 13 ft. *Middle*: Participant 25 (non-iteration) protected at 7 ft. *Right*: Participant 11 (iteration) protected at 5 ft

Fig. 9 *Left*: Participant 3 (iteration) successfully protected the egg at 5 ft. *Middle*: Participant 18 (iteration) protected at 2 ft. *Right*: Participant 28 (iteration) protected the egg only at 1 ft

Many participants used the materials and gestures to communicate about the features of their vessel. P20 said "I designed an outer boundary [hands around the prototype], using the [looks up at reference sheet] pipe cleaners... and I designed an inner boundary using the [look up at sheet] sticks."

5.2 Learning from Iteration

Most participants in the iteration condition made a concerted effort to learn and improve their designs with each iterative test. As P3 stated, "experimentation with materials is important, especially at the beginning, so you figure everything possible you can do with them. It is also really important to see what actually happens when it hits, 'cause with my first design I didn't realize it would hit so hard." Her main design insight was to have damping sticks protruding at different angles (Fig. 9, left).

P9 learned the vessels do not fall evenly: "What I didn't account for is, as it gets to higher heights, this will not drop straight down." P18 recognized a different problem with her design. "The main problem with the last design is that it wasn't covering the egg enough, so I was afraid it was going to fall out" (Fig. 9, middle). The iterative process helped participants identify issues such as creating drag, balancing the weight, managing the landing, and containing the egg.

Iterative testing does not always reveal the source of failure. P28's first vessel braced the egg with a square wooden structure. It broke at 1 foot. Then he added a platform underneath and parachute, while he kept the wooden frame (Fig. 9, right). Although, his design continued to fail from low heights, P28 never inferred a key problem: the wooden frame can easily jab into the egg, cracking it with very little force. However in the final interview he did say "I was thinking that I could use – for the holding bay – instead of the wood, I could actually use the pipe cleaners since they are a little bit softer."

5.3 Using Mental Simulation

The interview right before the final egg drop asked participants to envision how their concepts performed. P12 commented and gestured using his design, "When it falls, it's probably going to fall one way or another. Once it starts getting dropped from higher, it's going to bounce and flip maybe [shows how the vessel might flip over]." P14 projected his design would "land kinda crooked sideways." P27 was concerned her design would impact the floor on its side (Fig. 10). She also correctly observed that the parachute should keep her design from falling on its side.

5.4 Effects of Manipulating Iteration

In the iteration condition, many participants expressed frustration with having to drop so early and often. At one point during the task P16 says to himself: "What is sturdy enough to support an egg drop?" Then he sighs, takes a deep breath, and sits back in his chair looking frustrated. He felt pressured to come up with something under the tight time constraint. In the interview he said, "I thought five minutes was too soon to really have anything substantial" (Fig. 11, left). While the tight iteration cycles were stressful, his vessel scored 6 ft – average for the iteration condition

Fig. 10 Participant using her vessel to illustrate possible failure scenarios

Fig. 11 *Left*: Participant 16 (iteration) successfully protected the egg at 6 ft. *Middle*: Participant 21 (iteration) protected at 7 ft. *Right*: Participant 15 (non-iteration) protected the egg at 2 ft

and significantly better than the average non-iteration score. Other participants embraced the opportunity for iteration and really stress-tested their vessels, such as P22 who stood on the table to test his design.

In the non-iteration condition, participants were often ready to test their idea before the end of time period, as P15 said, "so if I'm done can I start?" Similarly, with 10 minutes left in the design period P25 declares, "Alright, I'm finished." It was not clear (at least to us) a priori that the multiple-iteration condition would be so much more engaging for participants than the single-iteration condition.

5.5 Iteration did not Lead to Divergence

While participants in the iteration condition were allowed to test multiple egg drops, they did not necessarily explore a variety of concepts. As P16 described, "I'm not a very good outside-the-box thinker, so I kinda just had one idea and I was going to try to make it work." P27, who had the best overall design, expressed a similar notion: "I went with the whole parachute idea...from the beginning. So, I had one core idea." Generally participants selected an initial design direction and iterated to improve on that idea.

More unexpectedly, some participants claimed that their chosen design seemed like the only possibility. P21 said, "For some reason this seems to be the only idea. There needs to be a platform and then as good of cushion as possible. I don't see any other way" (Fig. 11, middle). Likewise P20 asserted, "This is the best approach for such a design." Despite oft-mediocre preliminary tests and a wide range of possibilities available, many participants appeared fixated on their initial design concept.

5.6 Factors that Prevented Divergence

The short time period impacted why participants did not diverge. As P18 stated, "This is what I thought of first [holding his design], and I started thinking, 'well that's one idea what else can I do?' Then I said, 'nah, I better make this to make sure I will have time." P24 discussed the notion of changing to a new idea, "With time and with trials, I was sort of improving upon the first idea I had and not trying to scrap it and go on to a whole new idea." Participants may not have felt they had time to brainstorm different ideas, and once they got started, they found it difficult to justify changing to a new idea.

While many participants described how they had "one idea and just went with it" (P6), some participants indicated ideation occurred before prototyping. P27 talked about constructing "some sort of box with the sticks and involving rubber bands so the egg is in the middle." P24 said, "I think if I had more time I probably would have been more accurate, maybe even do some calculations." Participants may have considered ideas that were not pursued due to lack of time and perceived complexity. P4 commented: "There were a lot of different ideas I had originally... possibly even using the tissue paper like a parachute."

Participants' underlying assumptions affected their fundamental design choices. P15, like others in the experiment, assumed the egg had to drop by itself into a nest: "I just figured I was supposed to build a vessel to catch the egg on its own" (Fig. 11, right). P11's sense of personal pride in his "Turkish cone" perhaps dissuaded his willingness to pursue other concepts between iterations: "An [alternate] design may have been better... but I am proud of mine." (P11)

6 Conclusion

Participants entered the final fifteen-minute build period armed only with what they learned during the design period. Why did participants in the iteration condition outperform non-iterators? One interpretation says that participants in the iteration condition discovered more flaws and constraints, and tried more new concepts. Non-iterating participants could only speculate how their design would perform. Another interpretation says participants in the iteration condition became better carpenters; they often built the same construction multiple times and thus they tuned the craft. These interpretations are not mutually exclusive, as experimenting and discovering constraints are part of craftwork.

Why did participants in the iteration condition significantly increase their estimated performance on the design task? Unlike the non-iteration condition, the iterating participants received multiple benchmarks. Each iterative test contributed to their judgment of performance. Participants in the non-iteration condition also managed to correctly estimate their low performances, so it remains inconclusive whether the feedback alone leads to better self-estimates. Surprisingly, the non-iteration condition saw no rise in perceived performance despite working on the task for 40 min.

Why did iterating participants with prior experience far outperform all others? Prior exposure to the egg drop exercise gave participants a head start in forming initial design concepts, but why did they make stronger gains with feedback than preliminary ideas from newbies? One argument says that prior experience gives people an index of examples (or cases) and feedback merely aids people to sort through the good and bad ideas. Another argument says prior experience is not only about knowing examples; it's about knowing how to perceive and analyze feedback on proposed solutions. This finding suggests the possibility for scaffolding design expertise with domain-specific examples, along with various feedback perspectives. Future authoring tools, for example, could include domain-specific design exemplars, each with a host of expert feedback.

What factors influence the use of rapid iteration? We found some participants expressed anxiety from having to iterate too early and too frequently. The iteration condition demanded proficiency and imprecision. On the other hand, several of the non-iterating participants were unsatisfied because they could not immediately see how their design performed. Participants may favor longer iterations over short and early iterations to avoid duress; this emotional factor may affect design outcome.

Iterative prototyping does not necessarily lead to an exhaustive exploration of alternatives. Participants in both conditions of the study explored a narrow range of possibilities in the design space. The short time frame and uncertainty about more complex constructions influenced participants. Unlike many real-world design processes, the design period did not include structured time for divergent thinking. More interestingly, several of the participants talked about how they believed their idea to be the only possibility. Design research explains people often fixate on concepts, especially if they have invested energy and time into one path [11, 28].

External validity is a concern for any lab study. While most real world design ventures are often social in nature, we focused on individual designers in this preliminary study to avoid the potential confounds of groupthink and interpersonal relationships. Likewise, design problems are typically solved over the course of days or months. To control for external stimuli, we chose a time frame that only required a single uninterrupted session. Our choice of a design task placed value on having an objectively measurable outcome. In the real world, the problem space or "design brief" is often not set in stone; it gets defined along the way. That said, the egg drop design exercise might be in some respects representative of design tasks that do have clear goals (e.g., designing a bridge always has a clear objective: to insure that cargo and people can cross safely). As a whole, participants demonstrated a range of creative solutions to the egg drop problem. Just as in real design settings, the outcomes cannot be defined by success/failure/right/wrong, but by what concept best fits the current design context.

7 Future Work

Questions remain about how designers perceive the efficacy of prototyping. Do designers undervalue rapid iteration? Within a given timeframe, how do designers determine an iteration strategy? How do designers decide the frequency and temporal spacing of iterations? Do designers typically plan iterations or do they unfold organically? The literature on organizational research can help us hypothesize about the interaction between plans and situated prototyping practices [3, 24, 50, 56]. We hypothesize for example that planning for lots of rough iterations will achieve better results than planning fewer meticulous iterations.

Does the particular formation of iteration affect how designers explore concepts in a design space? Do designers benefit when explicit juxtaposition and reflection are built into iteration? The study indicated that iteration did not necessarily lead to more divergence; participants sought incremental improvements to their concept. We hypothesize exploratory techniques – such as performing analogy training [54] and creating parallel prototypes – can lead to more divergence between iterations and enable more explicit comparisons when processing feedback.

Do the benefits of iteration pertain to groups? While we know group brainstorming leads to unique ideas and serves organizational functions [47, 51], the advantages of team prototyping are less understood. What strategies emerge? Do participants prototype different ideas and later combine them? Do participants work together to understand the feedback? We hypothesize an interaction effect between groups and the presence of feedback; groups will get farther with iterative feedback than individuals because of their ability to collaboratively perceive and interpret feedback on prototypes.

Does iterative prototyping positively affect designer self-efficacy towards a design task? Do the "small wins" of iterative prototyping lead to greater confidence as the design process proceeds? Further, if iteration does have a positive effect on self-confidence (and potentially team confidence), how do these emotional wins contribute to the overall outcome? We hypothesize prototyping practices can have positive effects on individual emotions and team dynamics.

In the face of motivational barriers, what methods encourage the best practices for iteration? For example, if we believe anxiety hinders rapid iteration, we can test the relative merits of anxiety management and team building techniques. If we find participants make false assumptions about prototyping's return on investment, we can investigate how to structure the economic environment to encourage best practices.

Acknowledgements The Hasso Plattner Design Thinking Research Program funded this research. We thank Björn Hartmann, Jeff Heer, Daniel Schwartz, Barbara Tversky, and Terry Winograd for helpful comments on early versions of this paper.

References

1. Aronson, J.M. Improving academic achievement. Academic, 2002.
2. Athavankar, U.A. Mental imagery as a design tool. Cybernetics and Systems 28, 1 (1997), 25–42.
3. Austin, R., and Devin, L. Artful Making: What Managers Need to Know About How Artists Work. Financial Times Press, 2003.
4. Ball, L.J., and Christensen, B.T. Analogical reasoning and mental simulation in design: two strategies linked to uncertainty resolution. Design Studies 30, 2 (2009), 169–186.

5. Bilda, Z., and Gero, J.S. The impact of working memory limitations on the design process during conceptualization. Design Studies 28, 4 (2007), 343–367.
6. de Bono, E. Six Thinking Hats. Back Bay Books, 1999.
7. Brown, T. Change By Design. HarperCollins, 2009.
8. Buchenau, M., and Suri, J.F. Experience prototyping. Proceedings of the 3rd conference on Designing interactive systems: processes, practices, methods, and techniques, ACM (2000), 424–433.
9. Buxton, B. Sketching User Experiences: Getting the Design Right and the Right Design. Morgan Kaufmann, 2007.
10. Christensen, B.T., and Schunn, C.D. The role and impact of mental simulation in design. Applied Cognitive Psychology 23, 3 (2009), 327–344.
11. Cross, N. Designerly Ways of Knowing. Springer, 2006.
12. De Leon, D. Building Thought Into Things. European Conference on Cognitive Science, (1999), 37–47.
13. Dodgson, P., and Wood, J. Self-esteem and the cognitive accessibility of strengths and weaknesses after failure. Journal of Personality and Social Psychology 75, 1 (1998), 178–197.
14. Dweck, C. Mindset: The New Psychology of Success. Ballantine Books, 2007.
15. Dym, C.L., and Little, P. Engineering Design: A Project-Based Introduction. Wiley, 1999.
16. Erdogmus, H. The Economic Impact of Learning and Flexibility on Process Decisions. IEEE Software 22, 6 (2005), 76–83.
17. Ericsson, K.A., Charness, N., Feltovich, P.J., and Hoffman, R.R. The Cambridge Handbook of Expertise and Expert Performance. Cambridge University Press, 2006.
18. Finke, R.A., and Slayton, K. Explorations of creative visual synthesis in mental imagery. Memory and Cognition 16, 3 (1988), 252–7.
19. Finke, R.A. Creative Imagery. Lawrence Erlbaum Associates, 1990.
20. Gentner, D., and Stevens, A.L. Mental models. 1983.
21. Gero, J.S., and Schnier, T. Evolving Representations Of Design Cases And Their Use In Creative Design. In J. S. Gero, M. L. Maher and F. Sudweeks (eds), Preprints Computational Models of Creative Design (1995), 343–368.
22. Goffman, E. Frame Analysis: An Essay on the Organization of Experience. Northeastern, 1986.
23. Hartmann, B., Doorley, S., and Klemmer, S. Hacking, Mashing, Gluing: A Study of Opportunistic Design and Development. Pervasive Computing 7, 3 (2006), 46–54.
24. Hinds, P. The Curse of Expertise: The Effects of Expertise and Debiasing Methods on Predictions of Novice Performance. Journal of Experimental Applied Psychology 5, (1999), 205–221.
25. Hollan, J., Hutchins, E., and Kirsh, D. Distributed Cognition: Toward a New Foundation for Human-Computer Interaction Research. ACM Transactions on Computer-Human Interaction 7, 2 (2000), 174–196.
26. Houde, S., and Hill, C. What do prototypes prototype? Handbook of Human-Computer Interaction, (1997).
27. Hutchins, E. Cognition in the Wild. MIT, 1996.
28. Jansson, D., and Smith, S. Design Fixation. Design Studies 12, 1 (1991), 3–11.
29. Jones, JC. Design Methods. Wiley, 1992.
30. Karat, C. Cost-benefit analysis of usability engineering techniques. Human Factors Society, (1990), 839–843.
31. Kelley, T. The art of innovation. Profile Business, 2002.
32. Kershaw, T.C., and Ohlsson, S. Multiple causes of difficulty in insight: the case of the nine-dot problem. Journal of Experimental Psychology. Learning, Memory, and Cognition 30, 1 (2004), 3–13.
33. Kirsh, D., and Maglio, P. On Distinguishing Epistemic from Pragmatic Action. Cognitive Science 18, (1994), 513–549.
34. Kolko, J. Thoughts on Interaction Design. Brown Bear LLC, 2007.

35. Kolodner, J.L., and Wills, L.M. Powers of observation in creative design. Design Studies 17, 4 (1996), 385–416.
36. Larkin, J., and Simon, H. Why a diagram is (sometimes) worth ten thousand words. Cognitive Science 11, 1 (1987), 65–100.
37. Laurel, B. Design Research: Methods and Perspectives. MIT, 2003.
38. Lave, J. Cognition in Practice. Cambridge University Press, 1988.
39. Lim, Y., Stolterman, E., and Tenenberg, J. The anatomy of prototypes: Prototypes as filters, prototypes as manifestations of design ideas. ACM Transactions on Computer-Human Interaction 15, 2 (2008), 1–27.
40. Lim, Y., Pangam, A., Periyasami, S., and Aneja, S. Comparative analysis of high- and low-fidelity prototypes for more valid usability evaluations of mobile devices. Proceedings of the 4th Nordic conference on Human-computer interaction: changing roles, ACM (2006), 291–300.
41. Maglio, P., Matlock, T., Raphaely, D., Chernicky, B., and Kirsh, D. Interactive Skill in Scrabble. Lawrence Erlbaum (1999).
42. Maglio, P.P., and Kirsh, D. Epistemic Action Increases With Skill. In Proceedings of the Eighteenth Annual Conference of the Cognitive Science Society 16, (1996), 391–396.
43. Martin, R.L. Creativity That Goes Deep. Business Week, 2005. http://www.businessweek.com/innovate/content/aug2005/di20050803{_}823317.htm.
44. Merholz, P., Wilkens, T., Schauer, B., and Verba, D. Subject To Change: Creating Great Products & Services for an Uncertain World: Adaptive Path on Design. O'Reilly Media, 2008.
45. Michalko, M. Thinkertoys: A Handbook of Creative-Thinking Techniques. Ten Speed Press, 2006.
46. Miller, G.A. The magical number seven, plus or minus two: some limits on our capacity for processing information. Psychological Review 63, 2 (1956), 81–97.
47. Osborn, A.F. Applied Imagination: Principles and Procedures of Creative Problem Solving. Charles Scribner's Sons, 1963.
48. Schon, D.A. The Reflective Practitioner: How Professionals Think in Action. Ashgate Publishing, 1995.
49. Schrage, M. Cultures of prototyping. In Bringing design to software book contents. 1996, 191–213.
50. Schrage, M. Serious Play: How the World's Best Companies Simulate to Innovate. Harvard Business School Press, 1999.
51. Sutton, R., and Hargadon, A. Brainstorming groups in context: effectiveness in a product design firm. Administrative Science Quarterly, (1996).
52. Suwa, M., Gero, J., and Purcell, T. Unexpected discoveries and S-invention of design requirements: Important vehicles for a design process. Design Studies 21, (2000), 539–567.
53. Suwa, M., and Tversky, B. External Representations Contribute to the Dynamic Construction of Ideas. Proceedings of the Second International Conference on Diagrammatic Representation and Inference, Springer (2002), 341–343.
54. Thompson, L., Gentner, D., and Loewenstein, J. Avoiding Missed Opportunities in Managerial Life: Analogical Training More Powerful Than Individual Case Training. Organizational Behavior and Human Decision Processes 82, 1 (2000), 60–75.
55. Torrance, E.P. Torrance Tests of Creative Thinking. Personnel Press, Ginn and Co., Xerox Education Co, 1974.
56. Warr, A., and O'Neill, E. Understanding design as a social creative process. Proceedings of the 5th conference on Creativity & Cognition, ACM (2005), 118–127.
57. Ylirisku, S., Halttunen, V., Nuojua, J., and Juustila, A. Framing design in the third paradigm. Proceedings of the 27th international conference on Human factors in computing systems, ACM (2009), 1131–1140.
58. Zhang, J., and Norman, D. Representations in distributed cognitive tasks. Cognitive Science 18, 1 (1994), 87–122.

Part III
Tools for Design Thinking

An Instrument for Real-Time Design Interaction Capture and Analysis

Matthias Uflacker, Thomas Kowark, and Alexander Zeier*

Abstract How do designers leverage information and communication technology to collaborate with team partners and other process participants? Given the increasingly complex, distributed, and virtual setups of design environments and processes, answering this question is challenging. At HPI, we have developed computational data collection and analysis techniques to improve the efficiency and range of observations in technology-enabled design spaces. Using our software, we were able to capture and evaluate complex characteristics of online interactions in distributed design teams at quasi real-time. Besides new insights into the communication behavior of design teams, it could be demonstrated that communication activity signatures of high-performance design teams are significantly different than those of low-performance teams. The combination of new techniques along with quantifiable performance metrics provides a stable foundation for real-time design team diagnostics.

1 Introduction

It is incontrovertible that communication plays a central role in collaborative activities such as engineering and design (Maier et al. 2006; Minnemann 1991; Poltrock et al. 2003). The success or failure of complex projects is considerably determined by how design teams communicate and interact to request information, negotiate, generate ideas, make decisions, or resolve conflicts (Eckert and Stacey 2001; Hales 2000). A strong need exists for design teams and researchers alike to be able to inspect and observe team communication early and during project runtime. Acknowledging communication as an influential factor that determines team performance, communication behavior should be made measurable in order

M. Uflacker (✉), T. Kowark, and A. Zeier
Hasso-Plattner-Institute, University of Potsdam, 14482 Potsdam, Germany
e-mail: matthias.uflacker@hpi.uni-potsdam.de; Alexander.Zeier@hpi.uni-potsdam.de

* Principal Investigator

H. Plattner et al. (eds.), *Design Thinking: Understand – Improve – Apply*,
Understanding Innovation, DOI 10.1007/978-3-642-13757-0_8,
© Springer-Verlag Berlin Heidelberg 2011

to establish deeper insight into what characteristics are beneficial or detrimental for success. However, new techniques are required to efficiently study team interactions during the early stages of engineering design projects. The augmented virtualization and geographic dispersion of team environments raises demand for an adaptive, computer-supported design research methodology, which takes the increasing role of online communication into account.

The Design Loupes project develops new technology to instantaneously collect and process arbitrary team interactions in the course of virtual collaboration. In the effort to construct, apply, and evaluate an automated approach to design team observation, the work gives answers to the following research questions.

Research Question 1. How can design team interactions be chronologically modeled and represented in a computer-processable format?

The computer-supported analysis of team collaboration requires the formalization and recording of activities under observation. The first research question is asking for an appropriate data structure, which is able to maintain a temporal representation of the identified collaboration properties. The requirements for the formalization of generally informal activities are complex. To ensure applicability in the myriad of different scenarios, the data structure cannot be designed for a particular predetermined environment or project, nor must it interfere with the natural creative modes of the subjects under study. This raises demand for a generic data schema, which supports the flexible configuration of extensible, yet unambiguous and clearly defined semantics.

Research Question 2. What are the structural and dynamic properties of a software system that facilitates the real-time[1] capture and analysis of design interactions in a technology-enabled environment?

The second question addresses the architectural layout of a software system to handle the formalization process and to provide capabilities for real-time data inspection. The system design clearly needs to respond to the characteristics of prevailing design environments without interfering with the natural mode of collaboration. Multiple workspaces distributed in time and space, concurrent team interactions, and a diversity of media and groupware for virtual collaboration create demand for a scalable solution. Service-orientation defines an architectural paradigm to construct distributed and loosely coupled software systems that promote integrability, flexibility, and reusability (Erl 2005). The instantiation of a service-based software system to conduct computational observations and analyses in distributed and heterogeneous design environments presents a new direction in design research. What is the nature of the services to be provided and how can such a system be integrated into the design process?

---

[1] With regard to the ambivalent meaning of this notion in computer science, *real-time* refers here to the ability to collect and prepare data from user observations steadily and almost instantaneously, i.e., within the range of minutes.

In the background of these research questions, the following hypothesis is being formulated:

Hypothesis. Online interaction signatures of high-performance design teams are significantly different than those of low-performance teams.

Identifying significant correlations between properties of the formalized interactions and independently measured team performance is a necessary, but not sufficient requirement for the computational evaluation of design process qualities. A multitude of indeterminable factors are influencing the project outcome, preventing a complete and definite assertion by means of IT. However, correlations can provide indicators for what potentially impacts the design process and point to behavior that is worth to observe in more detail. With first indicators revealed, the presented approach would suggest itself as a platform for a design management dashboard to monitor those indicators at real-time. Testing this hypothesis was a major component of the Design Loupes project. Exemplary findings from a case study analysis are given at the end of this chapter.

2 Improving Design Process Instrumentation

The increasing proliferation of software services for computer-supported cooperative work (CSCW) and virtual collaboration has changed design environments and the way people communicate and share information. Groupware applications have moved to the Internet and the World Wide Web, providing an open interface to connecting people and information. In fact, communicating over the Internet has become standard and indispensable, especially in global organizations. About 62% of all employed Americans have Internet access and virtually all of those (98%) use email on the job (Fallows 2002). Web 2.0 services and other communication methods such as instant messaging are increasingly moving into the workplace (Shiu and Lenhart 2004). Storing and distributing project data in online services creates an unprecedented level of information availability. At the same time, the expansion of online instruments in the information handling and negotiation activities of design teams causes the digital footprint of communication to grow. This footprint can be leveraged to study communication structures during the early phases of innovation without interfering with the process. In combination with traditional empirical techniques, computational observation and analysis methods offer a powerful new approach to the study of team processes (Ashworth 2007).

Previous literature in design research has advanced the assessment and transparency of performance-relevant process variables, but instruments to evaluate computer-mediated team activities in real-time are still relatively uninformative and piecemeal (Dooley and Van de Ven 1999; Wang et al. 2002). There are two principal reasons for this significant lag of design process instrumentation. One is the growing complexity of continuously changing design environments. Distributed engineering design is an increasingly common phenomenon in professional practice and the ongoing emergence of new collaboration tools in design practice has led to a situation where research methodology to study the effects of technology use does not follow. Second, it is mostly unknown to which extent the technical level of communication can ultimately serve as an indicator for differences in design team activity and performance. What are relevant metrics in technologically mediated collaboration that might be observable surrogates for semantic level team interactions? If low-level data in the form of recorded interaction events can reveal beneficial or detrimental process characteristics, it can be used to monitor and manage design processes more effectively.

2.1 Challenges in the Development of Computational Design Research Instruments

Research in the IT-based analysis of virtual design team interactions has to deal with a number of non-trivial challenges that stem from human factors and the complexities inherent to creative environments. Design knowledge resides in processes, in the tactics and strategies of designing (Cross 2006). Hence, a major area of design research is methodology: "the study of the processes of design, and the development and application of techniques which aid the designer" (Cross 2006). If design methodology research is to be supported by computational data processing, the formalization of the subject under study is a necessity. Conceptual design, however, is deeply informal in its nature. It is inherently unstructured and ad-hoc on the level of individual activities. This renders the computational measurement, comparison, and prediction of complex process variables idiosyncratic (Dooley and Van de Ven 1999). IT systems that are to conduct empirical design observations must be built with universality in mind. They need to be configurable in a way which allows reacting appropriately to arbitrary social interactions and informal behavior. On the other hand, the systems need to apply well-defined and precise semantics in the encoding of the design process in order to ensure the validity of its formalization. Balancing between flexibility, adaptability, and formalism is one challenge in the design of a generic technological foundation for real-time team diagnostics.

A second dimension of complexity is spanned by a constantly transforming tool landscape in engineering design, which is and will remain heterogeneous. The unstructured and varying team activities in the different phases of iterated design demand for a diverse set of support tools with individual strengths and characteristics. Any analysis focusing on a single communication tool or homogeneous collaboration environment can therefore only comprise fractional and isolated parts of the information handling process. In order to complete this picture, capabilities to centrally monitor a broader range of distributed and concurrent communication activities over multiple channels are needed. Critical system requirements also stem from the complexities in design collaboration environments, which are increasingly distributed across multiple sites. Aggravating the effects of a heterogeneous tool landscape, geographically dispersed design teams further add to the clustering and partitioning of project information and interaction therewith. The distribution and concurrent nature of the subject under study needs to be appropriately reflected by the architecture of a system to support its observation.

2.2 Can Digital Traces of Communication Be a Surrogate for Team Behavior?

Fundamental to this work is the assumption that low-level data at the technical level of communication can be a proxy for the original intent of an interaction. The correlations between the formalized encoding of online communication and its semantic value in a collaborative environment are relatively unexplored. This problem is deeply rooted in the nature of communication itself. Shannon and Weaver (1949) nominate it to the category of semantic problems: how precisely do the observable symbols convey the desired meaning? (Fiske 1990)

Shannon and Weavers model of communication can be used as a basis to sketch out a non-interfering approach to communication capture (Fig. 1). While acknowledging the legitimate criticism for the static and linear nature of this model (cf. Mortensen 1972), its technological bias towards discrete units of information is tolerable as computer-mediated communication activities are targeted exclusively. Information is digitally encoded by a software system (encoder) and sent via a not further specified data connection (channel) to a receiving software system (decoder). Each of the three entities represents a potential information source for capturing team interactions. Depending on the sending and receiving software systems, public interfaces, log files, or other traces of interaction may be leveraged to unobtrusively tap into the information sharing process.

Recent studies give first evidence that data at the technical level of communication might be an observable surrogate for the semantic intent of a message (Milne 2005).

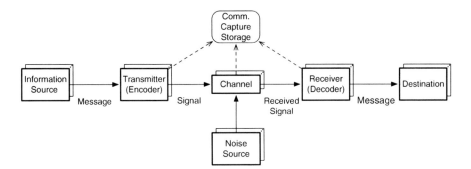

Fig. 1 Shannon and Weavers model of communication (Shannon and Weaver 1949), shown in a multi-instance setup to highlight the concurrent nature of communication. The figure visualizes three starting points for imperceptive communication capture. Note that the *dashed arrows* again resemble a communication process between an information source (a transmitter, channel, or receiver) and a capturing destination storage

If and how data in the form of recorded interactions could ultimately serve as an indicator for differences in design team activity and innovative performance remains a largely open question. If dependencies between observable patterns in team communication and objectively measured qualities of a design process can be identified, the envisioned instrument would qualify itself as an improvement to design research methodology.

3 A Real-Time Design Research Instrument

To implement real-time communication capture and analysis capabilities in real design environments, we articulate an extensible software architecture of distributed and loosely-coupled sensor and monitoring components. A collection of software services provides the functionality needed to incrementally capture and query detailed communication properties immediately during the course of collaboration. This establishes a central point of access to information about how design teams virtually communicate over time. The focus is on technology-enabled, distributed engineering design spaces, in which computer-mediated team interactions are necessary, common, and widespread.

This service approach to communication capture and analysis facilitates a symbiosis between design practice and research (Fig. 2). For design researchers, the system acts as an instrument to collect data. A number of client applications may continuously check for digital traces in the utilized communication channels and feed information about captured interactions to the services provided. At the same time, the services provide the functionality to measure trends and characteristics in the recorded events and to systematically explore the past and present of communication behavior in the observed teams. New theories in conceptual design methodology can be developed and tested, leading to a deeper understanding of relevant metrics in team communication. Completing the symbiosis, the set of services can be iteratively refined and adapted to form the basis for improved guidance, management, and design process support.

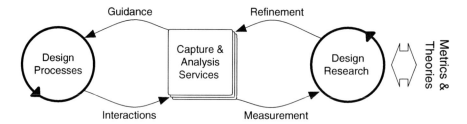

Fig. 2 A service-based approach to the concurrent capturing of heterogeneous communication artifacts can stimulate design research and support the design process through centralized access to communication properties. New insights into team behavior help to refine design tools and to optimize design process support

3.1 Capturing Design Team Activities

The development of an appropriate data model to describe the individual communication activities of design teams is a necessary first step for the analysis. While the observation of technology-mediated design activities has been the subject of many previous works, a more flexible and generic approach is required, which supports real-time application in the diversity of existing and future IT-supported design environments. The work introduces *team collaboration networks* (*TCN*), a graph structure in which the occurrence, attributes, and relationships of heterogeneous actors and information objects are represented over the course of a project.

Figure 3 gives an example of a team collaboration network with a set of four nodes ($V := \{a,b,c,d\}$). Nodes a and c each represent a person, b depicts an email that has been sent by person a, and d represents a wiki page that has been created by person c and which is referenced by email b (e.g., through a hyperlink). The model structure preserves the history of previous network states and maintains the traceability of collaboration activities. This way, the exploration of previous interaction behavior becomes feasible.

3.2 System Implementation and Testbed Integration

In a second step, we implemented *d.store*, a resource-oriented platform for team collaboration networks. The system provides a rich API for the continuous recording and evaluation of virtual collaboration activities in heterogeneous groupware applications. The services have been applied in an 8-month period of early stage concept

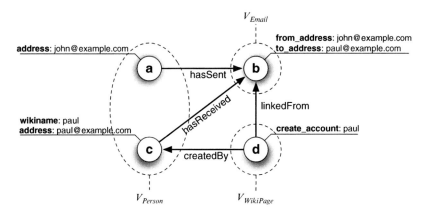

Fig. 3 Example of a team collaboration network, showing instances and different types of nodes, relations, and attributes. Team collaboration networks are used to describe associations between actors and information objects involved in a project-based design process

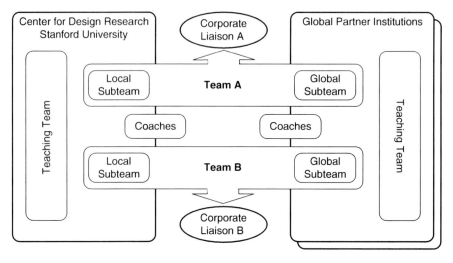

Fig. 4 Schematic representation of roles and process participants in the project-based engineering design curriculum "310"

creation in eleven engineering design projects and used to collect interactions through email messaging, wiki pages, and online shared folders. The generated networks provide the basis for the exploration of communication structures.

A project-based engineering design curriculum served as a testbed for the platform. Stanford University's "Mechanical Engineering 310 Project-Based Engineering Design, Innovation & Development" is a 9-month graduate level engineering course in which Stanford students collaborate with students at other universities around the world to develop innovative solutions to open-ended problems. Small distributed teams worked on real-world engineering design challenges posed by industry partners. The design tasks were purposely phrased broadly to challenge the students to determine, isolate and pursue a particular opportunity for innovation (Skogstad 2009). Figure 4 illustrates the general setup of the engineering design projects in 310 for the term 2007/2008. A total number of eleven teams were formed with students in Stanford and those of six partner institutions around the globe. Stanford's engineering graduates were partnering with students in product design, industrial design, or computer science, to foster inter-disciplinary teamwork and problem solving. The general team size was six, with three students representing a collocated sub-team both at Stanford (local) and global partner side. All teams had an equally sized budget at their disposal, which they could use to purchase materials or services and to craft prototypes.

Each of the globally dispersed teams was assigned with a design challenge given out by a corporate liaison. During the course, the students had to work together to identify needs, generate concepts, and create fully functional prototypes to show a potential path to innovation to the corporate sponsor. The project timelines have been structured into three major phases with a duration of approx. 3 months each. The first phase (*make it up*) starts with team building (local and global sub-teams come together for a short kick-off workshop) and is characterized by a high level of benchmarking, fact finding, and ideation activities. The second phase (*make it real*) aims towards the technological feasibility of the student's vision and the implementation and testing of their ideas. The third phase (*make it happen*) is about getting things done, making final decisions and presenting a functional solution at the end of the projects.

3.3 Case Study in Team Performance Measurement

The *d.store* platform supports the focused observation of specific communication parameters in unstructured interaction and virtual design collaboration. This functionality has been utilized to closely monitor specific patterns in the captured activities of the testbed projects presented before. In this case study, statistical correlations between the observed interaction properties and team performance measures are explored. We have captured more than 10,000 emails on the team distribution lists, over 800 wiki pages with approx. 4,000 edit events, and more than 8,000 activities in public team folders.

To test dependencies between the online interactions and performance-relevant process metrics, a number of performance measures have been empirically collected from the teams. One example is self-reported performance measures, which were surveyed after completion of the projects to quantify process performance from the perspective of the designer. The questions are taken from an established team diagnostic survey (Wageman et al. 2005). They provide a measure of three performance-relevant aspects of teamwork, which are controlled by the team and its members (Skogstad 2009). The aspects are (a) the quality of team task processes, a measure of team effectiveness, (b) the satisfaction with within-team relationships, a measure of the willingness to work together again in the future, and (c) the individual affective reactions to the team and its work, a measure of the individuals learning and well-being. Skogstad (2009) points out that the survey "provides a measurement of the design process quality from the designers point of view. It accounts for the fact that design performance must include more than just the project result, because no organization will survive if the designers are consistently unsatisfied."

Correlations are tested by linear regression analysis. The study considers collaboration patterns as dependent variables, which can be interpreted as a sign of applied design thinking principles or "designerly ways of interacting." Three basic principles that characterize a design thinking process are considered: (a) the constant involvement of end-users and customers, (b) interdisciplinary teamwork and knowledge sharing, and (c) a culture of prototyping. Directed by these interaction patterns in design thinking, the study compares performance measures with team communication signatures that may reflect according behavior in the virtual interaction space of designers.

4 Key Findings and Contribution

We briefly highlight the findings related to the hypothesis and the contribution of this research in terms of input to a common knowledge base and to the research environment.

4.1 Findings Related to the Hypothesis

Based on the team collaboration networks and the performance measures collected during the case study, we have tested the hypothesis that "online interaction signatures of high-performance design teams are significantly different than those of low-performance teams." We could identify statistically significant correlations in the online interaction behavior of the eleven design teams that assert this assumption. The findings suggest that those teams generally perform better, which put emphasis on external communication, team-internal information sharing, and diversity in the solution space through iterative prototyping. Accordingly, dependencies between independent team performance measures and the email and wiki-based team interactions can be made out in the data set. For example, a positive and significant correlation exists between the average team member satisfaction and the proportional amount of outbound email messages sent by a team, suggesting that the involvement of external sources of information (e.g., end-users and customers) has beneficial effects on team performance (Fig. 5).

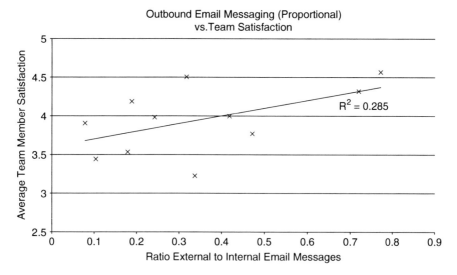

Fig. 5 One example for performance indicators found in the data set of a case study application: The proportional amount of outbound emails (compared to team-internal messages) sent by a team correlates positively and significantly with the average team member satisfaction

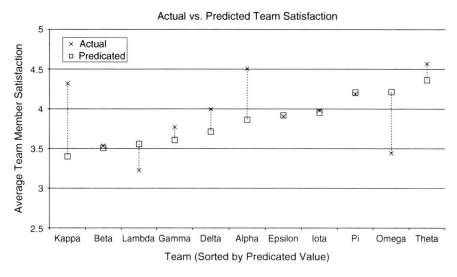

Fig. 6 The average team member satisfaction correlates even more significantly with a combination of two variables in the email-based team interactions: the ratio of external to internal messages sent by the team and the amount of emails received from the teaching team. The quality of the prediction is remarkable, considering the computational and automated nature of the data collection process

The quality of the prediction further increases when additional independent variables are incorporated into the regression model. In a second analysis, the number of emails a project team has received from the teaching team is factored into the regression equation. The results of the second linear regression analysis indicate that teams who receive more emails from the teaching team are statistically less satisfied with their project. A reasonable interpretation of this phenomenon is grounded on the remediating intervention of the teaching team in case of defects or conflicts in the collaboration process. The remarkable accuracy of the values predicted by the two-dimensional regression model is illustrated in Fig. 6.

Another inspection of the knowledge sharing behavior addresses the wiki spaces of the eleven observed projects. The team collaboration networks hold information about the point of time wiki pages have been created, edited, and hyperlinked to other resources of a project. This data allows insights into the structuring and coherence of information stored in a wiki system.

A graphical representation of the project wiki spaces has been created with data received from *d.store* services. Three examples are shown in Fig. 7. The structures represent the final topology of a project wiki space, which is defined by the hyperlink relationships between wiki pages and external resources of different types. This simple form of observation already reveals that design teams utilize wikis quite differently.

The wiki networks of the three teams (Theta, Alpha, Gamma) exhibit distinctive structures in the relationships of resources. Theta and Alpha show a relatively large number of wiki pages, each one covering a particular topic or subject-matter. Several

Topologies of Project Wiki Spaces

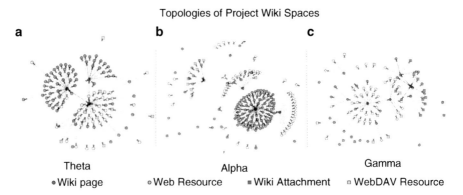

Fig. 7 Three graphical wiki space representations for projects Theta, Alpha, Gamma. Clustering and general connectedness of wiki pages may be an indicator for the quality of knowledge- and skill-related process criteria

pages obviously serve as indices to a bulk of other resources, forming clusters of closely related nodes and serving as hubs to other wiki pages or external information resources. In contrast, the topology of the wiki space of team Gamma is relatively lean. Not only is the total number of wiki pages considerably smaller, but also is the connectedness of the resources less pronounced.

Statistical relevant correlations to performance measures could not be revealed in these quantitative properties of wiki spaces. However, certain sub-scales of the team diagnostic survey indicate a relationship between process criteria of team effectiveness and the observed wiki structures. The instrument developed by Wageman et al. (2005) assesses, amongst others, the degree to which the team uses the full complement of member knowledge and skill. Based on the grading of knowledge- and skill-related statements (e.g., "Members of our team actively share their special knowledge and expertise with one another" and "Our team is quite skilled at capturing the lessons that can be learned from our work experiences") the scale contributes to the overall measure of the quality of team task processes.

The average results of this sub-scale in Theta, Alpha, and Gamma correlate with the visual impression that the breadth of information shared in a wiki system and increased connectedness of the resources contribute to the quality of a knowledge sharing process. This supports the assumption that wiki structures can partially reveal insights into knowledge sharing behavior and suggests a more detailed analysis.

4.2 Contributions to the Knowledge Base

The work presents a solution to a research problem rooted in the discrepancy between the informality of creative design processes and the formal requirements for their computational real-time analysis. Team collaboration networks constitute a model for representing and storing activities during project-based collaboration in a chronological manner. The networks can be configured and used to capture and compare the semantic properties of actors and information resources in multiple design projects. The results of an exemplary application suggest that the computational analysis of virtual design collaboration activities is expedient. Significant differences between the online signatures of low- and high-performing teams could be made out in the data set. The identified correlations with team performance measures substantiate the beneficial impact of fundamental design principles in the early stages of engineering projects.

Recently published studies build on the results of this work. Skogstad (2009) has developed a new theory about how designers gain insights needed to create novel solutions and how reviewers can have both positive and negative effects on the design process. Parts of the hypothesis testing are grounded on the interactions captured in team collaboration networks. Overall, the developed constructs for the observation of team communication provide a basis for achieving new insights into design aspects and performance-relevant properties of virtual collaborative processes. Future research projects may build upon this technological foundation and refine the results through additional case studies and improved software instantiations.

4.3 Contributions to the Research Environment

The contribution of this work to the field of applied design research is a flexible software tool, which provides services for the combined analysis of concurrent design activities in a direct and non-interfering manner. Tools and techniques have been developed, which support the study of the ever-widening variety of technologies and phenomena arising within distributed engineering team activity. The *d.store* platform decouples the data collection from the concurrent analysis and allows for streamlined and non-interfering team observations. The service-oriented approach simplifies the automated recording of distributed communication data and expedites the unobtrusive integration of team work analysis into existing and future research projects. A novel approach to real-time team diagnostics is established.

The same service-based approach that has been introduced to generate insights into the communication behavior creates new possibilities for supporting the management of design teams. With a more precise understanding of performance-relevant indicators, real-time awareness of potential drawbacks and process impediments is generated. This creates new starting points for the design and implementation of improved tools and dashboards for the management of design processes.

5 Conclusion and Future Work

We have developed an instrument for the real-time capture and analysis of multimodal team interactions in technology-enabled design spaces. The *d.store* platform provides a technological foundation to collect and monitor concurrent interaction events and distributed online communication in a graph-like representation named "team collaboration networks." The system has been applied in the conceptual design phases of eleven distributed, inter-disciplinary engineering projects over a period of 8 months. The online activities detected in the email archives, wiki spaces, and public team folders have been translated into team collaboration networks and provide a basis for the visual and quantitative examination of structures and trends in the interaction behavior of engineering design teams.

The results of a case study suggest that patterns in the online interactions of design teams can indicate performance measures. This is significant, because it demonstrates that design team performance can be approximated by objective collaboration metrics live and in situ. The findings give reason to a continued and intensified evaluation of design processes in IT-enabled collaboration environments. The outcome provides a technological basis and first statistical input to support this direction of current and future research activities.

Our work sought to expand the exploration window in empirical design research by enabling researchers to handle the increased complexity of design spaces. The work promotes a new paradigm in the conduction of real-time design team diagnostics, with probable implications for design theory and organizational process implementations.

The communication behavior of virtual engineering design teams has been the main focus of the initial *d.store* development, as well as the first applications of the platform in various case studies. A logical next step is the utilization of the platform for observations of different team types to determine if the previously made assumptions still hold true for other team structures and project set-ups. Therefore, the platform will be extended with the means to capture digital communication artifacts that are common for software development teams. Amongst others, this includes information about the usage of source-code management systems and application lifecycle management tools. A case study will be prepared that resembles a real-life software development process by having 80 students of a university lecture develop a single system in a collaborative effort. The students are divided into 13 sub-teams that are responsible for different, interdependent aspects of the system. By that, the project introduces a high level of urgency for inter-team communication and coordination. In order to observe the communication behavior and the progress of the teams, weekly meetings with tutor teams are obligatory. The project lifetime of 4 months is divided into four iterations. At the end of each iteration, an evaluation meeting takes place to determine how the teams fulfilled their tasks and how they adopted their development or communication behavior according to previously gathered experience. Those manual observations made by the tutors are the foundation for a post-hoc analysis of the team collaboration networks that are created within *d.store*. The digital traces are compared to the tutors' judgments in order to reveal patterns that possibly indicate problems within the intra- and inter-team communication.

References

Ashworth, M. J. (2007). *Computational and Empirical Explorations of Work Group Performance*. PhD thesis, Carnegie Mellon University, Pittsburgh, Pennsylvania

Cross, N. (2006). *Designerly ways of knowing*. Springer, Berlin

Dooley, K. and Van de Ven, A. (1999). Explaining complex organizational dynamics. *Organization Science*, 10(3):358–372

Eckert, C. and Stacey, M. (2001). Dimensions of Communication in Design. *Proceedings of the 13th International Conference on Engineering Design*, Glasgow, UK

Erl, T. (2005). *Service-oriented architecture: concepts, technology, and design*. Prentice Hall, NJ

Fallows, D. (2002). Email at work. *Pew Internet and American Life Project*, Washington, DC, USA

Fiske, J. (1990). *Introduction to communication studies*. Routledge, London

Hales, C. (2000). Ten critical factors in the design process. In *Failure Prevention Through Education: Getting to the Root Cause*, OH, USA

Maier, A., Eckert, C., and Clarkson, P. (2006). Identifying requirements for communication support: A maturity grid-inspired approach. *Expert Systems with Applications*, 31(4):663–672

Milne, A. J. (2005). *An Information-theoretic Approach to the Study of Ubiquitous Computing Workspaces Supporting Geographically Distributed Engineering Design Teams as Groupusers*. PhD thesis, Stanford University, Stanford, CA

Minnemann, S. (1991). *The Social Construction of a Technical Reality: Empirical Studies of Group Engineering Design Practice*. PhD thesis, Department of Mechanical Engineering, Stanford University, Stanford, CA

Mortensen, C. (1972). *Communication: The study of human interaction*. McGraw-Hill, NY

Poltrock, S., Grudin, J., Dumais, S., Fidel, R., Bruce, H., and Pejtersen, A. M. (2003). Information seeking and sharing in design teams. In *GROUP '03: Proceedings of the 2003 international ACM SIGGROUP conference on Supporting group work*, pages 239–247, ACM, New York, NY

Shannon, C. and Weaver, W. (1949). *The mathematical theory of information*, 97. University of Illinois Press, Urbana

Shiu, E. and Lenhart, A. (2004). How Americans use instant messaging. *Pew Internet and American Life Project*, Washington, DC, USA

Skogstad, P. L. (2009). *A Unified Innovation Process Model For Engineering Designers and Managers*. PhD thesis, Stanford University, Stanford, CA

Wageman, R., Hackman, J. R., and Lehman, E. V. (2005). Team diagnostic survey: Development of an instrument. *The Journal of Applied Behavioral Science*, 41(4):373

Wang, L., Shen, W., Xie, H., Neelamkavil, J., and Pardasani, A. (2002). Collaborative conceptual design – state of the art and future trends. *Computer-Aided Design*, 34(13):981–996

Tele-Board: Enabling Efficient Collaboration In Digital Design Spaces Across Time and Distance

Raja Gumienny, Christoph Meinel*, Lutz Gericke, Matthias Quasthoff, Peter LoBue, and Christian Willems

Abstract Design Thinking is an approach for innovative problem solving. A typical characteristic of this approach involves multidisciplinary teams and the extensive use of tangible tools such as sticky notes, whiteboards and all kinds of prototyping materials. When team members try to collaborate from separate locations their traditional way of working becomes nearly impossible. A number of computer supported collaborative work systems exist, but there still lacks acceptable support for teams applying methods like Design Thinking. We have created an environment that allows these teams to work together efficiently across distances, without having to change their working modes. The Tele-Board prototype combines video conferencing with a synchronized whiteboard transparent overlay. This unique setup enables regionally separated team members to simultaneously manipulate artifacts while seeing each other's gestures and facial expressions. Our system's flexible architecture maximizes hardware independence by supporting a diverse selection of input devices. User feedback has confirmed that the Tele-Board system is a good basis to further enable collaborative creativity across distances while retaining the essential feeling of working together.

1 Creativity Across Distances: Can We Make It Work?

Collaborative creative work is done best in co-located settings. People communicate with each other face-to-face, see each other's gestures and facial expressions, and directly manipulate all involved artifacts. Sticky notes, whiteboards, walls, pens, all imaginable handicraft objects, role-play and storytelling may all be used when creative methods such as Design Thinking are applied [1]. Bringing together the insights of research and different perspectives of a diverse team is a key factor for

R. Gumienny (✉), C. Meinel, L. Gericke, M. Quasthoff, P. LoBue, and C. Willems
Hasso-Plattner-Institute, Campus Griebnitzsee, P.O. Box 900460, 14440 Potsdam, Germany
e-mail: tele-board@hpi.uni-potsdam.de; meinel@hpi.uni-potsdam.de

* Principal Investigator

H. Plattner et al. (eds.), *Design Thinking: Understand – Improve – Apply*,
Understanding Innovation, DOI 10.1007/978-3-642-13757-0_9,
© Springer-Verlag Berlin Heidelberg 2011

successfully fueling innovation. In order to incorporate different cultural aspects as well, international teams are favorable. But how can teams reasonably use the above-mentioned analog tools if members are geographically dispersed, and time zones separate them by several hours? Can suitable digital equipment act as a comparable option to analog tools for teams using Design Thinking?

Discovering answers to these questions has been the objective of our project within the HPI – Stanford Design Thinking Research Program. We saw that Design Thinking teams at the Hasso-Plattner-Institute of Design at Stanford (d.school) and the HPI School of Design Thinking create successful products and concepts. Furthermore, the Design Thinking methodology is used at several design companies [2] and examples prove that it leads to successful results [1]. This kind of work, which is very different from standard office work, has a high potential for creating innovations in different industries. But we all know that in a globalized world development does not take place at only one location. Thus our vision emerged to enable people located at different parts of the world to work together as naturally and smoothly as they are accustomed to in their current environment.

A number of tools supporting remote collaboration already exist. For nearly 20 years research has been done to enable people to communicate and share artifacts across distances. In the last years, commercial products for remote collaboration also improved tremendously to enable easy video conferencing with various levels of quality and costs. But satisfactory support for distributed creative working does not exist yet, as shown by our evaluation of existing tools for remote collaboration. Most tools only support standard desktop work and are cumbersome to use in general [3]. In order to really meet the requirements of real-world Design Thinking teams we started by interviewing teams at the HPI School of Design Thinking and at SAP's Design Services Team and observing them in their workspace. We wanted to find out how people work with each other and how they interact with all involved artifacts. Our research resulted in identifying seven main Design Thinking working modes.

From these conclusions we decided to design and implement a new IT-tool which truly supports and optimizes collaborative creative work without getting in the way of the teams involved in the process. Recent development of touch enabled whiteboards, monitors and smartphones provided us with new opportunities for an intuitive use of hard- and software. Hence, we started to develop the Tele-Board system, an electronic whiteboard software suite which allows users to write digital sticky notes on tablet PCs, smartphones or directly on a whiteboard. Users can move the created sticky notes, cluster them and write or draw on the whiteboard. This digital implementation also includes additional features previously unrealizable by physical tools, such as resizing sticky notes or changing their color. All of the mentioned actions are synchronized automatically and propagated to every connected whiteboard client. To facilitate a real interactive session we included a video conference among the distributed team. The translucent whiteboard can be displayed as an overlay on top of a full screen video of the other team members (see Fig. 1). This setup lets everyone see what the others are doing, where they are pointing along with their gestures and facial expressions.

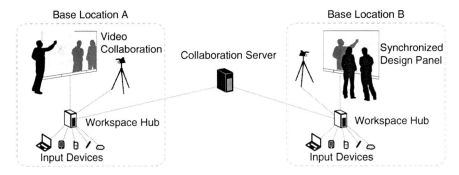

Fig. 1 Setup of the current Tele-Board prototype

In the following, we will present our findings on the Design Thinking working modes, describe the Tele-Board system and its architecture, and discuss user feedback we received in experiments and interviews. The chapter closes with an outlook on the following project year and further research topics.

2 Analyzing Design Thinking Working Modes

In order to formulate requirements for our tools, we needed to understand the way Design Thinking research teams work and interact, and anticipate what they would demand of an IT-tool aimed at supporting them. We observed and interviewed teams at the HPI School of Design Thinking and SAP's Design Services Team. Through our observations we found out that users have different needs in different situations. To classify these users' needs we identified seven working modes (see Fig. 2) which we consider the most important for Design Thinking. Of course these modes may be expanded by other modes as working techniques vary by organization and group.

The different working modes and their specific characteristics are the following:

Handwriting and drawing on a whiteboard. This working mode happens often and for various reasons during a design session. Some examples might be: noting facts or ideas, visualizing an idea or a process through rough sketches, or drawing a diagram to explain relations. Multiple colors and an eraser may be used, as well as printouts of pictures and other information. It is important that the whiteboard stands vertically to be seen easily by fellow team members. Each team member must have direct access to the whiteboard. Gestures are frequently used to support communicating an idea to other team members.

Writing a personal sticky note. Sticky notes are used to note down facts or ideas, sometimes including small drawings. The creation of sticky notes is often done individually and simultaneously by team members. Sticky notes may be added to the whiteboard either immediately or during a quick presentation phase. Differently colored sticky notes are used to keep track of the information's source. It is important

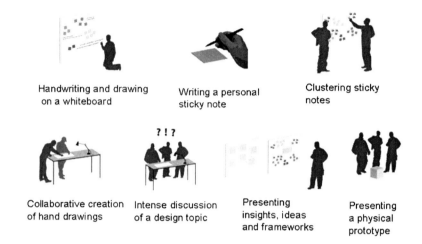

Handwriting and drawing on a whiteboard

Writing a personal sticky note

Clustering sticky notes

Collaborative creation of hand drawings

Intense discussion of a design topic

Presenting insights, ideas and frameworks

Presenting a physical prototype

Fig. 2 Working modes during Design Thinking projects

that sticky notes are relatively small so that team members use them to record only a single, concise fact or idea that can be grasped at a glance. It must be possible to write sticky notes on a horizontal surface to ensure comfortable writing and scribbling.

Clustering sticky notes. Usually, one or two team members stand in front of a whiteboard and cluster the team's sticky notes. A cluster is often defined by circling sticky notes with a whiteboard marker and applying a label. Other team members may instruct them from a distance. The team tries to group related research information or ideas that were generated during a brainstorming session. Moving sticky notes around must be easy, and all team members should be able to see each other's pointing gestures, as the whole group should find the best cluster representation together.

Collaborative creation of hand drawings. Often one person draws a design object in more detail, and the other team members give feedback. It is important that all people involved can see the drawing and may contribute to it. A horizontal setup is generally preferred to make drawing more comfortable.

Intense discussion of a design topic. The team meets to discuss a topic related to design artifacts, which are often laid out on a table. Visibility of team members' gestures, facial expressions and eye contact as well as related artifacts is crucial.

Presenting insights, ideas and frameworks. This working mode often involves a bigger audience. It is important to collect as much feedback as possible from the audience. The team uses design artifacts created in their team space mostly presented on a whiteboard using a vertical setup.

Presenting a physical prototype. For this working mode it is necessary to present a physical object from all sides. It might also include acting out an idea. Similar to the preceding working mode, an audience is involved.

The first three working modes (handwriting on a whiteboard, writing a sticky note and clustering) are essential for creative processes such as Design Thinking, and most suitable to be implemented in a digital solution. Therefore we aim to support working on a whiteboard with sticky notes, handwritten text, drawings and clusters. For distributed settings it is obvious that a digital representation of a whiteboard simplifies collaboration on design artifacts by all team members in all locations. It is necessary to support the visibility of gestures and facial expressions of team members in addition to hearing their voices.

3 Evaluating Existing Tools for Remote Collaboration

In the following we give a brief overview of existing full-fledged tools that are designedto support remote collaboration in the creative processes we evaluated. We considered commercial tools as well as some interesting scientific ideas and prototypes that make no claim to be complete. As a result of this evaluation we recognized that recent solutions do not realize the full potential that Internet and web technologies can contribute to support creative remote collaboration.

Commercial Products There are a variety of tools on the market which offer possibilities for collaboration between dispersed teams. However, most products focus either on video conferencing capabilities or on sharing artifacts. A commonly used tool that offers both functions is Adobe Acrobat Connect Pro,[1] formerly Macromedia Breeze, which is mainly a web-based conferencing system and so-called learning environment. It features the most common tasks in a meeting setup, such as audio and video conferencing, screen sharing and a simple whiteboard solution. Workspaces are called "pods" each with a specialized role (whiteboard, chat, etc.). Here lies the main drawback of the system: The integration between these components is insufficient. For example, pointing to certain parts of a sketch on a whiteboard is impossible in a video conference. Interviews with SAP, an intensive user of this software product, showed that most of the functionality is hardly used, such as the whiteboard component.

Telepresence systems such as those provided by Cisco[2] or Polycom[3] are the most elaborated high-end video conferencing systems on the market. High definition video and audio as well as special security features make it only suitable for big companies. Telepresence systems are basically an arrangement of hardware components. The best setup makes it possible to build up a virtual meeting room,

---

[1] http://www.adobe.com/products/acrobatconnectpro.

[2] http://www.cisco.com/en/US/netsol/ns669/networking_solutions_solution_segment_home.html.

[3] http://www.polycom.com/products/telepresence_video/telepresence_solutions/index.html.

so everyone in the meeting has the illusion of sitting together at the same table. A major drawback is the lack of integrated support for whiteboard interaction.

There are several commercial and non-commercial websites on the Internet which focus on enabling users to sketch ideas on digital whiteboards.[4] They all provide simple means to draw sketches and share them with colleagues. Real-time collaboration on the whiteboard is not supported and would be difficult to attempt, because none of these solutions offer support for audio or video conferencing.

What all of these solutions have in common is that they do not support the users in actual collaboration with each other. People cannot properly sketch their ideas and discuss them with remote partners. Because of this, an emotional disconnect is built up between the communicating partners.

Scientific Prototypes The first tools to support creative collaboration of spatially separated teams were *VideoDraw* [4], *VideoWhiteboard* [5] and *Clearboard* [6], developed in the early nineties. VideoDraw and Clearboard combine synchronous drawing and the ability to observe remote partners at the same time. A desktop-like setup combined with cameras is used to reproduce the drawings from one side on the other. VideoWhiteboard more closely fits the requirements of our working modes, as it transfers whiteboard content with the help of rear projection to the whiteboard of a remote person. Additionally, a shadow of the entire upper body of the remote person is transferred to see the gestures of the partner. Seeing only the shadow and not a real video of the other person is one limitation which Tang and Minneman point out themselves [5]. Even more importantly, one cannot manipulate the other persons drawings or show physical artifacts. This drawback also arises with the Clearboard system, although it is possible to see a real image of the other person rather than only a shadow.

Everitt et al. [7] also used shadows to mimic the remote person's presence. They augmented *The Designers Outpost* from 2001 [8], a collaborative tool for website design. Users apply digital sticky notes to sketch the structure of the planned website. Much research effort has been spent on computer vision techniques to digitalize paper sticky notes and keep them synchronous with their analog counterparts. In addition to vision-tracked shadows, Everitt et al. also used transient ink to convey deictic gestures. For example, participants drew arrows to show their remote partners where they would move a sticky note. The transient ink arrow disappeared after several seconds. The Designers Outpost hereby presented a very promising approach to work with sticky notes on a digital whiteboard. Representing gestures with shadows and ink improves remote collaboration. But as the authors already mention, the shadows cannot convey human characteristics. Facial expressions are not visible at all and the transient ink is not always used. Additionally, the system would need audio support for a real remote setup.

Another project with similar ideas is *Video Arms* [9] from 2006, which uses digitalization of arms to enable pointing in a remote setting. A computer vision approach is used to capture the arms of the people working, cut them out of the video image,

---

[4] cf. http://skrbl.com, http://thinkature.com and http://imaginationcubed.com.

and then reinsert a translucent version on both the remote and local screens. The main drawback of this solution is that the focus on body gestures is limited only to the arms. Eye contact and full body gestures are not transferred to the remote location. Hilliges et al. [10] present a brainstorming tool which supports writing digital sticky notes on an interactive, touch sensitive horizontal surface. At the same time the sticky notes appear on a vertical display to allow working at a whiteboard. The questions remains open as to how this holistic digital environment approach could be transferred to a distributed location setup, as it has only been implemented in co-located settings.

All aforementioned systems offer interesting functions for remote collaboration, but each of them also shows drawbacks, especially when used to support creative collaboration. Our goal is to overcome these drawbacks with our Tele-Board system, as described in the following section.

4 Our Tool: Tele-Board – A Digital Whiteboard for Remote Collaboration

The Tele-Board system aims at providing designers and researchers with a software suite to pursue the Design Thinking working modes we identified using digital hardware devices. It supports working over distance and under certain restrictions, such as being forced to interrupt and resume work at a different time or place. Tele-Board simulates whiteboard content like sticky notes and supports handwriting on electronic whiteboards. This also includes natural user interaction with the simulated objects, i.e., the ability to add, move or remove elements to and from the electronic whiteboard using touch input or digital pens. To support geographically dispersed teams, pairs of electronic whiteboards need to be synchronized over the Internet. User interaction on one electronic whiteboard should both influence the local and the remote whiteboard. Preliminary research has shown that such remote interaction should be accompanied by video transmission of the participating users, which provides remote whiteboard modifications with a human context. To overcome physical limitations of today's electronic whiteboards, and to support the working modes identified, Tele-Board also needs to support additional input devices other than electronic whiteboards. Hand-written notes play an important role in Design Thinking projects. In a digital setup, this can be achieved using pen enabled or touch enabled laptop computers and mobile phones. These devices can then be used to write sticky notes in a private environment. From these devices, users have to be able to transmit sticky notes to an electronic whiteboard.

Next, the general architecture of these components is presented, followed by an introduction to the server component which mediates content between devices. Also, we present results of our research on mobile input devices in the context of Tele-Board, and show how different video conferencing approaches can be integrated into the Tele-Board system.

4.1 Tele-Board: General Architecture

The Tele-Board architecture clearly separates objects and concepts taken from the Design Thinking domain from the computer software and hardware involved. We will present the data model derived from these Design Thinking concepts, the users interaction with the data model through physical hardware devices, and the software components facilitating data exchange between different devices and locations.

All activities in the Tele-Board software are centered around *projects*. A project can comprise all phases of a Design Thinking activity and can endure several months. During a traditional Design Thinking project, a fixed set of analog whiteboards is filled with sticky notes and handwriting over the course of several hours or days, and later be photo-documented or cleaned to be used for new content. These ready-to-use surfaces of physical whiteboards are called *panels* in the Tele-Board data model. Panels do not have to be cleaned after being used, but can be archived and restored, and an unlimited number of empty panels can be requested. The panels themselves can be filled with various *whiteboard elements*, such as sticky notes or handwriting.

Panels are viewed and modified through electronic whiteboards, which are connected to a dedicated presentation computer. Decoupling whiteboard hardware and the whiteboards content using the notion of panels adds flexibility, as potentially only one electronic whiteboard is needed to replace a traditional setup with multiple analog whiteboards, and a larger number of panels can be worked on. In addition to direct manipulation of a panel displayed on an electronic whiteboard, Tele-Board allows for indirect user input from mobile and special devices, such as mobile phones or laptops, preferably with touch or pen input.

The mapping of the Tele-Board data model onto these hardware devices is achieved by using the Tele-Board software, which consists of four components: a *whiteboard client*, a *sticky note pad*, a *server component*, and a *web application*. The web application serves as an entry point into the Tele-Board software, where users can browse and manage projects and associated panels, and start working on such panels by opening them on an electronic whiteboard. All components except for the web application communicate using the Extensible Messaging and Presence Protocol (XMPP), an XML-based protocol for message handling and routing. Using XMPP for synchronization of whiteboard content is a common approach.[5] The description of every whiteboard element is translated to an XML representation and synced to the remote location. Using an open protocol allows the sending of messages from very basic Internet-enabled devices such as mobile phones or smart phones. XMPP provides the participating components with the notion of sessions and users and fits fairly well into the desired Tele-Board ecosystem. Each electronic whiteboard is managed by the Tele-Board whiteboard client installed on the computer attached to the whiteboard hardware. Whenever a user modifies a panel

---

[5] http://coccinella.sourceforge.net/docs/MemoSVG_XMPP.txt.

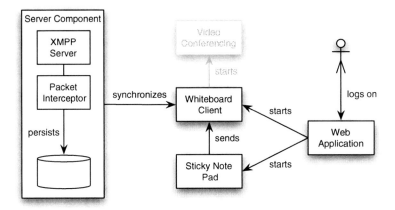

Fig. 3 Conceptual model of system components

opened in such whiteboard client, XMPP messages reflecting the modifications are generated and routed to the other participants in the session. When the whiteboard client receives such XMPP messages from other components, the electronic whiteboard is updated accordingly. On mobile devices, the sticky note pad component provides a user interface following the sticky note pad metaphor and allows the sending of handwritten sticky notes via XMPP to a specific whiteboard client. Typically this is the whiteboard client of the electronic whiteboard in the same room as the mobile user, but this is not a requirement. After receiving such input via XMPP, the whiteboard client will send update messages to the other participants' whiteboard client. All XMPP communication is processed by the Tele-Board server component. This server component adds additional session management aspects to the Tele-Board architecture which are not part of XMPP itself. These aspects include storing and restoring panel content, and more advanced Tele-Board digital features that go beyond the sticky note/whiteboard metaphor (see Fig. 3).

4.2 Tele-Board: Server Component

When participants are working on a panel using the Tele-Board system, XML representations of whiteboard elements transmitted to other participants are routed through the Tele-Board server component. In the server component, they are distributed to the recipients and are also stored for future history functionality in the XMPP server environment. The server-based components make it possible to interrupt and continue different sessions, and also to store the data to identify certain patterns of interaction.

The Tele-Board server component consists of two main parts: the plug-in for the Openfire XMPP server and a set of web services to process and visualize the history data. The plug-in encapsulates the stored history data and separates this from message routing in the XMPP server. The server plug-in is realized as a so-called packet interceptor. Each incoming message is read and parsed by the plug-in to decide how it should be treated. There are two possibilities: A message can be stored in the history data and forwarded to the recipients, or it can trigger an action and be prevented from being delivered to the other participants. The former case is used for every whiteboard exchange message, and occurs much more often than the latter, which is used for remote procedure calls to the XMPP server, e.g., to request the current whiteboard state upon application start-up. A sticky note updating its position will be logged to the history and the message will be delivered to the original recipients (e.g., the partner whiteboard client).

The data model used for storing the historical information is very basic. It is roughly a plain log made up of rows including the following: an object-identifier, a time stamp, a panel identifier, an action-code (such as NEW, CHANGE, DELETE), and XMPP-payload data describing the current object. This data structure provides a good trade-off between flexibility to reuse the data and detail of information. With this structure, every point in time and every creation, change or deletion of a whiteboard artifact can be reconstructed. That way, not only the latest state of a panel can be transmitted to whiteboard clients, but upon request older states can also be restored from the history database and viewed on a whiteboard client.

The web services can generate different kinds of information from the log data. It is possible to render a screenshot in several graphics formats and arbitrary resolutions from any point in time. Another option is to visualize whiteboard activities in their temporal order, including certain annotations such as whiteboard-clearing events, or to generate an overview of multiple charts that belong to one project and arrange them in their temporal order.

4.3 Tele-Board: Input Devices

Due to the average user's acquaintance with analog tools, supporting adequate input devices is clearly an important aspect of our work. Even rudimentary market studies show that development is increasing more rapidly than ever before. Not only sophisticated mobile devices, like smart phones such as Apples iPhone or recent Google Android phones, have emerged, but also the development of large scale touch-sensitive wall screens (digital whiteboards) has picked up. Convertible tablet PCs are making a comeback, with larger displays and multi-touch gesture support.

We dealt primarily with two deriving challenges:

- The selection of suitable off-the-shelf input devices for fast prototyping and early testing
- The design and implementation of a flexible and extensible software framework for the various user interfaces

Because we focused on the working modes concerning collaborative whiteboard interaction and the creation of sticky notes on personal note pads, there was the need to pick at least one digital whiteboard and a variety of mobile devices (phones, tablet PCs etc).

The optimal digital whiteboard would be very large but highly moveable and collapsible, could recognize an arbitrary number of pointers working simultaneously (multi-touch), and could distinguish finger input from pen input. Throughout our first year, we evaluated several product classes:

- SMART Technologies interactive whiteboard,[6] a stationary digital whiteboard screen for projectors that recognizes fingers and different pens
- SMART Technologies interactive display frame,[7] a touch-sensitive overlay for large plasma TVs, allows for dual-touch gestures
- Luidia Inc. eBeam,[8] a highly mobile device that can be used on arbitrary white walls, but only supports stylus input
- Promethean ActivBoard[9] series, a line of high resolution stationary digital whiteboards that support two pens simultaneously, but no finger input

We chose the SMART Technologies interactive whiteboard (SMART Board) as a compromise between feature richness and reliability. Its drawbacks can be disregarded for our project, as vendors will release more technically mature devices supporting multi-touch or dual-touch gestures.

Discussions on the work done by Johnny Chung Lee,[10] who uses Nintendos Wii Remote technology to realize a DIY multi-touch whiteboard, encourage us to consider this approach in future. System advantages would include lightweight implementation, thus better mobility, very good cost ratio and multi-touch capability.

Because mobile input devices act as the digital equivalent of basic personal sticky note pads when running our software, we decided to support as many systems as possible. Software for smart phones running iPhone OS, Android, Java Mobile Edition, Windows Mobile, and Symbian OS are planned to be available over time. This highlighted the need for platform-independent development and the usage of open standards wherever possible.

One example benefit of the open XMPP protocol standard is the availability of XMPP-capable chat clients for most existing platforms, as well as for all broadly used desktop operating systems and modern mobiles.[11] With these clients we were able to rapidly set up a first prototype of the overall system by only implementing the whiteboard client. Users can easily send messages from their personal smart phone using the respective instant messenger to chat to the whiteboard. The text appears on the board as written on sticky notes. Furthermore, the existing XMPP libraries for all common programming languages can be used for communication within the D-Tools 2.0 software suite. We designed an abstraction layer to decouple the different input devices and input types from our whiteboard client and sticky note pad applications (see Fig. 4).

---

[6] http://corporate.smarttech.com/products/SMARTBoards.aspx.

[7] http://corporate.smarttech.com/products/displayframe.aspx.

[8] http://www.e-beam.com.

[9] http://www.prometheanworld.com.

[10] http://johnnylee.net/projects/wii.

[11] http://xmpp.org/software/clients.shtml.

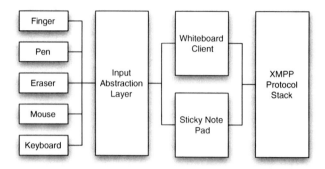

Fig. 4 Tele-Board input abstraction layer architecture

The input abstraction layer defines five basic types of input signals: touch inter-action with fingers, special device interaction with a pen or eraser, and mouse and keyboard input. A programming interface (API) is also available. The API allows Tele-Board applications to access raw input data, e.g., x/y coordinates, the value of a pressed key, or color of a pen. It can register observers for events triggered by the input devices, e.g., mouse clicked or finger down/up. From the other end, the ab-straction layer wraps the respective APIs of the physical input devices. Multi-touch gesture recognition will be implemented here.

The layer also enables the negotiation of parameters of input devices. For ex-ample, does it support finger and/or pen interaction? Does it support multi-touch or single-touch? How many buttons and colors are available? Applications can adjust their user interface according to the capabilities of connected devices.

This abstraction will allow us to integrate future digital whiteboard devices by just implementing a new interface. There will be no need to change any of the Tele-Board applications.

As development began, we implemented rudimentary adapters for the most generic input devices, namely mouse and keyboard. These adapters allowed usage of the whiteboard client on usual desktop PCs or laptop computers. Within the first year, we also finished the integration of the SMART Board API supporting touch interaction with finger and pen and differentiation of pen colors, as well as the per-sonal sticky note pad application for tablet PCs and other devices with pen input, e.g., the SMART Sympodium. More devices such as smart phones will be integrated in the next project phase.

4.4 Tele-Board: Video Conferencing and Remote Full-Body Gesture Overlay

Preliminary work has shown that remote collaboration on electronic whiteboards benefits from an accompanying video conference showing the remote team interact-ing with their whiteboard [11]. Video eliminates the problem of having whiteboard interactions by remote team members appear as actions made by a ghost hand. The Tele-Board system has been designed to support video conferencing from the beginning. This saves its users from well-known hindering factors and allows a clearer evaluation of the system's support for design thinkers. For our project, we wanted to focus on a reliable, cost-efficient video conferencing solution that does not impose additional entry barriers. For the current implementation we decided to use third-party video conferencing software such as Skype[12] because of its popularity and proven reliability.

Instead of separating video transmission screen areas from whiteboard content, the Tele-Board whiteboard client can overlay any video conferencing software in a translucent way to give the impression that the remote party is directly interacting with local whiteboard content. The video cameras can be positioned next to the electronic whiteboards, capturing the foreshortened whiteboard and the people in front of it (see Fig. 1). With this setup, people can face both the whiteboard and the camera at the same time. However, it comes with the trade-off that due to the camera angle on the electronic whiteboard, the screen area that can be used for the Tele-Board whiteboard client is roughly reduced by half (see Fig. 5). If the camera were to be pointed directly at the whiteboard to capture a flat image of it, the people at the board would naturally be shown from behind, which would reduce the communication experience between remote participants.

Fig. 5 Tele-Board remote system setup

[12] http://www.skype.com.

5 Tele-Board: User Feedback

During the whole process of prototype development, our goal was to minimize users' notice of the system's digital nature. To evaluate our success in fulfilling this intention we often asked colleagues with different scientific backgrounds to try out the system and give feedback on whether it felt natural to work with. Midway through the development phase we conducted a qualitative study with ten participants who had never heard of the system. All of them came from different educational backgrounds and have experience from the HPI School of Design Thinking. With the help of the study we wanted to understand how comfortable users are with different input devices, how the interplay between input devices and whiteboards works and how the general usability of the digital whiteboard was. As the study was specifically about whiteboard and input devices we did not include a video conference at this point.

Prior to the practical tests we asked the participants about their general behavior of writing sticky notes and applying them to a real whiteboard. We asked if they could imagine writing sticky notes with a digital device and about how important pen and paper were to them. Subsequently, the participants were asked to write sticky notes with a digital pen directly on the whiteboard and with a digital device similar to a tablet PC which sent them to the digital whiteboard. At this stage of development, our research prototype did not yet support digital pens. Hence, we used the Wizard of Oz method [12] to simulate it. Users wrote down their ideas on real sticky notes and hit a fake buzzer to send them. Simultaneously, a team member standing by with a laptop typed out the written message in a chat program and sent it. Afterwards the participants tried out all interactions we implemented in the whiteboard so far, such as moving, deleting and clustering sticky notes (see Fig. 6).

About half of the participants stated in the beginning that they would prefer using paper and pen over a digital device and kept their opinion after trying out the two different options. However, nearly all of them said that they would prefer the digital version if it was as fast and safe as paper and pen. Digital hardware and software are still not as precise and smooth as pen and paper, and people generally prefer analog artifacts for fear of data getting lost. Some users stated that they would not want to deal with a digital sticky note in addition to an analog one, as this might lead to confusion and eliminate the advantage of saving paper. Participants also emphasized

Fig. 6 Different tasks at qualitative user feedback study

that they could imagine using the digital version if it supported a wider range of standard computer system advantages like saving different versions, loading at any time or advanced documentation functions.

With regard to the interplay of input devices and whiteboard, we learned that a serious limiting factor of the digital sticky note pad application was its inability to determine where the sticky note would appear on the whiteboard. Users expressed that they either wanted to directly control where it would appear on their device, or would want to stand directly in front of the whiteboard with a portable device, so they could move the sticky note right after sending it. Concerning general usability the study also helped us to identify and improve various usability issues.

Using the input of this study we developed a next version prototype which we presented at the International Conference on Engineering Design (ICED) 09 at Stanford University and the Mensch und Computer 09 conference at the Humboldt Universität Berlin [13]. At both conferences the whole system was used, including videoconference between two whiteboards. In Stanford the audience participated by writing their own sticky notes; in Berlin our team gave a demonstration and members of the audience stood by to observe.

At both presentations the audience was enthusiastic about the combination of video and transparent whiteboard and the realistic feeling it conveyed. The ability to point at sticky notes and still keep talking to the remote partner was especially appreciated. Nevertheless, the video overlay was not very accurate yet and has to be improved. Participants also remarked that the whiteboard space is very small when using half of the space for the video. The restricted space on the whiteboard is clearly an important topic we have to concentrate on. When participants were involved in writing sticky notes at ICED09 we also noticed performance issues with our system. The more sticky notes were posted to the whiteboard the slower the reaction of the system was. It was difficult to move sticky notes around, and writing on the whiteboards became cumbersome. Since then we have solved many performance problems, but there is still room for improvement.

6 Outlook and Future Work

Findings of the first project year revealed many advantages of a digital solution applicable *not only* to distributed team settings. For example, in the physical world it is not possible to go back to different whiteboard states, and documenting can only be done by taking pictures of the analog whiteboards.

Existing research on computer supported collaborative work divides the topic into four parts, each demanding different requirements of tools [14]: The two defining factors are working synchronously vs. asynchronously and working in a co-located team vs. a distributed team (see Fig. 7).

Synchronous, co-located Design Thinking (Fig. 7c) is the preferred way for ideation and synthesis phases where it is important to directly communicate ideas and see the reactions of team members. Synchronous communication usually takes

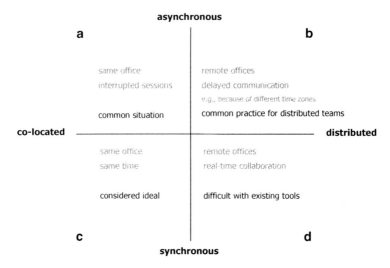

Fig. 7 The four dimensions of collaboration

place in co-located settings, because communication between distributed team members (d) is often troublesome with most existing tools. Asynchronous Design Thinking is especially important if time zone differences only allow a minimum number of overlapping working hours (b). Distributed teams define separate tasks and need to continue work where their partners left off. In this setting it is important to find out what has been done, i.e., have constant, easily accessible documentation of the other team's work, ideally created with minimal effort. Asynchronous communication also happens in co-located settings (a), e.g., if people work on different projects or other constraints don't let them work together. The requirements of a tool to support this are the same as in distributed settings. To narrow down the focus for our project we started by supporting synchronous and distributed Design Thinking sessions (d). The result is our Tele-Board system.

At the HPI School of Design Thinking, and especially in industry, gaps between source materials (files, printouts, media) and created artifacts from Design Thinking methods proved problematic. The same gap exists between Design Thinking results and documentation, needed for archiving or reporting to stakeholders. Working in a digital environment creates potential for retaining links from information artifacts that evolve from the methods of Design Thinking back to their original sources. It also allows enrichment of all items with metadata. This is the foundation to support generation of documentation and report files, such as presentation slides or statistical analysis with visualization. How to support both advanced workflows for Design Thinking projects and the generation of associated documentation, while still remaining very adaptable to the specific project context, is a future research topic for D-Tools 2.0.

Being able to go back and forth on the timeline and along the links between information artifacts enables the design thinker to view all gathered data from different perspectives and thereby gain a deeper understanding of the project context.

This will also help the team analyze the overall project progress and decision paths taken by the respective distributed sub-teams or by the team itself in earlier project phases. Additionally, the team can continue at any earlier state by branching whiteboard content. Further improvements might be achieved by detecting relevant time periods (hot spots), i.e., when project-critical decisions take place. Identification of those hot spots can help distributed teams working asynchronously when handing over their daily project progress to the remote team – for example by simply speeding up or even skipping the history playback between the hot spots.

Through our research in the first project year we found out that the synthesis phase is considered the most crucial part during a design process. Interviewees and test participants as well as other designers [15] stated that it is imperative that a common understanding of the research results is established. Only then the most important problems can be identified and addressed through iterations of the evolving design. Practical design thinkers claimed that synthesizing is already complex in co-located settings, and is hardly even possible for distributed teams.

We believe that digital tools can support designers in this complicated phase. With our current prototype it is already possible to rearrange and cluster sticky notes in order to classify research or brainstorming results. The clustering could be enhanced by other visualization techniques to create a common understanding by jointly creating data models such as mind-maps, flow-charts or other kinds of diagrams [15, 16]. Which tools would best support the synthesis phase must be investigated through observations of design teams and interviews with experienced design thinkers. The ideas triggered by our observations will be implemented and tested on our current prototype to find out which concepts work to improve the synthesis phase. All insights we gain through observation and testing can be valuable for the research on Design Thinking process phases. We want to investigate how important different types of visualizations are in the context of converging information and how they can be best applied to interactive tools.

In the next project phase we will conduct a user testing at the HPI School of Design Thinking and ask the students to use Tele-Board for their current projects. Thereby we want to understand how well a digital whiteboard system can be incorporated into a traditionally analog style of working like Design Thinking. Other interesting questions related to this study are: What impact does a digital system have on the whole process and on the team dynamics? Will people write more or less sticky notes, and does this have an impact on the creation of ideas? Does the system help structure and document ideas?

The Tele-Board prototype allowed us to demonstrate that it is possible to collaborate over distances and still employ creative working methods. Tele-Board provides digital support without being tied to the traditional desktop. It integrates life-size video with simultaneous manipulation of artifacts on a whiteboard. Forthcoming research will concentrate on enhancing the system for synchronous and asynchronous working in distributed and co-located settings. With this we bring remote collaboration closer to face-to-face communication while retaining all advantages of the digital world.

References

1. Brown, T.: Design Thinking. Harvard Business Review (June) (2008) 84–92
2. Lindberg, T., Noweski, C., Meinel, C.: Zur Entwicklung eines explorativen Forschungsansatzes zu einem überprofessionellen Modell. In: Stein, E.K., Walzel, F., eds.: Oberflächen/ Untersichten, Neuwerk, Zeitschrift für Designwissenschaft, Volume 1, pages 47–53 (2009)
3. Herrmann, T.: Design Issues for Supporting Collaborative Creativity. In: Proc. of the 8th Int. Conf. on the Design of Cooperative Systems, pages 179–192 (2008)
4. Tang, J.C., Minneman, S.L.: Videodraw: a video interface for collaborative drawing. ACM Trans. Inf. Syst. **9** (1991) 170–184
5. Tang, J.C., Minneman, S.: VideoWhiteboard: video shadows to support remote collaboration. In: Proc. of the SIGCHI conference on Human factors in computing systems: Reaching through technology, pages 315–322, ACM, NY, USA (1991)
6. Ishii, H., Kobayashi, M.: ClearBoard: a seamless medium for shared drawing and conversation with eye contact. In: Proceedings of the SIGCHI conference on Human factors in computing systems, Volume 92, pages 525–532, ACM, NY, USA (1992)
7. Everitt, K., Klemmer, S., Lee, R., Landay, J.: Two worlds apart: bridging the gap between physical and virtual media for distributed design collaboration. In: Proc. of the SIGCHI conference on Human factors in computing systems, Number 5, pages 553–560, ACM, NY, USA (2003)
8. Klemmer, S.R., Newman, M.W., Farrell, R., Bilezikjian, M., Landay, J.A.: The designers' outpost: a tangible interface for collaborative web site. In: UIST '01: Proc. of the 14th annual ACM symposium on User interface software and technology, pages 1–10, ACM, NY, USA (2001)
9. Tang, A., Tory, M., Po, B., Neumann, P., Carpendale, S.: Collaborative coupling over tabletop displays. In: Proc. of the SIGCHI conference on Human factors in computing systems, pages 1181–1190 (CHI 2006) (2006)
10. Hilliges, O., Terrenghi, L., Boring, S., Kim, D., Richter, H., Butz, A.: Designing for collaborative creative problem solving. International Conference on Creativity and Cognition, Washington, DC, USA (2007)
11. Fussell, S.R., Kraut, R.E., Siegel, J.: Coordination of communication: effects of shared visual context on collaborative work. In: CSCW '00: Proc. of the 2000 ACM conference on Computer supported cooperative work, pages 21–30, ACM, NY, USA (2000)
12. Maulsby, D., Greenberg, S., Mander, R.: Prototyping an intelligent agent through Wizard of Oz. Conference on Human Factors in Computing Systems (1993)
13. Gumienny, R., Böckmann, O., Willems, C., Quasthoff, M., Gericke, L., Meinel, C.: Verteiltes Design Thinking mit teleBoard. In Wandke, H., Kain, S., Struve, D., eds.: Mensch & Computer, pages 455–460, Oldenbourg (2009)
14. Rodden, T.: A survey of CSCW systems. Interacting with Computers **3**(3) (1991) 319–353
15. Kolko, J.: Information Architecture: Synthesis Technique for the Muddy Middle of the Design Process. In: 23rd International Conference on the Beginning Design Student Proceedings (2007)
16. Beyer, H., Holtzblatt, K.: Contextual Design: A Customer-Centered Approach to Systems Design. Morgan Kaufmann, CA (1997)

Physicality in Distributed Design Collaboration

How Embodiment and Gesture Can Re-establish Rapport and Support Better Design

David Sirkin

Abstract Geographically distributed design teams face barriers to effective collaboration that current communication technologies have difficulty mediating. We have found several key aspects, or building blocks, of effective, physically collocated interaction, which include: the exclusive physical presence of individual participants within the team workspace; the explicit and implicit body language signals that they exchange; and the ability to point to, and act upon, artifacts in a context that is shared with teammates. These provide the social and contextual clues that contribute to free-flowing, creative exchanges. However, when teams are distributed, they lose many, if not all, of these capacities. To re-establish them, we are introducing expressive, tele-operated robotic avatars into designers' workflows to provide a physical and social presence for distant team members. Our explorations going forward focus on employing physical avatars when design activity is most physical or tangible: during conceptual development, which occurs largely before ideas can be articulated with precision, and during prototype development, which generally occurs after a verbal or written exchange of ideas.

1 Introduction

1.1 Scenario: 'Remote' Collaborators

Philipp, a design engineer in California is prototyping a new remote control. Today, he is in his design loft figuring out the look-and-feel of an early-version craft paper model. With a quick glance over, his teammate Becky at a table nearby sees that he is turning to face her to ask a question. She turns toward him as well, and asks "What's up?" before he even has a chance to speak. "I'm working on the feel of this

D. Sirkin (✉)
Stanford University, Center for Design Research, 424 Panama Mall, Stanford, CA 94305, USA
e-mail: sirkin@stanford.edu

Principal Investigator: Mark Cutkosky

H. Plattner et al. (eds.), *Design Thinking: Understand – Improve – Apply*,
Understanding Innovation, DOI 10.1007/978-3-642-13757-0_10,
© Springer-Verlag Berlin Heidelberg 2011

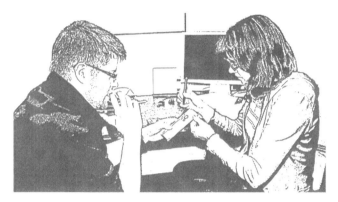

Fig. 1 A small, collocated design team works on a paper prototype of a remote control

part and don't know how well this button position works." "You mean right here?" as she points at the markings he's drawn on the side of the white paper box framed with tape and wood dowels. "Yes, my hands are larger than yours, so I can't tell if you can reach it." Becky carefully handles the fragile model and replies "It should be farther this way, and this much larger," as she puts new markings on the box in a slightly different position than the ones already there. Philipp asks "What about over here instead?" as he makes a new mark on the diagonal that runs between the two that are already there. "Yes, now it works for both of us," she replies, as she hands it over and turns back to return to her work (Fig. 1).

The next day, Philipp and Becky have scheduled a videoconference with Malte, a colleague who is working in Lulea Sweden. Sometimes, the difference in their time zones leads to early morning meetings for Philipp and Becky, or to late evening meetings for Malte, but today's schedule works for all three of them. Philipp starts out by showing Malte – rather, by showing the laptop video camera that Malte sees through – their prototype. Malte notices the markings on the sides and asks "Are those where you're putting the buttons?" "Yes, Becky and I thought the middle one would work best for most people's hands." Malte makes a face, but it is difficult for Philipp to interpret what it means through the screen. Malte's image is rather small – much smaller than it would be in person, and the window on Philipp's laptop that holds the video conference is only one among several that are visible; the others hold sketches of the next revision of the prototype and a document they are co-authoring. "Can you move it a bit more to the side?" he asks. Philipp doesn't know if he means that he should move the *button* to the side of the box – and if so, to which side – or that he should move the *box* to the side of the table, so Malte can see it better. So he asks. "Both, really," he replies. "But I meant the button, in particular. I have a prototype here with the button more to the side than yours. See?" He shows Philipp and Becky his prototype through the screen, but it appears to be larger and more refined than the one Philipp is working on. They are both finding it difficult to compare button positions or box sizes, because they cannot bring both models next to each other. "Maybe we could measure our prototypes and send the dimensions to each other for comparison." Malte does not have a measure nearby, so they all agree to schedule another conference for later in the day.

1.2   Constituents of Design Communication

In the preceding scenario, the first interaction was brief, efficient, and arguably more productive – at least for the time being – than the second. Let's walk through some of the differences between them.

In the first collocated session, physical proximity between teammates permitted their interaction to occur on the spur-of-the-moment, exactly when Philipp needed help. Each teammate was able to intuit when the other was about to act or speak, and to anticipate what would come next. They both used demonstrative phrases like "here" and "this" for easy reference, and supported their language use by pointing, which acted as an index into their shared contextual frame [1]. In contrast, in the second distributed meeting, the discussion had been scheduled ahead of time, so members met whether they needed help at that very moment or not. Philipp and Becky found it difficult to infer what the distant partner meant, either in what he said or expressed gesturally. Because their common frame of reference was gone, participants stumbled through, or chose not to use, the comparisons, demonstratives and pointing that had worked so fluidly when they were collocated. Such constituents of communication help participants to establish and maintain the common ground [2] – the coordinated, mutual understanding between what speakers mean and what addressees comprehend – that is so much a part of engaging and productive exchanges. That is, our *physicality matters*, and its advantages are difficult to secure when separated by a distance.

The constituents of design communication, and whether or not they are attained, can be viewed as a hierarchy. The first level represents the ultimate goal of, or rationale for, the interaction. In the broadest sense, the reason may be to improve designs or designers' understanding. For distant communications in particular, it may be to solicit the input of an expert, or to develop a cross-cultural perspective. Symptoms of these goals not being realized include design sessions that take on a tenor of coordination rather than collaboration, and engineers feeling that their time is spent in meetings rather than in design activities. The second level represents the communicative intent of the participants themselves. That is, what they intend to communicate, or learn, or resolve during the session. Symptoms of unclear intent include participants having disparate understanding of statements or ideas or events, possibly without even being aware of it at the time. Contributors include cultural differences or a lack of shared physical context, or common ground. The third level is composed of the specific elements that contribute to clarity and expressivity. These include: the proximity and orientation of participants to each other; the posture, bodily gestures and movements that they assume; and their facial expressions. Symptoms of a lack of clarity include designers having difficulty expressing themselves, or connecting with each other, or feeling that they or their partners are disengaged from the conversation.

In a sense, we are describing a form of 'trickle-up' collaboration. Participants are able to directly effect change at the third level, by developing a sensitivity to their own and others' physical presence and gestures. These actions influence their second level abilities to perceive context, share ideas and negotiate details.

And these abilities support the first level goals of productive working sessions and better understanding.

The remainder of this chapter discusses why collaboration breaks down in distance scenarios, some specific aspects of distance communication that contribute to these breakdowns, and how re-introducing physical presence can lower the barriers to truly effective distributed collaboration.

2 Understanding Collaboration in Design

2.1 Designers Use Their Bodies

What is actually going on in a collaborative design session? In addition to the verbal aspects of working together, which include talking, asking questions and discussing plans, designers use their bodies as an integral part of that work. At first, one thinks of the hands-on nature of design work: the way designers interact with tangible artifacts. But aside from sketching, building, manipulating and typing away at keyboards, designers use their bodies for *communicating*, both with collaborators and with themselves. The non-verbal aspects of working together play a central role in designers' abilities to perceive their local context, express themselves and exchange ideas. Non-verbal signals include facial expressions, visual gaze, posture, gestures and other bodily movements [3]. Many of these signals can also be further subdivided into more specific actions. Pointing at, or placing, objects and pantomiming observed or intended behaviors are all forms of bodily movement. These signals become communication when one person, who acts them out, influences another, who perceives them. *Explicit* signals are where the expression is intended; where it is in the foreground of the communicator's awareness. In contrast, *implicit* signals are in the background of consciousness [4]. Most signaling behaviors can be explicit or implicit, depending on the context. So a person's expression of surprise may be part of telling a story – say, demonstrating how a user might react to a new remote control – or it may be a genuine emotional response to being surprised. But both contribute to the shared frame – the common ground – between participants.

Design collaborators also make use of each other's proximate presence when they work and meet in person. They frequently rely on ad-hoc, informal discussions with participants who happen to be nearby and available. These sessions are brief, focused and content-rich; participants solicit input, confer on alternatives, raise and resolve questions. And they take place in local work areas, often at whiteboards. Kraut [5] has even noted that without such informal sessions, mediated by physical proximity, many R&D collaborations would not occur, or would break up before becoming successful. So the ways that designers use their bodies, and draw upon proximate colleagues, contribute to and support intuitive and creative exchanges within collocated teams. But similarly, the absence of these assets hinders design collaboration within distributed teams.

2.2   Design at a Distance

As design and engineering practice become more global – either to draw on the expertise of distant colleagues, or to interact with co-workers who are traveling – designers rely on the use of mediating communication technologies, rather than their bodies, to interact with each other. The intermediaries include the familiar: voice and video conferencing, email and instant messaging, and shared access to digitized sketches, documents and models. But rather than support designers' use of their bodies, these technologies, which try to bridge the distance between them, instead disable them. Two-dimensional video portals reduce their representations to a few square inches on displays often shared with other participants or with applications and documents. Their diminished facial expressions cannot relate emotion as effectively. They wave and gestures with their arms, and point with their fingers, but cannot penetrate into the space they are referencing. They cannot follow local action as well, because their position and perspective are fixed by someone else within the local hub of team activity. And their vision, hearing and speech may be spread among different devices around the room. Distant collaborators become disembodied.

To ensure that participants are available, distributed teams plan in advance and pre-set meeting times. However, the reasons that members have to meet are typically not pre-set, and arise in the moment when needed. Because these non-routine and ambiguous tasks, which rely on direct physical interaction and quick access to collaborators, are difficult to carry out with current technologies [6], the familiar approach to design activity becomes infeasible at a distance. As a result, distributed teams *perform* their work separately, within each distinct location, and only *confer* about that work between locations. Opportunities for second level clarity of communication, and its influence on first level goals of more productive sessions and deeper understanding, are lost. So how can we overcome such deficiencies and thoughtfully re-introduce elements of collocated design into the distributed collaboration experience? Before moving on to our explorations of this question, it will help to understand certain forms of local and distant interpersonal communication.

2.3   Modes of Communication

There are several ways that collaborators can arrange their communications with each other. Each way has defining characteristics that make it better suited to certain forms of social discourse and mediating technology. Figure 2 shows four modes of communication that we observe design practitioners assume during collocated and distributed sessions, extending the three modes that Nass and Mason [7] use to analyze communication within organizations.

In the first pane, called 1-to-1, one participant communicates with just one other. Examples include an active, co-present design task, or a face-to-face or telephone

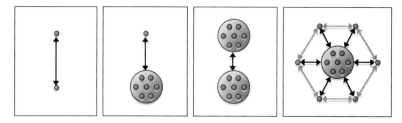

Fig. 2 Four modes of communication. The *left three panes* show 1-to-1, 1-to-many and many-to-many setups. In each case, there is a single channel of communication between the individuals or groups at each end of the connection. The *right pane* shows what we term 1-to-1-to-many. In this case, there is a separate channel for each individual to connect to the group, as well as a back-channel to connect to other individuals

conversation. In the second pane, called 1-to-many, one participant communicates with a small or large group of others. Examples here include a lecture or presentation, or a group meeting joined by a single distant participant. In the third pane, called many-to-many, one group communicates with another. This may occur when two teams speak to each other, either in person if collocated, or by voice or video conference if separated. Each of these first three modes may occur among members who are collocated or distant, and in each case, there is a single channel between the individuals or groups at each end of the connection. In the fourth pane, which we have termed 1-to-1-to-many, a single collocated group is joined by one to several individual participants, with each individual at a distinct location. This presents a *satellite* communication setup, which may include direct back-channel connections among the distant participants as well. The satellite setup is primarily used for distributed teams, and requires the effort of one or more support personnel to manage technology – including displays, cameras, microphones and audio mixers – as well as to moderate the remote discussion. Back channel communications may be via email, instant message, voice or video chat.

3   Explorations in Distributed Design

We have taken the design research approach of employing a variety of technology probes [8] to explore the issues surrounding physicality in design activity. Here we describe three studies that focus on the roles of embodiment and presence, agency and approachability, and gesture and expressivity. Note that these are in the third level of the collaboration hierarchy.

3.1   Study 1: Embodiment and Presence

While PC or laptop video chat suits close-proximity 1-to-1 conversations, and high-definition video conference rooms suit many-to-many teams, even the best

technologies available have difficulty supporting the physical interaction requirements of design engineering sessions. When room setup requires that local participants and those connecting remotely be a distance apart, video chat suffers because
cameras and microphones are setup for up-close use. But distant participants often
need to see whiteboards or video screens and hear local participants who are across
the room. Alternatively, video conference systems change the way several individual
participants at distinct locations are represented locally: each becomes bound within
a window that shares the screen with other individuals-within-windows. As a result,
the sense of personal presence and persona that is imparted by our distinct and
uniquely-addressable physical bodies vanishes. In these ways, distant participants
are *sensory impaired*, and they share this characteristic with each other. To address
these particular needs, we have begun to develop and employ physically present,
embodied, gesturing avatars at the local hub of design activity. An avatar is an embodied representation of one's self. Distant collaborators *inhabit* and tele-operate
these avatars, which serve as their stand-ins during team interactions. By filling the
gaps between what distant actors see and how they are seen, as well as what they
can do in their own environment and in the hub workspace, physical avatars give
them a *seat at the table*.

What are the implications of a persistent presence on group activities and mutual awareness? Over the last two years, weekly meetings of our distributed design
research community have seen an increasing number of global participants, forming what we now recognize as a 1-to-1-to-many setup. A noteworthy aspect of these
meetings is that activities vary between three categories of social exchange. Sessions
begin with informal socializing, continue with a more formal structured presentation, and conclude with a semi-structured dynamic Q&A dialog. These transitions
result in distant members, as well as their local counterparts, assuming several roles
in settings that vary from close-up individual chat, to presentation with overheads,
to room-scale group discussion. At the start of our explorations, distant participants
were perceived by the local group either as passive observers lurking on the fringe of
activity, or as visible collaborators who required significant effort to include in the
conversation. From the perspective of the distant participant, the local group was
barely aware of their existence. We found that introducing and arranging distinct,
physical avatars, shown in Fig. 3, so that local and distant participants could see and
interact with each other, increased their perceived sense of each others' physical and
social presence [9], and that this increase in visibility led to more frequent and on-
topic interactions. The sense of presence that the avatars helped to create was most
influential, perhaps not surprisingly, during close-up, informal exchanges, when the
conversation could become more in-depth and rich content could develop. At these
times, it was critical to be presented as a distinct individual.

With embodiments of each distant participant now joining in the local space, we
next set about providing them with further capabilities afforded by their newfound
physicality. Notable among these was a mannequin arm and hand, which could be
raised when someone wanted to join in on the conversation. But we were surprised
to find that people did not raise their hands very often. In trying to understand why
this should be the case, we found that it is not the social norm of the group to raise

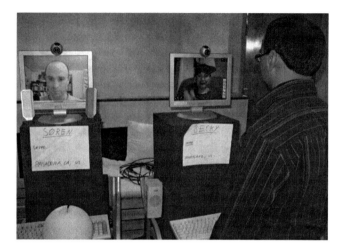

Fig. 3 Early physical avatars. This image shows two distant participants speaking with a local moderator by video chat. Their screen images are positioned atop kiosks at eye-level, and each has a personal camera, microphone and speaker for close-up conversation. Their names, location in the world, and instant messaging identity are shown so local participants can join them in the back-channel chat. A foam microphone ball, passed around by local speakers during Q&A dialog, is visible at the *bottom left*

hands to request to speak up – one just speaks up. But distant participants had limited abilities to see and hear, due to the rapidly prototyped, low-resolution capabilities of their avatars. Accordingly, they would miss some of the action within the local group. The resulting uncertainty created a reluctance to speak up, due to concern for interrupting another speaker who was not seen or heard.

3.2   Study 2: Agency and Approachability

To explore and better understand how physicality and motion can serve as indicators of a willingness to engage others and encourage interaction, we moved to a more public setting and focused on agency – the attribution of action to individual actors. We created an interactive touch-screen information kiosk, shown in Fig. 4, with either a virtually represented, or a physically attached, gesturing appendage, in the form of a waving arm. The virtual representation was shown directly on the information screen for the pilot study, and back-projected onto an opaque vertical screen for the follow-up. The physical arm was attached in a position that matched the projected location as closely as possible. At the end of the arm was either a graphic arrow that pointed down toward the kiosk or a humanlike mannequin hand. This arrangement permitted us to independently change conditions – virtual versus physical in one case, and graphic versus humanlike in the other – to learn how they influenced

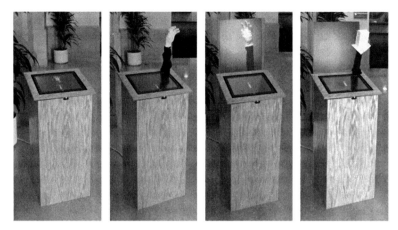

Fig. 4 Waving arms. A public information display that includes onscreen, projected and physical versions of a waving arm with either a graphic arrow or humanlike hand attached. The first image shows the onscreen–hand condition; the second shows the physical–hand condition; the third shows the projected–hand condition; and the fourth shows the physical–arrow condition. We ran the study in two stages: a pilot and a follow-up. The pilot did not include the projection screen (shown in the two left images), while the follow-up did (the two right images)

peoples' behavior. We carefully positioned the device in three semi-public areas at our research institution, so that people had a clear and consistent view of it while passing by.

We found that twice as many passers-by approached and interacted with the kiosk when they saw a physical, rather than onscreen arm, and 60% more interacted when they saw a physical, rather than projected, arm. But contrary to our expectations, the arrow condition generated slightly more interactions than the hand. Interviewees reported that the arrow was "more understandable" than the hand. While this result does not suggest that graphic elements should be preferred to humanlike ones in a general sense, it does imply that human likeness is not required to effectively indicate the availability of a communication device for interaction. Interview results also suggest that greater human likeness requires greater care in design. People have expectations of how human arms and hands should look and move; if a robot arm looks the part but does not act correctly, people will notice. The opportunity here is that people have few, if any, expectations of how graphic elements should move; by avoiding reliance on human likeness, the physical avatar designer has greater latitude in designing the behavior of remotely-actuated elements.

3.3 Study 3: Gesture and Identity

In their book *The Media Equation*, Reeves and Nass describe their finding that people treat communication technologies as social actors, whether or not they are aware of doing so [10]. They are polite, they reciprocate, and generally act as though computers are their teammates. So to what degree do the actions and gestures of a physical avatar acting as an intermediary between teammates enhance – or perhaps, complicate – the interactions between them? And do we find the same social actor behaviors when we look alternatively at explicit and implicit signals?

We are currently conducting a video-based study to learn how people interpret specific avatar gestures. The immediate goal of the study is to understand how these gestures correspond, or map, to the distant operator's communicative intent. With this knowledge, we can provide visual cues to accompany these intents, so that people who interact with avatars can latch on to familiar actions or nuanced expressions. So if a distant teammate becomes confused, should the avatar represent her state and if so, how would it do so? The longer-term goal is to apply this understanding to the design of tools and spaces that promote collaboration.

Some gestures seem to map directly to their associated behaviors. Examples include the way we turn our heads – and sometimes our entire bodies, if necessary – to look to the left or right, or how we lean forward and down to inspect some detail on a table more closely (as in Fig. 5), or that we naturally shudder when we laugh. Other gestures may not have such direct mappings. For example, how would we indicate that a distant teammate is confused, or is thinking for a beat, or is simply present and aware, without appearing idle and lifeless, or without her avatar appearing *uninhabited*? If you think about your experiences for a moment, you realize that unlike computers, people are not usually perfectly still for minutes, or even several seconds, at a time; their eyes scan the room, their chests rise and fall as they breathe, they shuffle their shoes. We are beginning to explore how distant participant tele-operated inputs should be matched to robotic avatar motion outputs – that is, when it is important to use direct mappings, and when it is important to use indirect ones. For instance, in many Indian cultures, it is customary to shake one's head from side-to-side to indicate agreement, but in the U.S., this gesture is interpreted as disagreement. Knowing this, an avatar might perform the task of cultural translation, converting a participant's head shakes on one side of a conversation to head nods on the other side. We expect that such actions will affect the clarity of communications as well as the avatar's perceived sociability [11].

Fig. 5 Avatar gestures. In this sequence of frames taken from a video shown to study subjects, a distant collaborator leans in toward the camera and peers into the local space, while the avatar screen moves forward and down, mirroring his actions. The sequence and timing differences between the images shown onscreen, and motions of the screen itself, influence whether study participants interpret the observed action as being controlled by the collaborator or by the avatar

Fig. 6 A robotic avatar at work. On the left is a robotic avatar in use during a design session. On the right is a closer view of its remotely controlled components. The remote participant who operates the robot uses onscreen buttons to make pre-programmed movements, such as "wave" or "point near emphatically," with its arm, and a handheld gesture-based controller to make front-to-back, left-to-right and tip-up or tip-down motions with its head, which includes a video screen, camera and microphone

For our initial study of these mappings, we recorded head-and-shoulders videos of male and female collaborators communicating through an avatar that can move its own "head" and "shoulders" (Fig. 6). The collaborators behaved in ways that they might during a typical conversation or working session. For instance, they looked to the left or right, leaned forward for a closer look, nodded their heads to agree or shook them to disagree, and expressed surprise or boredom. The twist is that in one case, the collaborator gestured while the screen remained motionless; in another case, the collaborator held a neutral expression while the screen performed motions similar to those the collaborator had made earlier; and in yet another case, the collaborator and avatar performed the same gesture in concert with each other. We then showed these videos to study participants and asked for their interpretation of what was happening and what, if anything, was being communicated. Our findings so far suggest that study participants have different ideas about the distinct identities of the collaborator and the avatar. That is, some of them interpret what they see as the actions of two separate actors, others only identify one or the other, and others conflate identities, without distinguishing between the two at all. Following from this, participants also have different interpretations of variations in sequence or timing between the collaborator's expressions and the avatar's motions. So if the avatar's motion precedes the collaborator's, participants may read what they see as the avatar *initiating* the action, rather than the reverse, which is what actually occurs.

Going forward, we expect to find that either the collaborator's expressions or the avatar's motions alone will be sufficient to convey less ambiguous messages, such as looking to the side or nodding, but neither alone will be enough to consistently convey subtler messages, such as thinking or boredom. However, we also expect that some combination of them will.

4 Plans and Issues for the Future

Our explorations going forward will focus on deploying more robust, field-hardened avatars for use within working design teams. In particular, we anticipate their use when design activity is most physical or tangible: during concept development, which takes place largely before either broad design ideas or specific details can be articulated with precision; and during prototype development, which generally occurs after the team, coaches and managers have verbally exchanged ideas and conferred. This will permit us to shift emphasis, from establishing proof-of-concept, to implementing with users who have real and immediate needs, and to understanding how to engage a robotic communication mediator on both sides of a global conversation.

For distant avatar operators, three issues stand out as critical to longer-term usability. First is the design of tangible and onscreen user interfaces, to provide intuitive control and a useful range of expression. Enabling technologies for control include video image recognition, which permit either facial expressions or bodily gestures to be used as input controls, and table-top or hand-held devices that reproduce the capabilities of the avatar's range of motion. Second are ways to provide greater sensory abilities, to assist distant participants in seeing, hearing and understanding action within the local team hub, and to more fully immerse them within that action. The first part of this implies the use of higher-resolution, zooming video cameras onboard avatars, as well as sensitive directional microphones. The second part opens the door to alternative inputs, such as force-feedback tactile sensors, so operators know when another person or object is in contact with the avatar, or proximity sensors, so operators know when they are near say, tables or walls. Third is understanding the issues of extension into, or *inhabitation* of, the avatar. Extension describes the way an operator feels like the avatar is more a part of his or her self, rather than a tele-operated device [12]. Greater extension is desirable if it improves the interaction, but only if it does not intrude on the operator's own sense of identity. For instance, we have yet to resolve whether physical avatars should be named independently of the distant participant who operate them. By observing teams using avatars, we expect to find out if people are inclined to say Malte or Avatar Malte, or something altogether different.

For the local hub team interacting with one or more distant participants through these avatars, the questions relate to what makes a robotic presence *comfortable* to be around in an ongoing basis. Much like extension is relevant for distant operators, the *transparency* of the avatar is relevant for the local team. A transparent interface lets one's perception of the avatar disappear into the background, leaving only an awareness of the distant collaborator whom it represents. A potential complication is how the team will respond if or when more than one person were to inhabit the same avatar at different times, or alternatively, if more than one person were to appear on the screen at the same time. Perhaps avatars could be matched one-for-one with individual collaborators, or modified for each individual user.

5 Conclusion

Schön states that designers design not only with their minds, but with their bodies and senses, which presents a challenge to their use of computers, which are sensorily deprived [13]. Physical avatars may help bridge the sensory void that currently separates global collaborators. Instead of filtering design communication through a series of technology portals, physical avatars provide a medium through which designers can establish their presence and communicate more directly.

5.1 Scenario: Continued

Somewhat later in the remote control design project, Becky is working in the loft when Malte, still in Sweden, waves her over using his new robotic avatar. When she approaches, he tells her "I just made some changes to the shape of the case and sent you the drawings, but they need more detail. I thought you could help me finish the design." Becky replies "Sure, let's see what we can do." As she steps over to their worktable to check out the new work, Avatar Malte follows just behind and settles in across from her. Malte glances around and sees Philipp at his desk, so he waves him over as well.

As Philipp and Becky start sketching out ideas among themselves, Malte's attention drifts and he starts doing other work. A few minutes later, Becky notices that Avatar Malte is looking out the window, so she gives a sympathetic glance, brings him into their huddle around the worktable, and puts an arm around him to make him feel included. "Come over here and take a look at this," she says. As Avatar Malte zooms his camera in to look more closely at a particular drawing, Philipp and Becky see him lean forward and look down, just as a person in the room might. They know exactly where Malte's attention is focused without having to ask or step away from their own work.

Malte uses a handheld touch-sensitive interface to help his avatar point and gesture his arm at the team's worktable. "I like these here and those over there, but…" Philipp can see from the tilt of Avatar Malte's head that he is confused about how to interpret some of their drawings. "Take a look at these instead," he says, as he draws in some more details. Finally, Malte nods his head and points towards a particularly promising idea that they can all move forward with.

Acknowledgements The author would like to thank the Hasso-Plattner-Institute – Stanford Design Thinking Research Program for funding this project; Professors Mark Cutkosky and Larry Leifer for supervising the research; and collaborators Dr. Wendy Ju for co-conceiving and running studies 2 and 3 and analyzing their results; Rebecca Currano for editing this chapter and contributing to the content of studies 1 and 3; Eric Kent for designing and constructing robot avatars and contributing to the content of studies 2 and 3; Neeraj Sonalkar and Malte Jung for co-development of study 1; and Samson Phan for guiding the design and safety of our robot avatars.

References

1. Clark, H. (2003) Point and placing. In: S. Kita (Ed.) *Pointing: Where language, culture and cognition meet.* Erlbaum, Hillsdale, 243–268.
2. Clark, H. (1996) *Using language.* Cambridge University Press, New York, Chapter 1.
3. Argyle, M. (1988) *Bodily communication.* Methuen, New York, Introduction.
4. Ju, W. and Leifer, L. (2008) The design of implicit interactions: Making interactive systems less obnoxious. *Design Issues: Special issue on design research in interaction design* 24(3), 72–84.
5. Kraut, R., Fish, R., Root, R. and Chalfonte, B. (1990) Informal communication in organization: Form, function and technology. In S. Oskamp and S. Spacapan (Eds.) *Human reactions to technology: Claremont symposium on applied social psychology*, Sage, Beverly Hills, CA, 145–199.
6. Olson, G. and Olson, J. (2000) Distance matters. *Human-Computer Interaction* 15(2–3), 139–178.
7. Nass, C. and Mason, L. (1990) On the study of technology and task: a variable-based approach. In J. Fulk and C. Steinfeld (Eds.) *Organization and communication technology*, Sage, Newbury Park, 46–67.
8. Gaver, B., Dunne, T. and Pacenti, E. (1999) Design: Cultural probes. *Interactions* 6(1), 21–29.
9. Lee, K. (2004) Presence, explicated. *Communication Theory* 14(1), 27–50.
10. Reeves, B. and Nass, C. (1996) *The media equation.* Cambridge University Press, New York.
11. Breazeal, C. (2002) Towards sociable robots. In T. Fong (Ed.) *Robotics and Autonomous Systems* 42(3–4), 167–185.
12. Takayama, L., Groom, V., Ochi, P. and Nass, C. (2009) I am my robot: The impact of robot-building and robot form on operators. *Proceedings of the 4th ACM/IEEE International Conference on Human-Robot Interaction*, San Diego, 31–36.
13. Schön, D. (1992) Designing as reflective conversation with the materials of a design situation. *Research in Engineering Design* 3(3), 131–147.

Part IV
Design Thinking in Information Technology

Bringing Design Thinking to Business Process Modeling

Alexander Luebbe and Mathias Weske*

Abstract Business process management is at the heart of organizations. It provides concepts and methods to capture, analyze and improve operational procedures in the daily business of organizations. The elicitation of process models is the first step in any process improvement project. Process models mediate communication between the different stakeholders involved, such as, for instance, business analysts, process participants, and software architects. Process models provide a shared understanding, so that everyone can contribute knowledge.

Based on design thinking principles, this paper develops a method that aims at improving business process modeling. To achieve this goal, we introduce physical building blocks and methodological guidance to fundamentally change the way people interact with process models. Tangible prototypes have been successfully used in design thinking, and initial experiments show that a tangible toolset is a promising approach to improve business process modeling and comprehension. The focus of this paper is on the insights we got during the cooperative research project, i.e., the research path we took. Finally, we explain our research method and outline the next steps.

1 Introduction

Business process management evolved as a organizational approach to structure and better understand work in organizations. The idea is to investigate procedures that drive the daily business operations of companies with the goal of improving them. As an example, a key process in an insurance company is the processing of insurance claims. Saving an average 5 min in the processing time of a single claim ends up saving considerable resources, given the high number of cases that an insurance

A. Luebbe (✉) and M. Weske
Hasso-Plattner-Institute, University of Potsdam, 14482 Potsdam, Germany
e-mail: alexander.luebbe@hpi.uni-potsdam.de; mathias.weske@hpi.uni-potsdam.de

*Principal Investigator

H. Plattner et al. (eds.), *Design Thinking: Understand – Improve – Apply*,
Understanding Innovation, DOI 10.1007/978-3-642-13757-0_11,
© Springer-Verlag Berlin Heidelberg 2011

company deals with. From a business process management perspective one can identify people that are involved, information that needs to be gathered, tasks that have to be performed and decisions that have to be taken to get a claim processed. Analyzing the process can reveal flaws or point to improvement potential.

Eliciting information and making process knowledge explicit is the role of business process modeling. The models are captured as visual diagrams such as depicted in Fig. 1. Process models map out roles, tasks, decisions, and information used. The visual elements have a distinct semantics which allows to represent complex processes in a compact way. That makes process modeling a powerful tool to share knowledge. Process models are the basis for discussions between the stakeholders involved, such as process participants that process claims in an insurance company, managers that have to ensure claim processing quality, the top management that is looking for optimization and software architects that shall support the work of the employees by providing adequate software systems.

In the next section we examine how process models are used today for communication between process analysts and the stakeholders of the process. From there we derive our research questions which we outline in Sect. 3. The main part reports on the iterative research process in Sect. 4. We describe our prototypes, the findings and how it drove the research process. The result is a tangible set of shapes for process modeling, called TBPM (for tangible business process modeling). In Sect. 5 we show what it is, explain how it works and outline some experiences we had when applying it in different settings. In Sect. 6 we have a look around in research and industry to find related approaches. In Sect. 7 we sketch our research method and point out the next steps towards a rigor validation. We summarize the paper in Sect. 8.

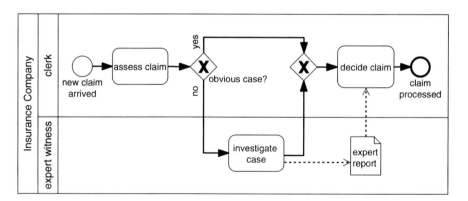

Fig. 1 Sample process model depicting a simple view on claim processing. It shows process participants: *clerk* and *expert witness*; Events: *new claim arrived* and *claim processed*; Activities: e.g., *assess claim*; a decision: *obvious case?*; and a document: *expert report*

2 Background: Process Models Mediate Communication

In 1993, Michael Hammer and James Champy published a book called "Reengineering the Corporation" [1]. At that time they were at the frontier of a new discipline that investigates how an organization works by looking at the work activities and their ordering, i.e., the processes. They shared best practice knowledge gained from projects in the 1970s and 1980s that achieved dramatic improvements by redefining processes. In each project a team of software specialists and domain experts would form a task force to reinvent the way crucial processes are done. By introducing software systems to store and access centralized information or automate calculation steps significant performance gains could be realized.

However, initially the problem was addressed from a technological side, resulting in solutions that lacked acceptance by end users. In this context, supporting working procedures with software systems was scientifically investigated in the 90s under the term *workflow management* [2]. As a result of these issues, Business Process Management (BPM) emerged as a discipline that provides a broader perspective by addressing organizational aspects as well as technological aspects [3]. It addresses the full business process management cycle: from analysis, to (re-)design, to implementation, to operations. Process models are essential artefacts in all of these phases.

To visualize the implicit knowledge, process models are created. These are compact drawings that capture the activities to be done, their order and the like (see Fig. 1). This idea can be traced back to flow charting techniques in the 1970s and it evolved over time. In particular, the IT had an interest in a compact and precise description of the process which usually serves as a requirement documentation for software implementation. To support the full cycle with software tools, formal, i.e., unambiguous process modeling were required. As a benefit, formal models can be used to configure software systems [4] and shorten the time needed for implementation.

Yet, the way process improvement projects are conducted has not changed much since Hammer and Champy. Specialists, usually process analysts, conduct individual interviews with stakeholders or hold workshop to elicit the process related information. We studied process elicitation and observed the path that a process model takes from the conversations with domain experts to the implementation at IT departments. The workshops usually use whiteboards, flip charts and post-its to capture process related knowledge. The quality of the extracted information relies heavily on the experience and skills of the process analyst. He must listen carefully, read between the lines, and extract the knowledge relevant to the process. At the end of a day, stakeholders leave the workshop. The process analyst creates a process model, an abstraction and reframing of all notes and impressions that he has collected throughout the workshop. The process model now becomes the central artifact that reflects the findings from the workshop and is used in all subsequent discussions and negotiations.

The stakeholders are asked to review the process model and provide meaningful feedback. This is a common theme. But the stakeholders are asked to evaluate and make judgements on a process model that they have never seen before. This, in turn, leads to additional efforts to explain the model and to resolve misunderstandings. In some cases domain experts reject process models. Because they are unable to "read" the model and conclude that their domain knowledge is not appropriately represented.

Problems in communication about the process lead to a significant loss of time and money. However, it is essential that all stakeholders reach consensus about the current and the desired situation before the process becomes implemented in a software system. Given these pain points in contemporary process modeling practice, we chose process elicitation to be our starting point in exploring how to improve the quality of communication between domain experts and process analysts.

3 Research Question: How to Improve the Quality of Communication

Given the current situation, we asked ourselves what could be done to improve the communication between the domain experts, those that implicitly have the process knowledge and the method experts, those that elicit the information and have knowledge about process modeling. As described in Sect. 2, the quality of communication is crucial to the success in those projects.

Additionally our research was driven by the following questions:

- How to create a shared understanding based on a shared representation?
- How to receive detailed feedback and detailed information about a process?
- How to enable people to reflect on their process and get new insights?
- How can we strengthen understanding of process models by domain experts?

4 Iterating Ideas

In November, 2008 a group of researchers from the Center of Design Research (CDR) at Stanford University and Hasso-Plattner-Institute (HPI) at University of Potsdam met for a first workshop. As part of the discussions and knowledge exchange, we as researchers from the Business Process Technology group told about aspects of process models for communication as described in Sect. 2. During the discussions the idea was born to explore more lively settings to let people experience the process rather than confronting them with a prepared model on paper. In this section, we report on the ideas, the prototypes we have build and the observations we made. Through constant iterations we developed a solution that we call TBPM, Tangible Business Process Modeling.

4.1   First Iteration

The very same day the idea was born, researchers from CDR and HPI performed a first prototype (Fig. 2). The goal was to explore the possibility of experiencing the process rather than discussing it. The group decided to do a role playing exercise. Our notion was that by playing it, we could come up with a general understanding of the process involving all partners. We chose a scenario based on the transactions surrounding a fictitious bicycle shop. This scenario assumed multiple stakeholders (customers, suppliers, fabricators, bank) simulating the process of ordering and buying a bicycle. When a customer ordered a bike, it had to be manufactured. When parts were missing the bike shop had to order new material from the suppliers. Money was transferred via the bank. To perform the role play, participants were provided with all possible material available at the D-School in Potsdam. That included but was not limited to post-its, Lego, whiteboards and the like.

We allowed about 1.5 h to get the people into playing mode, play the game and talk about the findings. In the spirit of the practices of innovative design development, we did not establish explicit rules. Instead, we wanted to see what the situation would suggest to us as a way of moving forward.

Observations and Learnings

All participants enjoyed playing. Creativity spawned alliances between suppliers, variable interest rates from the bank and new bike shop offers. However, we also observed some confusion about Lego pieces and what they represented. For example, one player assumed that a Lego piece was a bike part, another player a bicycle, and still another player assumed it was money. Negotiating meanings did consume some time. Painting or tagging the objects with a post-it makes it far easier to share a common understanding. Still confusion about objects and their associated meanings

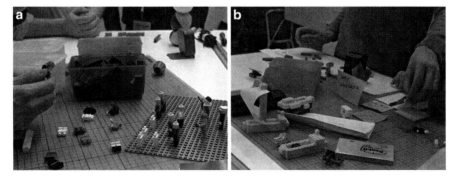

Fig. 2 Snapshots from the first prototype: Lego and arbitrary material was available to explore the experience of a process as a role playing game

were common during the game. The team realized that a well prepared set of objects with a predefined meaning might be more productive than freely choosable objects.

The most confusing issue was concurrency. Playing the game with several stake-holders at the same time added complexity to following and understanding the actions on the table. As we did not restrict the play, many different threats were active in parallel at a time. This made it hard to track the state of the interactions at the table. That also let to the effect that not one process instance was processed at a time, but many different instances were spawned. In other words, more than one bike order was in progress. Although this is a realistic setting, the team realized that the condensed nature of a role play was overcharging participants with impressions.

We concluded that there was a huge potential in playing out the process rather than modeling it. The level of engagement and fun was fascinating. Yet, further refinements were obviously needed to steer the actions on the table and allow for more traceable interactions.

4.2 Second Iteration

During the research retreat of the Business Process Technology group we decided to do another iteration of the game (Fig. 3). The goal was to incorporate the learnings from the first prototype and explore ways to channel communication. A special focus was on the message exchange between participants. Participants of the first iteration reported that they had difficulties tracing the information exchange. We prepared wooden whiteboard plates (dry erase) to capture conversations. They were passed equivalent to email threads with an evolving story. Alternatively, we prepared message cards. They had the size of a post-it and framed each message to have a sender, receiver, header and body. Both approaches aimed to channel and capture the communication at the table.

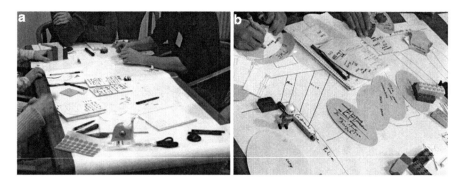

Fig. 3 Snapshots from the second prototype: Experimenting with different material to channel the conversations

We formed four different groups. Each group had the size of three to four people. We restricted the roles to the bike shop, customer, supplier and bank (in case of four players). We made all groups aware of the learnings from the first prototype and explained the alternatives to channel interactions at the table. Each group was free to choose their interaction channels. The groups had additional material such as Lego, paper and scissors to help themselves were needed. Also we handed two of the groups a ball. It represented a mutually exclusive token that would only allow one person to act at a time.

We allowed 1 h to get the groups into playing mode and play the game. Afterwards a moderated group discussion was hold to let the groups share their findings and collect suggestions for further investigations.

Observations and Learnings

Again the participants enjoyed playing the game. They used the preparation time extensively to identify with their role, e.g., a person build a bike from paper to identify with his role as a bike shop owner. On the other hand, the creative potential also unfolded many exceptional cases of the bike shop scenario that made it more interesting for the players. In other words, players were making up new problems to keep the game from the "boring" normal path. We concluded that the game would need objectives for the players that would motivate and therefore direct them.

An important aspect of this iteration was capturing of information that is passed between participants. The group using the wooden whiteboard plates reported that they took shortcuts instead of writing the whole information on the plate. The real information was passed verbally and the scripture on the plate served as a memory aid. That was okay for short-term memory recall but already at the group discussion after the game a lot of information was not recallable. Similarly, the group that used the message cards reported that message cards were barely useful. The written text did not reflected the full information. A long description would also be counter intuitive to the dynamics of the game. Also messages did not correlate which made it hard to trace answers. We concluded that written messages are not feasible to capture the dynamics of the interactions at the table.

The groups that used a ball in the game reported that this worked but revealed new problems. The concept of the ball was to sequentialize the actions on the table and therefore enable better tracing for the participants. While that worked as anticipated, sequential actions led to long idle times for other players. Thus, participants shifted their attention and when it was their turn, they were not up to date with the state of the game. Due to the length of the game and the potential depth of discussions, we concluded that we needed to find a way to allow participants to fade out their attention and still get back into the game.

When collecting feedback multiple participants independently reported that they would like to have a game master. That would allow them to test the limitats instead of carefully following guidelines. While playing, they would rather like to think about the content than about the rules of the game.

4.3 Third Iteration

Weeks later we did a new iteration. The goal was to investigate how we could make the role playing a more challenging game with an agenda (Fig. 4). For this iteration we limited the information exchange to post-its. We changed the setting of the game to an online auctioning scenario. Competing for the lowest price was considered a reasonably goal for the players. We had asked five HPI students and colleagues to act as stakeholders: online auctioneer, post office, bidder 1, bidder 2, and seller.

We shortened and guided the preparation phase. All participants were asked to fill in a sheet. It should help them to develop empathy with their role. As an example, we asked them about the motivation of their role. More importantly, we asked them to create the message post-its that they assumed to be needing later in the game. Every participant had a unique colored post-it set to codify the sender of a message.

In addition, we included a game master. It was on him to watch the actions of the game and ensure rule compliance. To capture the actions on the table, we used a dictaphone. It sequentialized the actions on the table, just as the ball did in the last iteration. More importantly, the dictaphone forced participants to take well defined moves (only an action spoken to the dictaphone was valid) and conveniently capture the flow of the game for the researchers.

Observations and Learnings

The preparation phase was quite helpful for the players to develop empathy for the users. The prepared activities on post-its were of value as such that they allowed participants to think about their role in the process. Later in the game, people used almost every post-it and rarely created new ones. Only one person had to recreate most of his post-its (the post office role) because his assumptions proved wrong during the game play. The post-its created during the game's preparation stage were rather restrictive during the actual gaming session. Almost all participants were strongly

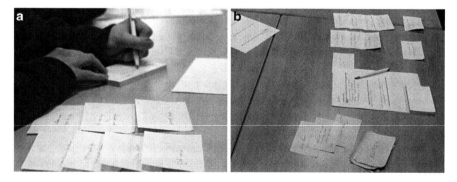

Fig. 4 Snapshots from the third prototype: Using prepared steps on post-its turned out to limit the scope of the game

motivated to fit these anticipated activities into the game. We concluded that the prepared post-its limited the thinking scope of the participants and changed the nature of the game from an explorative nature to a competitive nature. Unintentionally, the challenge became whether a participant could place all post-its later in the game.

A new observation was that the stream of post-its captured quite well the events of (inter)actions. It represented the state of the game which participants liked. They even asked for more details, like the time until the end of an auction to be represented on the table. Post-its were used now to capture a mix of information types such as messages, actions and money. This stream of post-its was an even better documentation of the process than the messages spoken to the dictaphone. Still, it was a stream of post-its and one had to read them all to get a picture of the process. We concluded that participants are able to map their process knowledge yet we needed a better framework to guide them.

In interviews after the prototype some participants reported that the setting was rather boring than fun. We concluded that the restrictions applied by us in this iteration were not compensated by the gameplay.

4.4 Fourth Iteration

From the last iterations we learned that group sessions with a gameplay environment need guidance and motivational factors (Fig. 5). We also learned that people wanted a shared representation of the process knowledge. In this iteration we took a step back to focus on the type of representation used to share the process knowledge. In order to simplify the task we looked at interviews with single process stakeholders. Our goal was to find out whether the individuals can map their process knowledge in a structured manner. Instead of letting everybody interact, one knowledge carrier should be enabled to map her process.

From previous iterations we knew that post-its and a certain framing like the message cards would probably help. When Jonathan Edelman from CDR visited HPI, he brought a set of white acrylic tiles based on systems modeling iconography. The

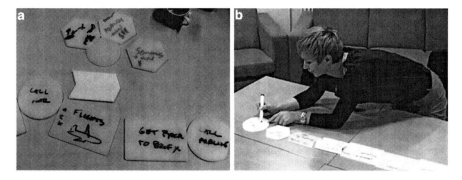

Fig. 5 Fourth iteration: Exploring acrylic tiles to let individuals map out their process steps

white acrylic afforded writing with a dry erase marker right on the piece, making the content easily changeable. The different shaping of the pieces imposed a certain semantics, meaning that only certain information would be hold on certain shapes. Furthermore, the pieces were made large enough to require gross motor coordination in order to manipulate them with the hands. We decided to test these tiles in interview situations.

As participants for the interviews we asked administrative assistants at HPI, Potsdam. We conducted three interviews in which we asked to describe the process of booking travel and accommodation for faculty members visiting a conference. The researcher conducting the interview tried to map the process together with the interviewee to the acrylic shapes.

Observations and Learnings

We found that the acrylic shapes worked well as a shared object that the interviewee and interviewer could talk about. Stepwise unfolding the process allowed the interviewee to follow the act of knowledge capturing and contribute her knowledge. In two out of three cases, the interviewee took the dry erase pen and started correcting or mapping information. We concluded that this is an easily accessible tool for everybody to get engaged with.

The elements used did not reflect the process modeling iconography, although they looked similar. In some situations this was a limitation as we could not frame all the knowledge to the concepts given in process modeling languages. We concluded that, given a full modeling language in plastic, domain experts could possibly map and frame the processes themselves.

4.5   Fifth Iteration

Equipped with learnings from the last iteration we designed a new set based on the same material (Fig. 6). We decided on the size, the shapes needed and the amount of elements per shape. Care was taken to design the pieces so they were big enough to write on them with dry erase markers and comfortably hold them in the hand. A complete set was made of 120 pieces. Yet, this set had only four basic shapes: activities, events, data objects and gateways (see Figs. 6 and 7). They reflect main artifacts of the Business Process Modeling Notation (BPMN) [5], the process modeling language of choice. Through markup of the shapes all language elements can be derived. In spite of that, we knew from empirical research publications [6] that only a few main elements are of interest for most practitioners.

We called this iteration the TBPM set, Tangible Business Process Modeling. The iconography moved nearer to the actual process modeling language and the resulting model. The table used for interviews would permit drawing on it. Thus, we could capture orders of activities, associations, annotations, and responsibilities by drawing on the table itself.

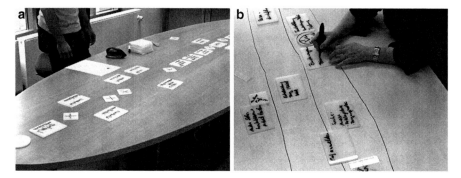

Fig. 6 Fifth iteration: First run using an acrylic set that represents BPMN [5] iconography

Again we interviewed office assistants for standard processes such as travel planning and conference organization. We used structured interviews and the TBPM toolkit. We wanted to see whether the domain experts would accept the tool and how they would apply it.

Observations and Learnings

People were reluctant to use the TBPM toolkit at first. Throughout the interviews we found it effective if the interviewer listens and models the first steps of the process while explaining the concepts behind the objects. After the interviewer has mapped the first steps, the interviewees started writing on the blocks themselves. The first steps also set the level of granularity for all other discussions. We concluded that an introduction to process modeling is quite easy if done by a working example.

We did not explicitly introduce the concept of control flow or gateways in BPMN. Intuitively, interviewees accepted a logical order if steps were laid out from left to right. Parallelism and alternatives were both captured by putting activities one over another. Only in processes where both concepts occurred together, gateways were introduced (see Fig. 6 left). In general, we introduced as few process modeling concepts as possible to reduce distraction from the problem itself. We concluded that these people are able to frame their knowledge and create process models themselves.

5 Experiences with the TBPM Toolkit

As off now, we have done more than fifty interview situations using the set from the fifth iteration (Fig. 7). We can say from our experience: it works . The semantics associated with the different shapes focus the discussion at the table and push the participants to frame their output to fit into the concepts of process modeling. We could even transport the idea to group modeling sessions as initially intended. The analogy to children's blocks dramatically lowers the barrier for non-process

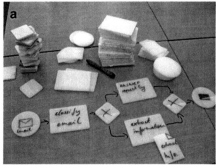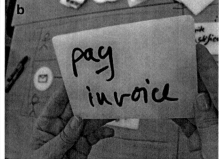

Fig. 7 The tangible business process modeling (TBPM) toolkit – turning the table into a chess-board for process modeling

modelers to use the toolkit, participate in process modeling, and contribute their knowledge. Everybody at the table can easily create, delete, arrange and rearrange objects. The immediate mapping of the implicit knowledge allows people to re-flect the process with their knowledge. Subsequent discussions are more precise as people can point at the part of the process that they are talking about. The pro-cess mapped down at the table represents the knowledge gathered. That is not to say, that methodological guidance is obsolete. We are still working out the details of a proper introduction and moderation techniques for both: interviews and group modeling sessions.

As such, we have conducted a series of case studies. As an example, we compared TBPM interviews with traditional structured interviews and interviews supported by post-its. We found that TBPM interviews take much more time because the inter-viewees have to frame their knowledge. As a benefit the result is already a process model. That relieves the interviewer from interpreting the interview and creating his own process. Using post-its in interviews did not provide such a process framing. We have have published papers on TBPM [7, 8] and presented it to profes-sionals. We got positive feedback and further ideas for refinement of the method and toolkit. We expect to do some more refinements of the toolset as a result of further learnings from investigations using TBPM.

6 Related Approaches

TBPM can be characterized as a form of participative modeling. The participation of users is widely seen as a crucial success factor in all types of projects that touch an organization. Larger IT projects are this type of project [9]. As described in Sect. 2 the current best practice is to listen, e.g., in interviews, and to give limited influ-ence to predefined design decisions, e.g., in workshops [10]. Model building in conjunction with end users usually happens in moderated groups [11, 12], in which a modeling expert translates the input into a model that is discussed with the audience.

Participative modeling in enterprise environments has been largely investigated by Anne Persson [13, 14]. Persson's work looks at the situational factors for adoption. She recommends to asses the organizational context, assess the problem at hand and acquire sufficient project funding for enterprise modeling [12]. For modeling sessions a facilitator and a tool operator is proposed. They should guide the participants to model goals, organizational entities and processes. In those sessions the process is modeled by an expert using an software tool. Participants can see how the process evolves and participate by providing input. We argue that TBPM fosters another level of participation because the participants do not have to channel their input through a tool operator. Also, the direct interaction with the process creates a different notion of responsibility for the result. Nevertheless, Persson's recommendations [12] serve as a good guideline for group modeling sessions.

There are more examples of related approaches that follow similar ideas. Especially, consulting companies have developed similar concepts. The nearest related approach we could find (as of now) is a consulting practice used by Unity,[1] a company that applies the OMEGA method [15, 16]. The OMEGA method is a proprietary process modeling method embedded in a "strategic production management" approach. The consulting methodology suggests the use of paper cards that reflect the iconography of the modeling elements to be used in workshops. The cards are available in different sizes depending on the use case: moderated group modeling at a pin-board (size of TBPM shapes) and group driven modeling on a table (size of business cards). Unfortunately, only little public knowledge exists [17] about the Unity methods to engage users. Much of it is hidden as best practice in consulting and was never scientifically investigated.

7   Research Methodology

At a first glance this project is no research, is it? Why is this science and not just another invention?

When we started investigating how to achieve more user involvement we did not know how the solution would look like. We did not even have a clear research question as outlined now in Sect. 3. The ideas that popped up were investigated by immediate prototyping. A prototype does not have to represent the overall situation but the particular aspect to be investigated. Thus, it was fair to start with a wild game to investigate the fun factors that made people be engaged. Also it was fair to try process modeling with system modeling objects to investigate whether acrylic tiles afford user participation. The early prototyping approach allowed many iterations with low effort. Indeed, this started as a side project and only little time as available throughout the first year to investigate the issue. We call this first step the initial *Learning Cycle* (see Fig. 8). The theme is to test out ideas as early as possible to get feedback. Documenting iterations and reflecting on the lessons learned is an

---

[1] http://www.unity.de/.

Fig. 8 Sketch of the research method employed for the TBPM project

important aspect of the *Learning Cycle*. Observations might be easily captured but learnings need time to settle. Over time memories fade and good documentation of the original impressions might yield new insights even weeks and months later.

What we ended up with is a *Working Solution* as described in Sect. 5. We published a paper to the Design Thinking Community [7] about our early findings which concluded the initial learning cycle. We also published a paper to the Business Process Management Community [8] in which we outlined early hypotheses about why TBPM works. Learning is still ongoing and refinements to the *Working Solution* are very likely.

Refining the hypotheses and setting up a laboratory experiment are the next steps towards a *Scientific Investigation* of TBPM. The goal of a rigor scientific investigation is not to show that TBPM works. The goal is to investigate why it works. We hypothesize some reasons and we plan to test them. We seek to understand better how different aspects such as tangibility, accessibility, shared model ownership and moderation work together. From that investigation we can draw more general conclusions. We call these *Transportable Findings* (see Fig. 8) which are applicable to more domains and different problems.

8 Summary and Outlook

In this chapter we have motivated the search for new ways to allow end users to share their process knowledge. We seek to empower them to create and give meaningful feedback to business process models. We documented the prototypes and the learnings that let to a solution which we call TBPM, Tangible Business Process Modeling. It is a tactile set of inscribable acrylic that can be used to model processes on the table. Unlike current practice this approach allows more people to directly interact with process models, frame their knowledge as a process and participate in process modeling sessions. We have published scientific papers [7, 8] to spread the word and gather feedback from the scientific community. In the next step, we set up experiments to investigate how and why TBPM is working. This will lead to more general findings that can be transported to other areas as well.

Acknowledgements We are very grateful to Jonathan Edelman who was constantly involved in our research activities. His insights from his own media model research were crucial to steer our learning cycles. We also thank Gregor Gabrysiak for his support in the early stages of the TBPM development.

References

1. Hammer, M., Champy, J.: Reengineering the corporation: A manifesto for business revolution. Collins Business, NY (2003)
2. Lawrence, P.: Workflow handbook, WfMC. Wiley, NY (1997)
3. van der Aalst, W., Hofstede, A., Weske, M.: Business process management: A survey. Lecture Notes in Computer Science, pages 1–12, Springer, Berlin (2003)
4. Smith, H., Fingar, P.: Business process management: The third wave. Meghan Kiffer Press, FL (2003)
5. OMG: Business Process Modeling Notation, Version 1.2. Final Adopted Specification. Object Management Group (2006), http://www.omg.org/spec/BPMN/1.2/
6. Zur Muehlen, M., Recker, J.: How much language is enough? Theoretical and practical use of the business process modeling notation. In: Proceedings of the 20th International Conference on Advanced Information Systems Engineering (CAiSE 2008), Lecture Notes in Computer Science. Volume 5074, pages 465–479, Springer, Berlin (2008)
7. Edelman, J., Grosskopf, A., Weske, M.: Tangible business process modeling: A new approach. In: Proceedings of the 17th International Conference on Engineering Design, ICED'09 (August 2009)
8. Grosskopf, A., Edelman, J., Weske, M.: Tangible business process modeling – methodology and experiment design. In Mutschler, B., Wieringa, R., Recker, J., eds.: 1st International Workshop on Empirical Research in Business Process Management (ER-BPM'09). Volume 1, pages 53–64, Springer, Ulm, Germany (September 2009)
9. Krallmann, H., Schönherr, M., Trier, M.: Systemanalyse im Unternehmen. Oldenbourg (2007)
10. Byrd, T., Cossick, K., Zmud, R.: A synthesis of research on requirements analysis and knowledge acquisition techniques. MIS Quarterly 16 (1992) 117–138
11. Kettinger, W., Teng, J., Guha, S.: Business Process Change: A Study of Methodologies, Techniques, and Tools. Management Information Systems Quarterly 21 (1997) 55–80
12. Stirna, J., Persson, A., Sandkuhl, K.: Participative enterprise modeling: Experiences and recommendations. Lecture Notes in Computer Science, Volume 4495, page 546, Springer, Berlin (2007)
13. Persson, A.: Enterprise modelling in practice: situational factors and their influence on adopting a participative approach. PhD thesis, Dept. of Computer and Systems Sciences, Stockholm University (2001)
14. Persson, A., Stirna, J.: An explorative study into the influence of business goals on the practical use of enterprise modelling methods and tools. New Perspectives on Information Systems Development: Theory, Methods and Practice, Kluwer, NY (2001)
15. Fahrwinkel, U.: Methode zur Modellierung und Analyse von Geschäftsprozessen zur Unterstützung des Business Process Reengineering. PhD thesis, Univ.-Gesamthochschule Paderborn (1995)
16. Heinz Nixdorf Institute: OMEGA: Object-oriented method strategic redesign of business processes. In: Changing the ways we work: shaping the ICT-solutions for the next century: Proceedings of the Conference on Integration in Manufacturing, page 381, Göteborg, Sweden, 6–8 October (1998)
17. Gausemeier, J., Plass, C., Wenzelmann, C.: Zukunftsorientierte Unternehmensgestaltung–Strategien, Geschäftsprozesse und IT-Systeme für die Produktion von morgen. Hanser Fachbuch (2009)

Agile Software Development in Virtual Collaboration Environments

Robert Hirschfeld*, Bastian Steinert, and Jens Lincke

Abstract Agile processes are gaining popularity in the software engineering community. We investigate how selected design practices and the mind-set they are based on can be integrated into Agile software development processes to make them even stronger. In a first step, we compared Agile methodologies with interaction and product design methodologies and discovered that both fields have much in common with respect to their underlying principles and values. Based on our findings and by applying both methodologies, we improved collaboration support for geographically-dispersed software development teams. We designed and implemented ProjectTalk and CodeTalk as part of our XP-Forums platform. Independently of their geographical location, team members can create and maintain user stories with ProjectTalk. CodeTalk enables team members to efficiently communicate their concerns regarding development artifacts in an informal manner.

1 Introduction

Agile software development processes are increasingly followed in software development projects that deal with complex domains and require continuous interaction among developers and with customers and prospective users. Agile approaches such as Extreme Programming [3] or Scrum [13] are people- and code-centric. Based on a high-quality code base throughout the entire project, developers can respond almost instantly to customer needs and requests. Teams can quickly make progress in providing the desired technical solution due to short development cycles and incremental explorations.

R. Hirschfeld (✉), B. Steinert, and J. Lincke
Software Architecture Group, Hasso-Plattner-Institute, University of Potsdam,
14482 Potsdam, Germany
e-mail: hirschfeld@hpi.uni-potsdam.de; bastian.steinert@hpi.uni-potsdam.de;
jens.lincke@hpi.uni-potsdam.de

*Principal Investigator

H. Plattner et al. (eds.), *Design Thinking: Understand – Improve – Apply*,
Understanding Innovation, DOI 10.1007/978-3-642-13757-0_12,
© Springer-Verlag Berlin Heidelberg 2011

Design Thinking [6, 12] as a process has interesting aspects to offer – not only to designers, but also to software engineers. In our project, we will extend agile development processes with elements from the Design Thinking approach to make them even stronger. Our enhancements will explicitly support both developers and customers to explore divergent alternatives and to converge on a decision or solution whenever necessary and possible.

There is also the trend that project teams tend to disperse around the world. Distributed development is getting more common, requiring team members to resort to means other than face-to-face communication to organize themselves, to collaborate, and to keep in touch regardless of geographical location.

Teams following agile software development processes or employing Design Thinking methodologies are usually small compared to the ones adhering to more traditional approaches. Team members collaborate closely via continuous and informal interactions rather than via large formal documents and schedules planned far ahead. This kind of collaboration is difficult to achieve in distributed settings, for example, when trying to gather expertise from team members. We will use and improve our extended agile software development process to design and implement better ways of communication for efficient and effective information exchange in distributed teams regardless of their geographical distribution, allowing them to collaboratively immerse in their tasks.

We both improve the tools we have developed so far, such as ProjectTalk for managing user stories and planning activities collaboratively, and expand our tool suite as necessary and desirable for improved interaction. We aim for a solution that allows a seamless transition between asynchronous and synchronous collaboration styles and which provides support for user-specific views at different levels of detail. We will focus on communication that is essential for keeping distributed teams in sync and for allowing a high degree of transparency on their core development activities.

Our approach is twofold (Fig. 1): First, we extend state-of-the-art agile development processes with elements of Design Thinking to allow software developers to benefit from the mind-set of design. Second, we employ our extended software development process to design and implement tools supporting this process keeping everyone collaboratively involved.

In the following, we outline our motivation to extend agile development processes and to provide appropriate tool support within a virtual collaboration environment. We then describe current findings regarding desired extensions to agile methodology. Thereafter we present our results gained with respect to tool support for distributed development teams – an application and an extension to a programming environment have been developed.

2   Motivation and State of the Art

Agile software development processes are iterative and incremental, embracing change and evolution, and promoting design simplicity and high software quality. In this section, we first describe important aspects of agile methodologies and then

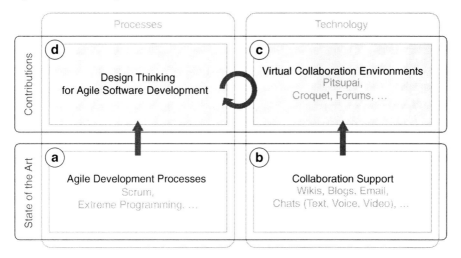

Fig. 1 Conceptual project map

discuss our objectives to enrich these methodologies with elements from industrial and interaction design methodologies. After that, we discuss the increased need for collaboration support as design and development teams tend to disperse around the world.

2.1 Design Thinking for Agile Software Development

Most agile software development processes [1] are people- and code-centric in that they foster interaction between project participants, grounded on short and many iterations, each of which resembling a full development cycle including planning, analyzing and prioritizing requirements, designing, and testing. Risk is minimized by producing a running system in every such iteration in a short period of time.

The most popular representatives of such processes are Scrum [13] and Extreme Programming (XP) [3]. Scrum is a high-level process framework that defines roles and practices. The Scrum process skeleton (Fig. 2a) has two main cycles: The long cycle (30 days) represents a development activity that leads to an increment of the product to be built, based on the requirements and the budget allocated for their implementation. It groups several short cycles (24 h each) that cluster daily activities of the team members inspecting each other's activities, proposing next steps, and suggesting corrective actions if necessary.

Compared to Scrum, XP is a more disciplined method. It focuses on the strict application of programming techniques representing best practices, on clear communication, and on teamwork. XP assumes short development cycles that allow for early feedback based on actual code. Automated test suites represent an executable specification of the system to be built, which is co-evolved with the system itself.

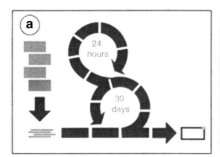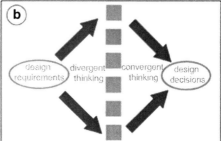

Fig. 2 (a) Scrum backlog and process skeleton; (b) Divergent and convergent thinking

We regard agile processes as solution-oriented since they encourage developers to advance only in small increments that are all based on sound technical decisions only, without enough opportunities to approach the same problem from different perspectives. Unfortunately, this does not leave much room for exploring both problem and design space.

In our project, we investigate how elements from Design Thinking such as divergent and convergent thinking (Fig. 2b), need-finding, brainstorming and sketching, and the preservation of ambiguity can be integrated into agile processes like Scrum and XP.

2.2 Collaboration Support for Distributed Development Teams

Both Design Thinking and agile software development projects rely on small teams working closely together. Informal direct communication and physical tools and artifacts such as whiteboards, sticky notes, and story cards are preferred means of expression and interaction. For that to work, team members need to be co-located to take full advantage of the benefits offered by these tools and artifacts.

Due to organizational structures and economical concerns of modern organizations, distributed development is getting more popular, requiring geographically dispersed project teams to collaborate across space and time. Geographically distributed teams have difficulties to apply the tools and artifacts preferred or required when following Design Thinking and agile development methods. This requires teams to resort to means other than face-to-face communication to organize themselves, to collaborate, and to keep in touch and sync.

We argue that there is a need for virtual collaboration environments as a shared place for project participants to meet, to work, and to collaborate as informal as they are used to. One key challenge addressed in our project is the computerization of these informal but important tools and artifacts without either loosing their advantageous properties, or by compensation for their potential loss. We will compensate for such losses with advantages offered by the new media of virtual environments, using their power and nearly unlimited space to go beyond the possibilities and constraints of the physical world.

Examples of tool support to be provided by our virtual collaboration environment include whiteboards that are unbound in screen estate, persistent, and searchable even after some of the design phases are finished. This way, early design decisions are available to the program maintainers when needed. Furthermore, we want important relationships between design and development artifacts to be made explicit and preserved for continuing efforts and future reference. Code editors, for example, can be annotated with the alternatives considered in previous convergent/divergent design phases.

3   Design Thinking for Agile Software Development

Relying on a natural approach to learning, that is comparing the new with facts and knowledge already understood and internalized, we examined design-related topics on innovation, need finding, interaction design, and creativity techniques from a software engineering perspective, allowing us to better understand and integrate new interesting elements into agile development processes. First results of this comparison between design methodologies and agile software engineering topics reveal many commonalities.

In this section, we describe these commonalities concerning the underlying values. We then present two different approaches to combine design activities with development activities and discuss pros and cons with respect to the principles of both fields.

3.1   Common Values

Recognizing similarities between agile and design methodologies has been our motivation for investigating the combination of XP and elements from Design Thinking. We studied literature on Design Thinking and interaction design from a software engineering perspective, and identified many commonalities with respect to the values of respective methodologies; values referring to underlying principles of the methodologies, the principles upon which concrete techniques are based.

- **Wicked Problems.** Software development projects are confronted with *Wicked Problems* [5]. Originally described in [21], the term *Wicked Problems* refers to problems that are not well understood and thus difficult to describe. The problem becomes, however, clearer as one moves ahead to the solution of the problem. The closer one gets to the solution, the more one can understand and describe what the actual problem is. In the field of design, it is reported that design teams usually face this kind of problem [4]. Moreover, solving a problem that is understood well may not be referred to as a design activity.

- **Close Interaction.** People interacting closely with each other exchange a lot of knowledge and opinions, which in turn supports making progress. For this particular and other reasons, agile processes such as XP strongly suggests a close interaction amongst all team members as well as with the customer. The value of close interaction results in recommendations of concrete practices such as on-site boards, pair programming, collective planning sessions, collective code ownership, or small but regular releases [3, 13]. Close interaction is also a key aspect of design activities. Many designers work with their customers using different methods to elaborate their understanding of the domain from multiple perspectives. As another example, the collaboration of team members having different areas of expertise and experience further supports the exploration of the problem and solution space; it eases the creation of a multitude of divergent ideas and supports their connection and composition.
- **Go for Feedback.** Iterative and incremental development is the foundation of all agile methodologies [14]. In each iteration a next running version of the system is created and delivered, bringing value to the customer and allowing for feedback on this running, executable prototype that is used in real work settings. Being close to design processes in this respect, XP recommends to have actual users on-site; this enables early and direct feedback during the workout and implementation of all details of the higher-level concepts and ideas. Programming is also an activity resulting in feedback. Developers get feedback on their understanding of the program domain and about the quality of their implementation [3]. For similar reasons, designers are encouraged to create many prototypes and to work with them, getting feedback on the forms and materials, for example, or feasibility constraints. Early prototypes should further be tried out by users of the target group in target scenarios, striving for valuable feedback on aspects such as usability.

3.2   Approaches to Combine Design and Development Activities

The development of a software product involves a multitude of different activities. While some activities may assigned more to design than to development and vice versa, they cannot be clearly separated. This would require precise definitions of both design and software engineering methodologies that are not available. Moreover, design in the broadest sense can be considered as the entire process of creating a new product from understanding the needs over multiple prototypes to the final product; software development usually refers also to the entire process including aspects such as requirements engineering and user interface concepts [20, 23]. For that reason, we also examine interaction design as one specific candidate of design methodologies that deals with understanding user needs and elaborating interaction concepts to meet these needs. Interaction Design involves activities of the following categories: inquiry (the study of the existing), exploration (the study of the possible), composition of the existing and the potential, assessment, and coordination [15].

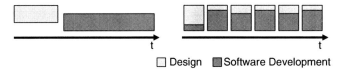

Fig. 3 Approaches to combine design and development activities; a waterfall-like approach, and an iterative and incremental approach

While agile methodologies value user feedback, they are usually not very specific about useful techniques for understanding the users' needs and developing respective user interface concepts. However, the design of the interface to the users gets more important and software vendors have started to attach more value to it [17, 19] This was a main reason for researchers to conduct case studies investigating how companies integrate design activities into the overall software development process [7, 9, 27]. Basically, there are two different approaches to combining the work of interaction designers with the work of software engineers; both are depicted in Fig. 3.

The left side of Fig. 3 shows a waterfall-like approach: conducting design activities first and handing over the resulting concept to a development phase. It is the task of the designers to understand the problem domain of the users. Based on that, they develop several concepts addressing the users' needs, work the concepts out, and align them to each other. The overall and finalized design represents the requirements on the system that is to be realized by the software developers in a subsequent stage.

The right side of Fig. 3 depicts an alternative approach that is based on the notion of iterative and incremental development. Over multiple iterations, designers and software developers simultaneously work on the design concepts and the code base respectively. This approach is built on the observations that getting all requirements right first is rarely possible, that requirements can and will change during the project lifecycle, and that the understanding of the problems evolves as we get closer to their solution.

The iterative and incremental approach implicates that the overall design is neither final nor complete until the end of the project and can be changed at any time during the course of the project. The problem domain and the corresponding set of requirements has to be separated early in the project so that designers and developers can work on a prioritized subset of requirements and problems in each iteration. On the one hand, changes to the design result in additional development effort. On the other hand, the iterative approach allows for taking advantage of new insights gained during the ongoing project development. With that, this approach allows both designers and developers to embrace change in most if not all all different aspects relevant to the project. It is based on the notion that learning is a natural consequence of making progress and reflecting on it.

The executable or running systems delivered after each iteration bring value to the customer and thus form trust based on their early return of investment. Furthermore they provide the opportunity to obtain and incorporate feedback from real work usage settings. Getting feedback early and often is an important aspect of both

Design Thinking and agile development methodologies, and prototyping techniques such as sketching and paper prototyping support the exploration of alternatives and eases getting insights and making progress. The main goal of a prototype is to reveal misconceptions and to improve the understanding of the problem domain. In this sense, each version of the software system delivered after an iteration can be considered as another kind of prototype. In contrast to a sketch, for example, it has a higher resolution, but it allows for getting different aspects of feedback, in particular the adequateness of the current solution in the target settings, when real users work with the application in real work situations.

4 Virtual Collaboration

Close collaboration and communication is vital in XP projects – amongst team members and also with customers. Development teams tend, however, to disperse around the globe and thus have to resist to means other than face-to-face communication. In our project, we integrate and develop tool support for distributed development teams to allow for informal communication and efficient collaboration despite geographical dispersion. We describe the results of our efforts during the last year in this section. Amongst others we have developed ProjectTalk an application that supports collaborative planning activities in distributed teams. ProjectTalk's design allows for working with story cards in a similar way as it is possible with physical artifacts, by still providing the advantages of a digital solution (4.1). Co-present users can interact with ProjectTalk simultaneously without synchronizing on an input device, for example. All users are further enabled to act on their own behalf (described in 4.2). This functionality represents a contribution to the collaboration community and is described in detail in [24]. We also have developed CodeTalk [25], an extension to an development environment that enables distributed developers to have conversations about source in an informal and efficient manner (described in 4.3). Along with other tools, such as ProjectTalk, CodeTalk was used in several development projects and showed its usefulness. We have written and submitted a research paper on the approach of CodeTalk to informal conversations about source code.

4.1 Bringing Physical Artifacts to Digital Environments

XP similar to design processes heavily relies on co-location of all teams members and on physical tools for communication and organization such as index cards and whiteboards. *User Stories* are the central artifacts in XP teams. They form a concise description of the customer's requirements written in everyday language. *User Stories* are elaborated in concerted planning sessions with the customer and persisted on index cards. These cards are usually managed by pinning and moving them on a whiteboard, being visible for the team and indicating progress of the project.

Bringing all these information from the physical whiteboard into the digital world promises a multitude of new possibilities, such as having unbounded space or support for full text search. In addition, having these artifacts digitalized provides a good basis for supporting and encouraging close collaboration in teams working geographically dispersed. Prospective collaboration software should thereby incorporate as many strengths of physical setups as possible.

Learning from others about the flaws and strengths in this and other respects, we extensively benchmarked existing software solutions supporting agile processes. As one important result, it turns out that a main challenge is the design for interaction with huge amounts of information within limited dimensions of a computer screen. Many solutions have decided for tabular representation of *User Stories* actually causing a feeling of information overload. All solutions distinguish between viewing and editing information and usually offer a number of forms to alter contents of *User Stories*. This design does not harmonize well with the card metaphor and requires a decent number of clicks for simple usage scenario.

By trying out available solutions and actively working with them, we became aware of that the design of the tools influenced the project team in working with user stories; depending on available space, team members cut descriptions down to single bullet-points or fill out many different fields of the forms making stories too formal and complex.

Getting closer to a solution candidate meeting the needs, we continuously designed user interface concepts, created various prototypes, implemented the prototype concepts, and used the implemented version during our daily work. The left column of Fig. 4 depicts prototypes of different concepts developed in the course of our project. The right column shows corresponding versions of implementation called *ProjectTalk*. The last picture at the bottom left shows a new prototype for ProjectTalk that is currently implemented. This current version includes some innovative user interface concepts for easily browsing large amounts of project artifacts.

We argued in Sect. 3 that the early use of the application, which is to be enhanced over the project time, is important for getting feedback from actual users already working with the application during their regular activities. Applying this theory, we used ProjectTalk from early on for planning the next version. This continuous work with ProjectTalk help us to understand important aspects regarding its collaborative use.

4.2 Multi-user Multi-account Single-Screen Interaction

Integrating Single Display Groupware (SDG) concepts [26] with more traditional groupware, such as Wikis or project management software, requires re-considering the way of interacting with and designing for users. ProjectTalk integrates SDG concepts, enabling co-present team members to collaborate using the same application instance. Users are provided with separate input channels allowing them to contribute with the need to synchronize. While users often have an account and

Design protoypes   Prodect screenshots

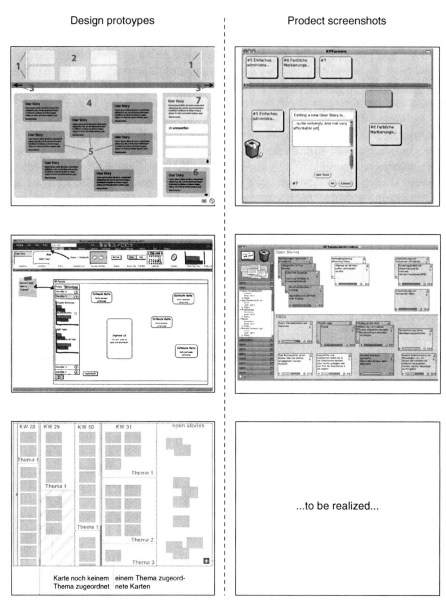

Fig. 4 User interface concepts (*left column*) and screenshots of corresponding applications

interact with the application in a way specific to their account, traditional SDG concepts do not allow users to act on their on behalf. In this subsection, we describe the issues resulting from this limitation and present our approach to handle them, which was implemented in ProjectTalk.

4.2.1   Merging Characteristics of Asynchronous Groupware and Single Display Groupware

By employing SDG concepts, we provide XP teams with interaction characteristics similar to working with physical tools (Fig. 5). XP teams traditionally rely on these physical tools such as index cards and whiteboards for communication and organization purposes. Bringing all these information from the physical whiteboard into the digital world would enable a multitude of new possibilities, such as having unbounded space or support for full text search. Additionally it enables remote collaboration, because virtual whiteboards, unlike physical ones, can be shared over computer networks.

Using physical tools such as whiteboards and index cards, team members are able to act independently of one another without the need to synchronize on pens, for example. Traditional applications, however, only support interaction with one user at a time. The need to synchronize on application control impedes spontaneous interaction and reduces social dynamic in comparison to a physical whiteboard. Therefore we enable multiple users to interact with the application independently. To further increase the dynamic of a session, users are able to join or leave a session at any time. We also incorporated screen sharing technology to support distributed XP teams. Remote team members can share planning sessions, for example, and interact with the same shared screen.

When multiple users interact with a single screen, traditional applications are unable to distinguish acting users. These restrictions of current concepts lead to issues concerning authorization and traceability. Figure 6 depicts a typical multi-user single-screen scenario. In this scenario, the application is unable to make a reasonable decision whether the user is privileged to perform the desired action as the application does not know who the the currently acting user is. By using current approaches, all users actually act on behalf of a host user, the one who logged in before. This gives all acting users the same privileges in the described scenario.

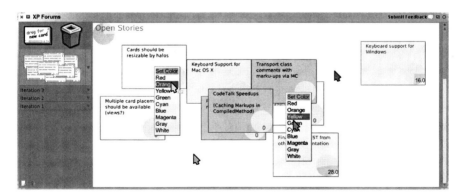

Fig. 5 Screenshot of the application: Multiple users, represented on the screen by colored mouse cursors, interact with a virtual whiteboard. Every user may open their own context menu

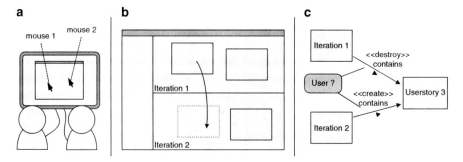

Fig. 6 Two users collaborate on a shared screen, each user having its own cursor (**a**); one user moves a user story from one iteration to another (**b**); this user action leads to a change in underlying object structures (**c**). If the application is not provided with sufficient context information about the currently acting user, it is unable to validate privileges correspondingly

The inability to distinguish multiple acting users does not only lead to undesired modifications, but also to unintended restrictions of users. When, for example, users want access to previous projects for analysis purposes, they might be unable to open the projects as the host user is not privileged for accessing this information. As another consequence of application actions not being linked to the acting user, tracing data of user action become unreliable. It is impossible to find out who modified certain important information.

The examples described above show that it is necessary to distinguish users concerning their security context and to execute every action users want to perform in their respective context. In particular, the following questions come up:

- How might an application be designed to allow multiple interacting users logging in and logging out?
- How should the user credentials be managed?
- How might UI events be distinguished by acting users?
- How might the application make use of this distinction and link application actions to users?
- How should applications be designed to deal with multiple interacting users having different privileges?

4.2.2 Platform Support for Multi-user Multi-account Interaction

An application featuring multi-user single-screen interaction requires special support in the application's platform such as handling the events from multiple, similar input devices independently from each other. In addition, if multiple remote users should be able to work in same way as local users, and if UI actions should be linked to the users, an adequate concept representing the users and their actions is needed.

The concept of *Hands* has shown as a meaningful approach to represent and manage user interactions. *HandMorphs*, or *Hands* for short, are part of the object-oriented GUI framework Morphic [16]. Hand objects obtain their event data from the corresponding input stream autonomously. By using this concept, additional input streams can be integrated; multiple hands, that is, mouse pointers and cursors, can be controlled by different input sources. Current operating systems, however, support only one system cursor and input events from different devices are merged into one input event stream. To bypass the operation system's behavior [28, 30], we developed special support for Squeak's virtual machine (VM). The design of our VM extensions allows attaching and detaching input devices during the application's run-time. Hand objects further abstract from concrete input sources and provide a defined interface to applications. Thus, it is transparent to the application, whether the hands are controlled from a local device or via a VNC connection.

Finally enabling applications to link users to actions, we extended the concept of *HandMorphs* and allow for impersonation. Our extensions to *HandMorphs* manages required user information and provide an interface to applications. Application objects have access to the currently active HandMorph and can ask this HandMorph for credentials of the currently acting users. If the HandMorph is not yet associated with an user, it opens a dialog asking the user to provide username and password. Based on that information, the HandMorph is then associated with the corresponding user.

4.2.3   Application Support for Multi-user Multi-account Interaction

Our extensions to the application platform, described above, enable applications to link users to actions. This in turn allows all users for acting on their on behalf. We describe how ProjectTalk makes use of this functionality here. The integration of SDG concepts further requires application developers to handle the upcoming additional issues regarding authorization. Additionally, content and functionality that is specific to certain users or roles must be offered in new ways as the users interacting with the shared display may have different privileges. Both kinds of user, user-specific content and authorization, have been addressed in the design of ProjectTalk, and is presented in this subsection.

ProjectTalk realizes multi-user multi-account single-display interaction by accessing the information of the user that triggered the current event processing and links this user to HTTP actions. It consists of a client and server component that synchronize on shared data using the HTTP protocol. A user interface action that involves modification of data in the client results in one or more HTTP request to the server. The application platform provides access to that particular *HandMorph* object that represent the input the channel of the user that initiated the current event processing. This *HandMorph* object is also called *ActiveHand*. The *ActiveHand* is accessed by the client HTTP-communication layer, retrieving the associated user and using corresponding credentials for the HTTP requests to the server. With that, ProjectTalk links HTTP request, which form the primary action of the client, to users enabling them to perform all actions on their own behalf.

Supporting our approach to multi-user multi-account single-display interaction, application developers have to consider additional authorization issues. A groupware that provide role-specific behavior is often designed in a way that users see only the functionality they have access to. In a project management software, for example, only administrative users are able to create new projects; users without these privileges cannot see this functionality. If multiple users interact with a single screen at the same time, the different users might have different privileges. It has to be respected that some amongst all co-present users sharing one display are not allowed to perform actions that are offered.

This mismatch can be handled in three different ways. One way is displaying the collective set of functionality all users have access to. Unfortunately, users would be limited and could not use all features they are allowed to. Another approach is presenting every feature available to at least one user. As a result, users can activate actions they are not allowed to perform. Applications have to handle denied access explicitly and be able to recover from this error. The last possibility is to (re-)design the application so that, for instance, users are provided with menus specific to their privileges.

The application design of ProjectTalk combines the second and the last option. For example, some users will not be allowed to modify user stories or move them between iterations. Still, all users have read access to these user interface components; users unprivileged to perform a modification will experience a failure and receive a corresponding message. The menu for opening projects exemplifies the last option. For each user accessing the menu, it provides specific content – only projects the user is a member of.

The handling of denied access gained special attention in ProjectTalk, so that this concern is not scattered over the entire application code. A typical user interface action results in one or more HTTP request to the server. If the acting user is not authorized to read or write specified resources, the server will return with an unauthorized error. An HTTP error is responded and converted into an application specific *NotAuthorized* exception. The exception is handled in the implementation of the model proxy objects. The proxy objects provide application specific interfaces that are implemented generically. The proxy objects store object properties and synchronize modifications with the server. If the server processes the request successfully, the modification will be applied to the corresponding description property of the user story's proxy object, and bound views will get notified about the change. Otherwise, the modifications are discarded, the stories will show the old description, and the user will receive an error message.

The implementation of both handling denied access and linking actions to users is integrated well in the design of ProjectTalk. Both concerns are well-separated from application specifics and the extensions can be integrated easily into other applications.

4.3 CodeTalk: Conversations About Code

This subsection describes CodeTalk, our approach to enable efficient informal communication about source code. CodeTalk, which was implemented in Squeak Smalltalk [11]. CodeTalk allows developers to mark and annotate single expressions, whole lines, or entire methods in the source code. It works similar to text processing applications and tools that are capable of adding comments to PDF files. The markup and annotations are shared along with the source code using regular source code management support.

4.3.1 The Need for Communicating About Code

Developers often talk about the source code of the system to be developed and extended. The source code itself is the most important artifact during the development process, in particular in agile development processes. Developers usually care much about it and prefer, for example, simple and elegant solutions over complex ones that are more difficult to understand and maintain [3]. The system naturally evolves and is extended; so, software developers spend much time reading code.

However, parts of the system may be difficult to comprehend raising the need to request support from the originators; an algorithm might be very complex or the intended run-time behavior might be difficult to infer [29]. Programs can also be written in different styles making them more or less easy to understand [18]. This leads to another kind of communication amongst developers having the source code itself as the topic. During code reading developers also often discover source code that needs to be revisited and improved; for example, variable or selector names can be too general and thus not very meaningful [18]. Developers might further have ideas to simplify the system's design [3, 8] or even detect potential failures in algorithms. While these issues are often discovered during regular coding activities, developers may not have enough time or background knowledge [22] to refactor the respective parts of the system or to validate their theory of a failure and fix it if necessary. Also, developers rather might to continue working on their primary task at hand [10]. So, an efficient mechanism is needed to make the discovered issues explicit and share their insight with peers.

4.3.2 Informal Communication via Markups

Current approaches to communicate about source code include *source code comments* and external communication tools and protocols such as email and instant messaging. However, both have limitations and do not provide adequate means to support informal spontaneous communication about source code. But this kind of communication is important; it helps to ensure a high code quality and helps developers to become better in their profession. This has been our motivation to design and develop a new approach to support this informal ad-hoc communication.

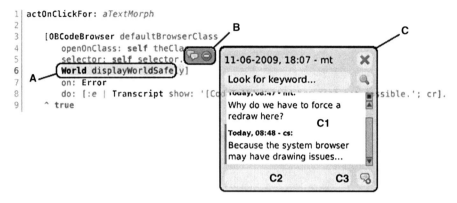

```
1 | actOnClickFor: aTextMorph
2 |
3 |     [OBCodeBrowser defaultBrowserClass
4 |         openOnClass: self theCla
5 |         selector: self selector.
6 |       World displayWorldSafe y]
7 | A    on: Error
8 |         do: [:e | Transcript show: '[C                                sible.'; cr].
9 |       ^ true
```

Fig. 7 *Right*: Code with markup (A), inline morphs (B) and the chat (C); *Left*: marked methods

Developers might, for example, discover a message send calling an expensive operation. Figure 7 shows an example method in a typical code browser in Squeak. The statement selected in the figure enforces a full redraw of the entire scene graph, which can be a quite time-consuming operation. Developers might be skeptic about the necessity and mark the selected code as critical using a context menu or a keyboard shortcut. This will highlight the statement with a red background color. To additionally describe their opinion and thoughts, developers add then a note in the dialog that will be displayed next to the marked section, as shown in Fig. 7.

This new annotation functionality CodeTalk was integrated into the standard development environment, in particular into the tools for browsing and editing the code. So, developers can informally annotate a piece code whenever necessary during their regular code activities. The region of interest in the source code can directly be marked and annotated with an explanation.

Annotations are an integral part of the source code and as thus they are exchanged along with the source code itself. When developers commit modifications applied to their working copy, they will also submit all annotations currently in the code base to the source code repository, as depicted in Fig. 8. The critical question about the statement that force a complete redraw is now part of the newly created source code revision.

When team members update their working later, they will retrieve the newly added annotation along with source code modifications. They will notice the question regarding the redraw statement, and the authors of that code might either remember a reason for forcing the redraw or they might not. In the latter case, they might consider removing the statement, test the application to validate the assumption, and commit the modification. As the annotations are connected to the source code they reference, the annotations would be removed together with the referenced statement in the described scenario.

If in the other case, enforcing the redraw is well-founded, developers can change the type of annotation, from critical to normal, and answer the previous question. Our extensions to the code browser enables developers to directly reply to questions or remarks in annotations so that a chat can evolve (Fig. 9).

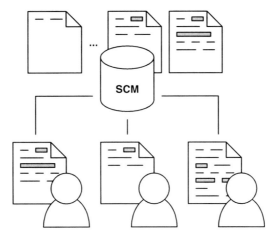

Fig. 8 CodeTalk's markups (*gray*) are shared through the SCM

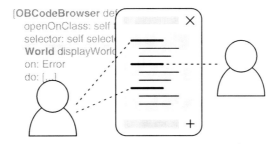

Fig. 9 A new conversation about code evolves

Talking about source code often involves other sources located outside the currently discussed context: Sometimes developers come across methods that seem to be very similar, but they do not have the time or knowledge to perform the necessary refactoring. CodeTalk allows developers to mark that issue and to reference the other method in their comment. For example, the chat in Fig. 10 replaces the occurrence of "`String >> #findTokens:`" automatically with a hyperlink that browses to the method "`findToken:`" in the class "`String`". The link below points to a method "split" that does not exist and is therefore drawn in red.

The primary concept of CodeTalk is to separate the discussions about the source code from the source code itself, while keeping the connection to each other. This separation allows for individual support for the different concerns; specially designed tools can ease the creation and exchange of annotations and can provide a better awareness of these issues. The direct connection between source code and annotations indicates that they belong together and, thus, encourages developers to keep both in sync. This may prevent the problem, that occurs when the code gets updated with accidentally ignoring the corresponding comment.

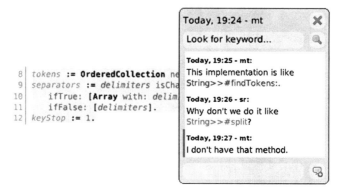

```
 8  tokens := OrderedCollection ne
 9  separators := delimiters isCha
10     ifTrue: [Array with: delim
11     ifFalse: [delimiters].
12  keyStop := 1.
```

Today, 19:24 - mt   ✕

Look for keyword...   🔍

Today, 19:25 - mt:
This implementation is like
String>>#findTokens:.

Today, 19:26 - sr:
Why don't we do it like
String>>#split?

Today, 19:27 - mt:
I don't have that method.

Fig. 10 Method links enable convenient source code navigation

		Team 1	Team 2	Team 3	Team 4
	Number of Methods	745	605	700	828
	Number of Revisions	178	174	246	335
Number of Markups	**All Over Time**	103	25	82	43
	Maximum	5	9	22	17
	At Project End	0	1	2	3
	Average Lifetime	33	18	27	63

Fig. 11 Summary of markup usage from selected teams

4.3.3 Case Study

CodeTalk has been used by several development during a case studies that was carried with 80 students in our *Software Engineering I* lecture. Students formed 16 different teams, ~5 each, that were asked to develop applications in Squeak. The teams used an agile software development process such as *Extreme Programming* [2]. The project's time frame was about 3 months. After the end of the projects, we analyzed the source code of all revisions of all groups for markups. As shown in Fig. 11, the analyzed projects are of similar size consisting of about 600–800 methods. While one team created 20 annotations, other teams created up to 100 annotations.

Figures 12 and 13 indicate a continuous use of CodeTalk during the course of the project. At the end of the projects development teams cleaned up all markups, hopefully handling the described issues before. Note that the source was inspected by teachers at the end of the project. The average lifetime of annotations was 20–60 revisions, approximately a fifth of all revisions created during the project time.

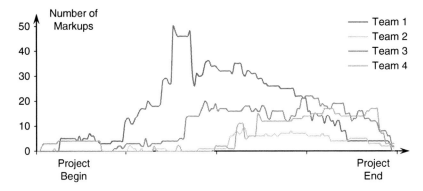

Fig. 12 Absolute number of markups in the source code over whole project development time

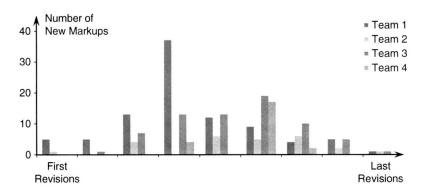

Fig. 13 Number of new markups in several development parts

Annotations created during the projects include the following examples:

- "That is somehow totally crap. The instance variable *separatorMap* seemed to be good for defining the place of these separating things for each category ..." (from German: "Das ist irgendwie total Mist. Die Instanzvariable *separatorMap* dacht ich wär gut, um fär jede Rubrik festzulegen, wie die Trenndinger stehen müssen ...")
- "Looks paradoxical! ..." (from German: "Irgendwie paradox! ...")
- "Where should the layout code be included, this seems not to be a good place?" (from German: "Wo soll das Layout stehen? Hier ist vielleicht nicht der beste Platz.")
- "onClick + callback =>nonsense"
- "Yes, there is a better way to do this :-)"

Developers started to use CodeTalk occasionally in the beginning of the projects and used it more often later on (Fig. 13). It seems that the need for conversations increases with the size of the code base. We further think that developers regard annotations as part of the source code and understand critical annotations as an indicator for insufficient code quality. All remaining annotations were addressed to the end of a project, to make it ready for release. The example annotations listed above show that developers like to use a colloquial style for communicating about source code related issues. While we have no evidence whether the teams would have discussed a similar amount of issues without CodeTalk or not, we think CodeTalk actually encourages this kind of conversations, which is important to bring all flaws to light.

Gathering additional personal opinions, we also conducted interviews with two teams. The teams reported that markups were used to write down tasks. This included planned refactorings of bad source code and new features that needed to be implemented. Additionally, the *critical* markup was occasionally used to point out bad coding style. Markups were also used for personal notes, especially as ToDo-items. Those teams that made heavy use of CodeTalk actually had a strong need for asynchronous communication, as many team members contributed from many different location and at different times for several reasons. The students argued that they used CodeTalk mainly due to convenience; it allows for staying in the current environment and context instead of switching tools.

5 Summary and Outlook

In this report, we present the objectives and first results of our project *Agile Development in Virtual Collaborative Environments*. We first describe and argue for our twofold research approach, investigating both design and agile software development processes and accompanying tools to support geographically dispersed teams in applying these processes. We then present commonalities between Design Thinking and agile development methodologies with respect to their underlying principles. Two different approaches to integrate design activities in agile development processes are discussed. Thereupon we describe efforts and findings regarding the technological support for distributed development teams; the application *ProjectTalk* and the development environment extension *CodeTalk* are presented. ProjectTalk has been designed and developed for collaboratively managing user stories and planning activities; it particularly supports co-present team members by allowing them to act on their own behalf when simultaneously interacting with shared tools. CodeTalk realizes an informal yet efficient approach to communicate about source code collaboratively and over time.

With our first insights being very encouraging as they support our original hypothesis that agile software development will benefit from elements of Design Thinking, our next involve introducing other elements and values of Design Thinking and balancing them with respect to the elements and values of the original agile software development practices are still very challenging. Therefore, we will reflect on our experiences, revisit our design decisions, redefine our theory and then apply it in subsequent projects in several iterations. Design Thinking and agile development seem to have much in common, also because both rely on skilled, motivated, and professional individuals and teams working creatively together. We will elaborate models of both methodologies to improve our understanding of both their similarities and their differences.

We plan to use and improve our extended software development process to design and implement new ways of communication support that enable distributed teams to collaboratively immerse in their tasks and that encourages efficient and effective information exchange regardless of the team members' geographical location. We will both improve and extend the tools we have developed so far aiming for a solution that allows a seamless transition between asynchronous and synchronous collaboration styles and which provides support for user-specific views at different levels of detail. We will focus on communication that is essential for keeping distributed teams in sync and for allowing a high degree of transparency on their core development activities.

References

1. Agile Alliance. Manifesto for Agile Software Development. http://agilemanifesto.org/, 2001
2. K. Beck. *Extreme Programming Explained: Embrace Change. ISBN 0201616416*. Addison-Wesley, MA, 1999
3. K. Beck and C. Andres. *Extreme Programming Explained: Embrace Change*, 2nd edition. Addison-Wesley Longman, CA, 2004
4. R. Buchanan. Wicked Problems in Design Thinking. *Design Issues*, 8(2):5–21, 1992
5. P. DeGrace and L. Hulet Stahl. *Wicked Problems, Righteous Solutions*. Yourdon Press, NJ, 1990
6. C.L. Dym, A.M. Agogino, O. Eris, D.D. Frey, and L.J. Leifer. Engineering Design Thinking, Teaching, and Learning. *IEEE Engineering Management Review*, 34(1):65–92, 2006
7. J. Ferreira, J. Noble, and R. Biddle. Agile Development Iterations and UI Design. In *AGILE '07: Proceedings of the AGILE 2007*, pages 50–58. IEEE Computer Society, Washington, DC, USA, 2007
8. M. Fowler and K. Beck. *Refactoring: Improving the Design of Existing Code*. Addison-Wesley Professional, MA, 1999
9. D. Fox, J. Sillito, and F. Maurer. Agile Methods and User-Centered Design: How These Two Methodologies are Being Successfully Integrated in Industry. In *AGILE '08: Proceedings of the Agile 2008*, pages 63–72. IEEE Computer Society, Washington, DC, USA, 2008
10. E. Horvitz, C. Kadie, T. Paek, and D. Hovel. Models of Attention in Computing and Communication: From Principles to Applications. *Communications of the ACM*, 46(3):52–59, 2003
11. D. Ingalls, T. Kaehler, J. Maloney, S. Wallace, and A. Kay. Back to the Future: The Story of Squeak, a Practical Smalltalk Written in Itself. In *OOPSLA '97: Proceedings of the 12th ACM SIGPLAN conference on Object-oriented programming, systems, languages, and applications*, pages 318–326. ACM, NY, USA, 1997
12. T. Kelley and J. Littman. *The Art of Innovation*. HarperCollinsBusiness, NY, 2001
13. S. Ken. *Agile Program Management with Scrum*. Microsoft Press, WA, 2004
14. C. Larman and V.R. Basili. Iterative and Incremental Development: A Brief History. *Computer*, 36(6):47–56, 2003
15. J. Löwgren and E. Stolterman. *Thoughtful Interaction Design*. MIT, MA, 2004
16. J.H. Maloney and R.B. Smith. Directness and Liveness in the Morphic User Interface Construction Environment. In *UIST '95: Proceedings of the 8th annual ACM symposium on User interface and software technology*, pages 21–28. ACM, NY, USA, 1995

17. G. Meszaros and J. Aston. Adding Usability Testing to an Agile Project. In *AGILE '06: Proceedings of the conference on AGILE 2006*, pages 289–294. IEEE Computer Society, Washington, DC, USA, 2006

18. P.W. Oman and C.R. Cook. Typographic Style is More Than Cosmetic. *Communications of the ACM*, 33(5):506–520, 1990

19. J. Patton. Hitting the Target: Adding Interaction Design to Agile Software Development. In *OOPSLA '02: OOPSLA 2002 Practitioners Reports*, pages 1–ff. ACM, NY, USA, 2002

20. K. Pohl. *Requirements Engineering: Grundlagen, Prinzipien, Techniken*. dpunkt, Heidelberg, 2007

21. H.W.J. Rittel and M.M. Webber. Dilemmas in a General Theory of Planning. *Policy sciences*, 4(2):155–169, 1973

22. T.M. Shaft and I. Vessey. The Relevance of Application Domain Knowledge: Characterizing the Computer Program Comprehension Process. *Journal of Management Information Systems*, 15(1):78, 1998

23. I. Sommerville. *Software Engineering*, 5th edition. Addison Wesley Longman, CA, 1995

24. B. Steinert, M. Grünewald, St. Richter, J. Lincke, and R. Hirschfeld. Multi-user Multi-account Interaction in Groupware Supporting Single-Display Collaboration. In *Proceedings of the 5th International Conference on Collaborative Computing: Networking, Applications and Worksharing (CollaborateCom 2009)*. IEEE Computer Society, Washington, DC, USA, 2009

25. B. Steinert, M. Taeumel, J. Lincke, T. Pape, and R. Hirschfeld. CodeTalk – Conversations About Code. In *Proceedings of the 8th International Conference on Creating, Connecting and Collaborating through Computing (C5 2010)*. IEEE, La Jolla CA, USA, January 2010

26. J. Stewart, B.B. Bederson, and A. Druin. Single Display Groupware: A Model for Co-present Collaboration. In *CHI '99: Proceedings of the SIGCHI conference on Human factors in computing systems*, pages 286–293. ACM, NY, USA, 1999

27. D. Sy. Adapting Usability Investigations for Agile User-centered Design. *Journal of usability Studies*, 2(3):112–132, 2007

28. E. Tse and S. Greenberg. Rapidly Prototyping Single Display Groupware Through the SDG-Toolkit. In *AUIC '04: Proceedings of the 5th conference on Australasian user interface*, pages 101–110. Australian Computer Society, Darlinghurst, Australia, 2004

29. A. Von Mayrhauser and A.M. Vans. Program Comprehension During Software Maintenance and Evolution. *Computer*, 28(8):44–55, 1995

30. G. Wallace, P. Bi, K. Li, and O. Anshus. A Multi-cursor X Window Manager Supporting Control Room Collaboration. Technical report, Princeton University, Computer Science, Technical Report TR-707-04, 2004

Towards Next Generation Design Thinking: Scenario-Based Prototyping for Designing Complex Software Systems with Multiple Users

Gregor Gabrysiak, Holger Giese*, and Andreas Seibel

Abstract Design thinking is at its best if tangible prototypes can be used to capture and validate end user needs and envision new products and services. However, today such tangible prototypes are not feasible in a cost-effective manner for complex software systems with multiple users and their complex behavior. To overcome this problem, we developed a scenario-based prototyping approach for complex multi-user software systems that uses executable software engineering models including structural as well as behavioral aspects. Simulation turns these models into tangible virtual prototypes for end users that visualize the complex behavior and capture feedback interactively. In this chapter, we elaborate our concept for cost-effective scenario-based prototyping, report on a first prototypical implementation of the approach for the validation of multi-user processes with end users, and discuss our initial findings and learnings that we gained from first experiments with the implementation.

1 Introduction

Design thinking projects typically aim at single user systems, such as a physical product or a piece of software, in which case often the graphical user interface and its interaction with the end user is in the center of attention [33].

Design thinking can be characterized by the intertwined set of activities shown in Fig. 1. The careful collection of information about the problem in the activities *Understand*, *Observe*, *Point of View* provides the basis for envisioning and evaluating possible solutions in the *Ideate*, *Prototype* and *Test* activities. The design thinking process is a highly interactive and incremental process, driven by people with

G. Gabrysiak (✉), H. Giese, and A. Seibel
System Analysis and Modeling Group, Hasso-Plattner-Institute for IT Systems Engineering
at the University of Potsdam, Prof.-Dr.-Helmert-Str. 2–3, 14482 Potsdam, Germany
e-mail: Gregor.Gabrysiak@hpi.uni-potsdam.de; Holger.Giese@hpi.uni-potsdam.de;
Andreas.Seibel@hpi.uni-potsdam.de

* Principal Investigator

H. Plattner et al. (eds.), *Design Thinking: Understand – Improve – Apply*,
Understanding Innovation, DOI 10.1007/978-3-642-13757-0_13,
© Springer-Verlag Berlin Heidelberg 2011

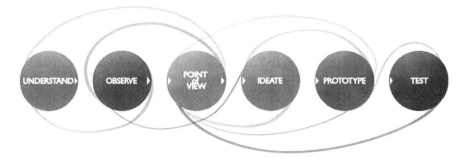

Fig. 1 The design thinking process is highly iterative [22, p. 114]

different backgrounds and experiences. This heterogeneity is important to capture as many viewpoints as possible during design, not only the ones of technical experts and engineers. Through these diverse backgrounds, prototypes are essential in establishing a common understanding between these different persons.

In computer science, models play a key role in designing complex systems. A model is an artifact that abstracts all aspects of the final system that are considered irrelevant to allow observations of the relevant aspects only [30]. But modeling is not restricted to computer science.

If the aim of the design process is a physical product, prototypes can be made of paper, wood or some other physical material that is easy to work with. A wooden prototype of a cup holder, for example, serves as a model, since end users can use the wooden cup holder to observe behavior that is similar if not the same with the final product. Prototypes allow studying the aspects of the physical product that the design process is interested in. End users can grab the prototype, experience and judge it to propose ways to improve it. This works well, because the prototypes are tangible. They are quite similar to the final product in the sense that they expose similar behavior and allow observations that are relevant to improve the design.

When designing a graphical user interface (GUI) of a software system, the situation is somewhat different. The reason is that the final product is not as tangible as a physical product. We can argue that the GUI is still the most tangible aspect of a software system, and that might be a reason why it is often in the center of design thinking processes related to software. However, a GUI is a rather individual, end user specific view onto a software system. For multi-user software systems, GUI prototypes are not suitable for expressing the *big picture* or the insights and needs leading to the prototype's design.

To make the user interface tangible and invite feedback from users already early during the process, paper prototypes are developed, so called low fidelity prototypes. These paper prototypes allow design thinkers to discuss with end users about the behavior of the final system. Once the user is satisfied with the low fidelity prototype, a high fidelity prototype is developed, e.g., using Flash[1] technology.

---

[1] www.adobe.com/flashplatform/ (Accessed 2 Nov. 2009).

This prototype is a mock-up of the final product. Thus, it enables the discussion of more detailed UI issues. However, the same is today not possible for complex multi-user software systems and their behavior which is not only dependent on how individual end users interacts with their respective GUI, but mainly on how they interact with each other. Finally, the design is completed, and engineering takes over.

With respect to modeling, a paper prototype of a graphical user interface serves as a model. The same is true for high fidelity Flash prototypes, which allow for even more detailed observations. In many engineering disciplines, simulation and prototypes are employed on a regular basis to better understand the problem at hand and identify innovative solutions. It has also been advocated that for complex problems and organizations simulation and prototyping can help to recognize design conflicts early, can invite people to play innovative *what if* games, and that the feedback from simulations of prototypes can in particular stimulate innovations [26].

For software, the pioneer Fred Brooks [6] also stated long ago that "the hardest single part of building a software system is deciding what to build" and that often prototypes can be more articulate than people concerning the what. However, the wicked nature of complex software, respectively, the *requirements* have prevented us from realizing the full potential of prototyping and simulation for complex software, especially when dealing with multiple users. When multi-user systems are in the center of attention, many usage scenarios can be obtained during the design thinking process. These scenarios can be regarded as process instances – they need to be related to each other and analyzed. For instance, it is crucial to find inconsistencies between the scenarios [15, 16] or to validate them by stepping through the respective processes. Scenario and process modeling as well as simulation techniques are important concepts to study the relationships between usage scenarios. Additionally, scenarios are also a suitable representation for "prototyping things you can't pick up" [7, pp. 92–95]. Information about artifacts involved in the process can be extracted from these scenarios as well. This allows to, e.g., relate state modifications of artifacts to activities within the process, assign relevant documents to stages within a process, and even to deduct responsibilities between artifacts and end users.

Another key problem for designing complex multi-user systems is *traceability*. The information collected by the different team members is usually not well captured and linked with the envisioned solutions in form of prototypes. Therefore, the evaluation of ideas is often restricted to the prototype alone and cannot be navigated back to the original source of the design decisions such as interviews or background information. An evolutionary prototyping approach [3] might help to avoid such information loss by documenting the feedback and the resulting modification of the used prototype for each step along the way. Losing this information is a limitation for an effective test of prototypes within the team or with end users.

The consequences of losing information are even more dramatic when it comes to engineering the product envisioned by the design thinking team. When engineering takes over, the decisions that have led to the design are not readily available. The design process and the engineering process are somewhat de-coupled through such handovers. This exposes a severe problem, since engineers might make engineering decisions that are not in line with design decisions. This is due to the fact that they are not aware of the rational behind design decisions. Therefore, design and engineering must be better linked. This means that design artifacts that document the design process and its decisions need to be available during engineering. They must not only be available, but they must be related to the very aspects of the design that they are responsible for.

In the following pages, we first outline our project setup in Sect. 2. Afterwards, Sect. 3 discusses current research results. This includes a description of the needs we found, our concept of how to support design thinkers, and the prototypical implementation of the concept. Our learnings are then presented in Sect. 3.5 and discussed in Sect. 3.6. Other approaches, which can be found in the domain of Requirements Engineering, are presented in Sect. 4. Finally, Sect. 5 summarizes the first year and gives an outlook on the next project year.

2 Project Setup

This section is separated into two parts. It starts by presenting our research method, which is closely aligned to the design thinking process. Afterwards, our initial research question and hypotheses are discussed in Sect. 2.2. Then, this section concludes with an outlook on the expected impact of our research.

2.1 Research Method

Our research method is based on the design thinking process as shown in Fig. 1 and guided by our research hypotheses presented in Sect. 2.2. We start by gathering insights about the problem domain, trying to *understand* how practitioners of the design thinking process use it for multi-user software systems and how virtual prototypes can improve this process. Afterwards, we *observe* and interview practitioners from our project partner D-LABS GmbH to gain needs. The following synthesis leads to a *Point of View*, which we can base our *ideation* on. Then, we *prototype* our concept to evaluate our hypotheses applying *tests*, i.e., experiments. The prototype will then be modified according to the insights we gather during these test sessions in multiple iterations.

2.2 Initial Research Hypotheses

The general question that guides our research is "How can we support design thinkers working on solutions for complex multi-user software systems?" As mentioned before, scenarios are a suitable means to capture and communicate how multiple users work together. Also, prototyping is a powerful tool in the design thinkers' toolbox, which enables the realization of divergent ideas, presenting them, and to experience them. These ideas embodied in prototypes can also be judged, enabling design thinkers to converge again. By combining these two concepts, we formulated Hypothesis 1.

Hypothesis 1 *By introducing the idea of prototyping scenarios to create a common understanding and validate the scenario as well as the underlying assumptions, it is possible to get more reliable, i.e., commonly agreed upon results.*

During the validation of requirements and insights, end user feedback is invaluable. However, confronting them with models in notations they have never seen before is futile. So, in order to improve the validation of insights, the quality of the feedback gathered during validation sessions needs to be increased. Consequently, we formulated Hypothesis 2.

Hypothesis 2 *By being able to present a scenario-based prototype, it is possible to gather quality feedback, which end users would not provide using common validation techniques.*

Also, validation sessions are quite time consuming and expensive to conduct. In order to help with this problem, we want to evaluate Hypothesis 3.

Hypothesis 3 *We can derive tangible prototypes from software engineering models for complex multi-user software systems that are suitable for end users and all design thinkers in a cost-effective manner.*

2.3 Expected Impact

By finding a suitable answer to our research question and our hypotheses, one of the most powerful tools from the design thinkers' toolbox can be made available for developing complex multi-user software systems as well. While it is currently not feasible to thoroughly validate insights in a cost-effective manner, we hope to integrate an incremental, cost-effective prototyping approach in order to produce more reliable and better results not only during the validation and synthesis of insights, but throughout the whole life span of a design thinking project.

3 Research Results

This section presents the results of our research during the last year. Firstly, insights about our industry partner D-LABS are presented in Sect. 3.1. Then, the *needs* that we identified will be described in Sect. 3.2. Based on these needs, our *concept* of how to support design thinkers working with complex multi-user processes will be discussed in Sect. 3.3. A prototype of this concept is presented in

Sect. 3.4. As mentioned in Sect. 3.5.1, this prototype was already used in qualitative validation experiments. The resulting learnings of these experiments are presented in Sect. 3.5.2 and discussed in Sect. 3.6.

3.1 Understand and Observe

Our project partner D-LABS[2] is a start-up company located in Potsdam (Germany). They provide expertise in design thinking for complex multi-user software products to customers as a service. Their projects are run based on a catalogue of design methods. The portfolio they offer includes trainings in these methods, however their main focus and expertise lies in running software design projects. D-LABS covers the requirements engineering stage of a project. To do so, they start by *understanding* the problem domain through a 360° View. Afterwards, they start end user research through *observations* and *interviews* as shown in Figs. 2 and 3.

The succeeding synthesis phase during which the *Point of View* (PoV) is created, iterated and refined is the most important one, since the ideation of solution concepts relies on the correctness of these agreed-upon findings. Based on the ideation, the prototyping stages usually start with paper prototypes, which are iterated till a prototype of the graphical user interface is created. In order to maximize the re-use capabilities of their results, apart from a detailed documentation of how they got there, D-LABS also provides re-usable software engineering artifacts using e.g., Flash or the .Net Framework.[3]

The Point of View is quite important for a design thinking project. It contains the most important needs and insights that have been gathered from end users about object of study. However, in multi-user processes, there are different end users or

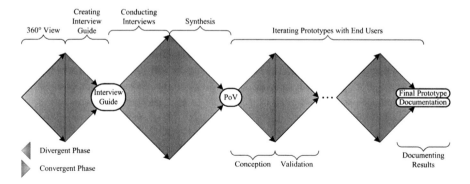

Fig. 2 The D-LABS process separated into its divergent and convergent phases

---

[2] Web Site of D-LABS GmbH: www.d-labs.com/english/ (Accessed 2 Nov. 2009).

[3] http://msdn.microsoft.com/netframework/ (Accessed 2 Nov. 2009).

Fig. 3 Not only the design thinkers need to understand the gathered insights, but also the end users

participants who have diverse, potentially opposed needs. In order to help design thinkers in this context, they need support to capture and validate and manage all of these needs and different *roles* to later on decide which ones to emphasize.

Usually, there are only few validation sessions due to the high costs of traveling to the end users and validating insights or prototypes with them. This stresses the importance of the interviews and the validity of the insights gained from them. While it is always possible to talk to certain end users to correct minor mistakes, e.g., different names were used for the same process artifacts, it is rarely feasible to gather all end users in order to establish a common understanding of the process.

3.2 Point of View

While all tools and methods of design thinking can be used for complex multi-user software systems, some of them do not scale well for such a scenario. Therefore, they have to be adapted to fit the needs of this domain.

For multi-user processes, this implies the necessity to validate insights and assumptions as cost-effectively as possible. Traditional validation techniques are too expensive to be used in multiple iterations, since these mostly rely on bringing multiple end users together to present them the current state in order to gather feedback on this state as depicted in Fig. 4. Validation sessions also need to provide tangible artifacts of some kind in order to ease the end users' understanding. Otherwise, the end users are decoupled from the assumptions gathered from them or the ideas that are generated based on these assumptions. The possibility of conducting validation sessions remotely helps to circumvent potential travel costs. An incremental approach,

Fig. 4 To validate insights and requirements, feedback can be gathered by presenting and translating the current state for end users

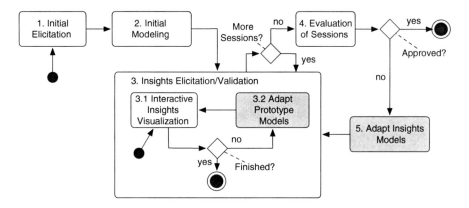

Fig. 5 Iterative insights elicitation/validation process

which provides means for validation sessions through multi-user sessions as well as single-user sessions might also help to emphasize the validation of certain subsets of insights.

3.3 Ideation

Based on the insights we gained from our research question and the resulting hypotheses, we came up with a concept for scenario-based prototyping for designing complex software systems with multiple users. This concept is shown in Fig. 5.

In the beginning, as with all software projects, initial insights have to be elicited (1). These initial assumptions can then be captured using formal requirements models (2). Formal models offer helpful capabilities such as being able to pinpoint inconsistencies automatically or to propagate modifications consistently.

These models enable an interactive simulation of the captured insights with a domain specific animation on top, which behaves like a real prototype, allowing the end users to experience how they were understood (3). Thus, the end users interact with the *prototype models*, which are semi-automatically derived from the current state of the insights gathered by the design thinkers.

During such a simulation session, all end user interactions with the prototype simulation are recorded (3.1) and incorporated into the prototype models (3.2). After multiple sessions, a software engineer needs to evaluate the recorded interactions (4) to judge the end users' approval of the prototype models' current state. This also represents a measurement of how well the end users share a common understanding of the insights gathered by the design thinkers. If the approval is still not satisfactory, the insight models can also be adapted (5) more or less automatically.

Further details of our concept are discussed in the respective subsections of Sect. 3.3 by means of examples.

3.4 Prototype

In this section, we explain the current state of the implementation of our concept based on the process in Fig. 5. The prototype was first presented in [10]. It has been build on top of the Eclipse environment and a model-driven development platform developed in our group. Therefore, in relation to this effort a concept to efficiently maintain traceability in a model-driven engineering domain have been developed [27]. Other extensions of the employed platform provide more flexible means for developing simulators based on EMF[4] models [4, 18, 19], simulators for interactions in distributed service oriented systems[5] and some efforts for migrating some required features to the Eclipse platform [4].

3.4.1 Initial Elicitation

Traditionally, insights are initially elicited using interviews, which appear to be the most effective technique for a wide range of domains and situations [8]. This is also the best practice used by our industrial partner, D-LABS (cf. Sect. 3.1). For the prototype, however, the initial elicitation is out of focus. It is assumed, that initial interviews were conducted and that the results are already available.

---

[4] Eclipse Modeling Framework, www.eclipse.org/modeling/emf/(Accessed 2 Nov. 2009).

[5] Gregor Gabrysiak's master's thesis, *Modeling and Simulation of Reusable Collaborations for Embedded Systems with Dynamic Structures*, 2009.

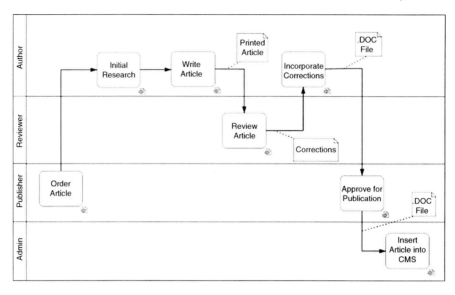

Fig. 6 An initially synthesized process based on insights from interviews

3.4.2 Modeling the Insights

Based on these interviews, design thinkers have to identify activities, a preliminary causal order of activities, abstract roles these activities are assigned to, and scenarios with interactions. These findings are synthesized into requirements models, which in our domain are role-based business processes. Figure 6 shows an example of such a model, which is an initially synthesized process of *ordering an article* initiated by a role named *Publisher*. Currently, the used insight models are based on a subset of BPMN[6] elements, enriched with additional semantics.

Roles are an important concept in our approach because they are an abstraction layer between individual end users and views on the prototype. Each role can be related to a different view that reflects the aspects that are important to the respective end users, e.g., views may differ in their level-of-detail or whether information is hidden, visible, or even highlighted.

3.4.3 Insights Elicitation/Validation

It is important to validate insights incrementally since the elicitation is a highly subjective, creative, and dynamic process. This implies that insights, which are initially elicited, may be incomplete, inconsistent, or even incorrect [23]. To overcome this issue, our approach allows multiple end users, or an individual one, to reflect on existing insights. Furthermore, the approach supports finding new insights

---

[6] Business Process Modeling Notation, www.omg.org/spec/BPMN/(Accessed 2 Nov. 2009).

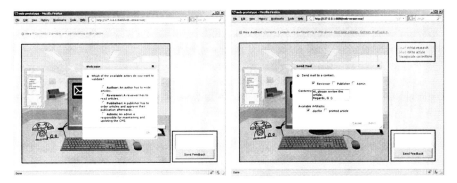

Fig. 7 Two screenshots of the employee visualization - Connecting to a Session (*left*); Playing a Session (*right*)

by conducting a simulation session based on prototype models, which have been automatically derived from the given models capturing the insights. In general, there is a conceptual overlap between these models. Nevertheless, prototype models have additional execution semantics. The derivation of prototype models is configurable. The configuration depends on the view of the role, the role itself and the level-of-detail that should be shown to the end user playing a role. The level-of-detail depends on the intention in terms of which domain specific aspects should be validated, e.g., whether activities in the prototype models are in causal sequential order or not ordered at all. The latter approach enables a less restrictive simulation and thus could help the elicitation of alternatives within the process.

For example in case of an employee view, only the context of the employee is visualized by using a generic workplace visualization (Fig. 7). In this view, end users can interact with other roles or software systems by triggering domain specific primitive actions [20], e.g., phone-calls, visits, or e-mails. The simulation uses the role as a parameter to control which interactions are shown to or highlighted for the end user. Instead of creating a customized GUI for each project like in [21], the domain specific views can be re-used for different derived prototype models.

Since conducting these validation sessions cost-effective is also an important aspect, providing them remotely by visualizing them in a web browser saves travel costs and simplifies sessions for multiple users.

Figure 7 shows two screenshots of the interactive visualization. (Left) shows the initial screen where one of the four available participating roles of the process can be chosen. (Right) shows a screen during a simulation session of an end user playing the *Author* role. In this figure, the *Author* prepares an e-mail for the *Reviewer* including a document, which has to be reviewed.

Currently, our tool supports only one view during the simulation. While this view is appropriate for end users who directly participate in the business process that is elicited, other views have to be integrated to include other groups of stakeholders as well (cf. [1]), e.g., the potential maintainers of such a complex multi-user software system.

When an end user triggers one of these domain specific primitive actions, it may lead to new activities and interactions, which have to be considered as new insights that were not elicited before. Roles that are not played by a stakeholder during a simulation session are automatically simulated. Simulated roles do not only react on interactions, but also initiate interactions with other roles and therefore other stakeholders.Initially, simulated roles do only interact with generic patterns coming from the prototype models, i.e., a stakeholder who plays the *Reviewer* role receives an e-mail from the simulated *Author* role with the content: "`review article.`" However, the authenticity of a simulation session increases over time. For example, as soon as an end user plays the role *Author*, the exact wording of this e-mail is saved and might be re-used in further simulation sessions (see Fig. 7b). Thus, interacting with simulated roles feels as if the interaction takes place with another player. This feature *plays-in*to the prototype models and, furthermore, can be more or less automatically incorporated into the insight models (3.2 in Fig. 5).

3.4.4 Evaluation of Sessions

Based on recorded interactions, which emerged during simulation sessions, a domain expert can evaluate the session and the findings gathered. Each action during each simulation is recorded and mapped back directly onto elements of the underlying insight models. The interactions of stakeholders that are recorded during simulation sessions can be analyzed quantitatively and qualitatively.

Quantitatively, it can be examined, e.g., how many stakeholders actually used a specific communication primitive to finish a specific activity (cf. Fig. 8). More importantly, it is possible to verify the identified process by observing the path that stakeholders agreed upon throughout the simulation sessions. Based on these results, changes to the insight models can be approved or discarded. Qualitatively, it is possible to see which recorded interactions diverged from the identified path through the considered process, thereby revealing conflicts or alternatives within the process, which might have been ignored otherwise.

3.5 Tests and Learnings

To evaluate our hypotheses, we need to establish an experiment design, which can prove or falsify our assumptions. An initial experiment design is presented in Sect. 3.5.1. Our findings and learnings are then discussed in Sect. 3.5.2.

3.5.1 Experiment Design

During the last months of the first project year, we conducted a pilot study on the feasibility of our approach, comparing our results to validation sessions merely based on a BPMN model representation and a method expert explaining it to an end user.

Analysis Protocol

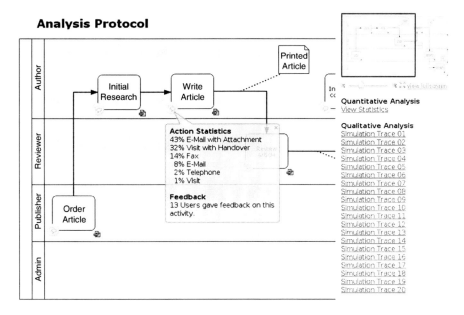

Fig. 8 Quantitative visualization of multiple simulation sessions of the role *Author*

Within this pilot study, we elicited two (partially complex) multi-user processes from three university assistants and validated these processes 8 weeks later. This delay was chosen to ensure that our validation results were based mainly on the everyday experiences of participating in these processes instead of memories from the interview during the elicitation session. The experiment design will be the foundation for follow-up experiments during the second year of the project.

3.5.2 Experiment Results

During our evaluation sessions, we made different observations that led to many insights. First of all, apart from usability issues of our prototype, our approach is feasible. Feasible in a way that allows us to generate interactive simulations for end users, enabling them to experience how they were understood. The process that is replayed for and with different end users allows them to experience the content of a model that would require a bi-directional translation by a modeling expert otherwise. Bi-directionally is mandatory, to ensure that gathered feedback can be used to modify the model.

During the validation sessions, we enforced the active enactment of tasks within the interactive visualization, which is much less abstract than talking about how to do these tasks. The explanatory sessions produced feedback with additional comments on already captured activities, while the usage of the prototype led the assistants to enact refined tasks and comment on priory unknown decisions within the already captured tasks. This is an indication of the barrier(s) that modeling notations pose, even when explained. The graphical distance between two notation elements within a model is relatively small and usually does not represent the mismatch of semantic information or abstraction levels that they might convey.

Additionally, the explanatory sessions had no means of *synchronization* between the presented model and the flow of comments that were gathered. The assistants started uniformly by pointing on the initial activity in the model and moving their finger along as they commented on the process. However, two of them stopped at certain activities, looked up to the ceiling and proceeded further through the process without moving their finger accordingly. This is a strong indication for a missing synchronization between what they told us and the current state of the process that they were walking through mentally. When using the interactive simulation, the end users are always in a well-defined state of execution of the process. Hence, their direct input can always be mapped to these states.

However, we also noticed that end users were not willing to comment within the tool, but rather prefer to talk directly to other persons in the same room. Therefore, we have to adjust the experiment to include remote telephone sessions to test how we can either promote the usage of textual input into the prototype as well or to capture and automatically synchronize an audio stream to the output of our interactive simulator.

Not surprisingly, the willingness to use our simulator was not consistent throughout each session. Depending on whether or not all tasks can be achieved within the interactive visualization, the motivation declined or stayed the same. For instance, the tool had no means of signing documents, since this capability was not deemed necessary for the assistants according to the elicited processes. However, one of them demanded this capability, which led to a decreased, perceived usefulness of our tool.[7]

3.6   Discussion of Results

First of all, we have to deal with a fidelity problem ourselves. Although our focus lies on providing a prototype to experience a multi user process prototype, the usability of our prototype must suffice for end users playing through a simulation to have all the degrees of freedom they need. Thus, confronting them with an unstable or incomplete version of the prototype leads to two problems: they cannot "see" the underlying process to validate it and they rather comment on the implementation than on the model. Thus, all experiments were rather explorative in nature and yield no empirically significant results. Still, the feedback during these sessions indicate, that we are on the right track. Or, as an experimentee said during our second iteration in June 2009: "one might perform the [necessary actions] using a better version of this [tool]."

---

[7] By now, this capability is realized using drawing canvas as overlays in our tool.

Apart from this, we were able to generate tangible prototypes semi-automatically based on formal models (Hypothesis 3). While we have feedback indicating some success towards our other hypotheses (1 and 2), we still need to empirically evaluate them.

4 Related Work

In [2], the authors argue that *prototyping* should be used already during requirements elicitation to enable users to provide feedback to something *tangible*. There are several approaches that use *tangible artifacts* to improve the communication and to create a common understanding, e.g., CRC cards [5] or even recent approaches such as Tangible Business Process Modeling [9], which was developed within our Design Thinking Research Project. While these approaches are valuable and important, they all share one major drawback. All participants need to be in one location at the same time. Achieving this can be expensive or even infeasible in case of distributed teams.

In terms of software system prototypes, [3] identifies three different kinds of prototypes. While *Explorative Prototypes* are commonly used at the beginning of a project to test people's reactions on new concepts, *Experimental Prototypes* are produced to evaluate whether a concept fulfills the end users' expectations. On the other hand, *Evolutionary Prototypes* combine both approaches. Through multiple iterations, the prototype matures till the final prototype can be considered as the final result. Design thinkers mainly use either explorative or experimental prototypes. However, our approach uses evolutionary prototype models that are modified incrementally. Generally, prototypes are quite suitable for creating something tangible for stakeholders. Their feasibility, on the other hand, depends on the costs of their creation.

Approaches related to our simulation of assumptions that need to be validated can be found in the Requirements Engineering domain. In [28], the authors argue that *formal models* should be employed to be able to detect inconsistencies, conflicts or missing requirements more easily through formal verification. By using formal requirements models, it is also possible to execute, simulate, and thus validate them directly. In [25], ten commercial tools for simulating requirements were evaluated and compared. Due to their formal notations, all of these approaches are aimed at requirements engineers instead of the stakeholders. Thus, while inconsistencies can be found, the correctness of requirements can hardly be determined.

To include stakeholders directly into the validation of their requirements, the area of *Requirements Animation* emerged [32]. Gemino [12] presents an empirical comparison of requirements animation and narration. The preliminary findings included that the presentation of information can be as important as the content. However, different animation approaches for different groups of users exist. While some of these approaches merely visualize the state of the formal requirements in their formal notation, e.g., in [28], other approaches try to present a real world mapping of the requirements, e.g., [24].

It is important to note, that stakeholders are an invaluable sources of knowledge, but only as long as they provide feedback within their individual application domain. Thus, presenting them formal requirements models reduces their understanding of the content, thereby inhibiting their feedback. In [24], domain specific control panels visualize the state of the simulation in the stakeholders' domain of expertise, thereby easing the stakeholders' understanding. However, it focuses rather on single user control systems by monitoring the input of stakeholders without allowing them to extend the model during the simulation.

In [21], an approach to not only simulate the formal requirements model (called *play-out*), but also to enrich it with new details (named *play-in*) is presented. Besides the formal model in from of live sequence charts, also a prototypical GUI of the software system can be used to animate the simulation as well as capturing the user feedback to enrich the formal models by playing in new additional scenarios. Generally, scenario-based approaches such as [29] or [31] emphasize on synthesizing requirements either from multiple play-in sessions or records of valid system behavior. However, while partially using requirements animation, these approaches are aimed rather at requirements engineers than at end users.

Both, formal requirements models and prototyping offer many advantages. However, existing work either focuses on the one or the other. Existing requirements modeling approaches with animation and/or play-in result in sever limitations for the resulting interaction with the stakeholders. Either no focus on particular stakeholders can be set (cf. [32]) or the approaches are limited to animation only.

5 Summary and Future Work

We conceptualized how end users can be involved more directly in the validation of insights. Our concept relies on the simulation of formal models with an interactive suitable, i.e., domain-specific visualization on top. Allowing end users to directly provide feedback about the model during such a simulation can be used iteratively to evolve the underlying model till all end users share a common understanding on the validated model. This concept has been realized in a prototypical implementation that we used to conduct initial experiments. These qualitative explorative experiments emphasize the feasibility of our approach. We also received feedback which indicates that our approach is suitable for eliciting requirements which are likely to be overlooked otherwise.

During the second year, our focus lies on conducting different experiments for validating the approach in different settings, ranging from using the tool as part of lectures as well as using it in industrial settings. Along the way, our prototype will be enriched with new features, such as support for multiple modeling notations including graphical editors and another interactive visualization on top of the simulation in order to compare the impact of different levels of details on the feedback. Also, the simulation engine will be modified to offer more degrees of freedom for the end users during the simulation. Apart from these simulation capabilities, the modeling part of the prototype will be modified to allow using different modeling notations (cf. multi-paradigm modeling [13] and modeling notations [17]). Advanced techniques to transform and synchronize between different modeling languages (cf. [11, 14]) will be used to enable the co-existence of these different languages and paradigms.

Acknowledgements The authors are grateful for the input of Alexander Renneberg (D-LABS GmbH), Nico Rehwaldt, and Thomas Vogel, Jonathan E. Edelman, Alexander Großkopf, and Mathias Weske.

References

1. I. F. Alexander.   A taxonomy of stakeholders: Human roles in system development. *International Journal of Technology and Human Interaction*, 1(1):23–59, 2005
2. S. Andriole. Fast, cheap requirements: Prototype, or else! *IEEE Software*, 11(2):85–87, 1994
3. D. Bäumer, W. R. Bischofberger, H. Lichter, and H. Züllighoven. User interface prototyping – concepts, tools, and experience. In *ICSE '96: Proceedings of the 18th international conference on Software engineering*, pages 532–541. IEEE Computer Society, Washington, DC, USA, 1996
4. B. Becker, H. Giese, S. Hildebrandt, and A. Seibel. Fujaba's future in the MDA jungle – fully integrating Fujaba and the eclipse modeling framework? In *Proceedings of the 6th International Fujaba Days*, 18–19 September 2008
5. R. Biddle, J. Noble, and E. Tempero. Reflections on crc cards and oo design. In *CRPIT '02: Proceedings of the Fortieth International Conference on Tools Pacific*, pages 201–205. Australian Computer Society, Darlinghurst, Australia, 2002
6. F. P. Brooks, Jr. No silver bullet essence and accidents of software engineering. *Computer*, 20(4):10–19, 1987
7. T. Brown. *Change by Design: How Design Thinking Transforms Organizations and Inspires Innovation*. HarperBusiness, NY, 2009
8. A. Davis, O. Dieste, A. Hickey, N. Juristo, and A. M. Moreno. Effectiveness of requirements elicitation techniques: Empirical results derived from a systematic review. *IEEE International Conference on Requirements Engineering*, pages 179–188, Minnesota, USA, 2006
9. J. Edelman, A. Grosskopf, and M. Weske. Tangible business process modeling: A new approach. In *Proceedings of the 17th International Conference on Engineering Design, ICED'09*. Stanford University, Stanford, CA, USA, August 2009
10. G. Gabrysiak, H. Giese, and A. Seibel. Interactive visualization for elicitation and validation of requirements with scenario-based prototyping. In *4th International Workshop on Requirements Engineering Visualization, 2009, REV 2009*. IEEE Computer Society, Washington, DC, USA, 2009
11. J. Gausemeier, H. Giese, W. Schäfer, B. Axenath, U. Frank, S. Henkler, S. Pook, and M. Tichy. Towards the design of self-optimizing mechatronic systems: Consistency between domain-spanning and domain-specific models. In *Proc. of the 16th International Conference on Engineering Design (ICED)*. Paris, France, August 2007
12. A. Gemino. Empirical comparisons of animation and narration in requirements validation. *Requirements Engineering*, 9(3):153–168, 2004
13. H. Giese and S. Henkler. A survey of approaches for the visual model-driven development of next generation software-intensive systems. *Journal of Visual Languages and Computing*, 17(6):528–550, 2006

14. H. Giese and R. Wagner. Incremental Model Synchronization with Triple Graph Grammars. In O. Nierstrasz, J. Whittle, D. Harel, and G. Reggio, editors, *Proc. of the 9th International Conference on Model Driven Engineering Languages and Systems (MoDELS), Genova, Italy,* volume 4199 of *Lecture Notes in Computer Science (LNCS),* pages 543–557. Springer, Berlin, October 2006

15. H. Giese, F. Klein, and S. Burmester. Pattern Synthesis from Multiple Scenarios for Parameterized Real-Timed UML Models. In S. Leue and T. Systä, editors, *Scenarios: Models, Algorithms and Tools,* volume 3466 of *Lecture Notes in Computer Science (LNCS),* pages 193–211. Springer, Berlin, April 2005

16. H. Giese, S. Henkler, M. Hirsch, and F. Klein. Nobody's perfect: Interactive synthesis from parametrized real-time scenarios. In *Proc. of the 5th ICSE 2006 Workshop on Scenarios and State Machines: Models, Algorithms and Tools (SCESM'06), Shanghai, China,* pages 67–74. ACM, NY, May 2006

17. H. Giese, T. Levendovszky, and H. Vangheluwe. Summary of the Workshop on Multi-Paradigm Modeling: Concepts and Tools. In *Models in Software Engineering: Workshops and Symposia at MoDELS 2006, Genoa, Italy, October 1–6, 2006, Reports and Revised Selected Papers,* volume 4364 of *Lecture Notes in Computer Science.* Springer, Berlin, 2007

18. H. Giese, S. Hildebrandt, and A. Seibel. Feature report: Modeling and interpreting EMF-based story diagrams. In *Proceedings of the 7th International Fujaba Days,* 16–17 November 2009

19. H. Giese, S. Hildebrandt, and A. Seibel. Improved Flexibility and Scalability by Interpreting Story Diagrams. In T. Magaria, J. Padberg, and G. Taentzer, editors, *Proceedings of the 8th International Workshop on Graph Transformation and Visual Modeling Techniques (GT-VMT 2009),* 2009

20. P. Guyot and S. Honiden. Agent-based participatory simulations: Merging multi-agent systems and role-playing games. *Journal of Artificial Societies and Social Simulation,* 9(4):8, 2006

21. D. Harel and R. Marelly. *Come, Let's Play: Scenario-Based Programming Using LSC's and the Play-Engine.* Springer, New York, 2003

22. H. Plattner, C. Meinel, and U. Weinberg. *Design Thinking (German).* Number ISBN-13: 978-3868800135. mi-Wirtschaftsbuch, 2009

23. K. Pohl. *Requirements Engineering: Grundlagen, Prinzipien, Techniken (German).* dpunkt, Heidelberg, 2007

24. C. Ponsard, N. Balych, P. Massonet, J. Vanderdonckt, and A. van Lamsweerde. Goal-oriented design of domain control panels. In S. W. Gilroy and M. D. Harrison, editors, *DSV-IS,* volume 3941 of *Lecture Notes in Computer Science,* pages 249–260. Springer, Berlin, 2005

25. R. Schmid, J. Ryser, S. Berner, M. Glinz, R. Reutemann, and E. Fahr. A survey of simulation tools for requirements engineering. Technical report, University of Zurich, 2000

26. M. Schrage. *Serious Play: How the World's Best Companies Simulate to Innovate,* 1st edition. Harvard Business School Press, MA, 1999

27. A. Seibel, S. Neumann, and H. Giese. Dynamic hierarchical mega models: comprehensive traceability and efficient maintenance. *Software and System Modeling,* 9(4):493–528, 2010

28. C. Seybold, S. Meier, and M. Glinz. Evolution of requirements models by simulation. *International Workshop on Principles of Software Evolution,* pages 43–48, Kyoto, Japan, 2004

29. C. Seybold, S. Meier, and M. Glinz. Scenario-driven modeling and validation of requirements models. In *SCESM '06: Proceedings of the 2006 International Workshop on Scenarios and State Machines: Models, Algorithms, and Tools,* pages 83–89. ACM, NY, USA, 2006

30. H. Stachowiak. *Allgemeine Modelltheorie (German).* Springer, Wien, 1973

31. S. Uchitel, G. Brunet, and M. Chechik. Synthesis of partial behavior models from properties and scenarios. *IEEE Transactions on Software Engineering,* 35(3):384–406, 2009

32. H. T. Van, A. van Lamsweerde, P. Massonet, and C. Ponsard. Goal-oriented requirements animation. *IEEE International Conference on Requirements Engineering,* pages 218–228, Kyoto, Japan, 2004

33. T. Winograd, editor. *Bringing Design to Software.* ACM, NY, 1996

9 783642 137563